The Wines of Austria

Philipp Blom was first introduced to Austrian wines in the early 1990s while studying in Vienna, and since then they have become something close to an obsession for him. In this book he presents a persuasive case for these stunning wines, already discovered by collectors in the USA and soon to be asserting themselves on the international stage. As far as Philipp Blom is concerned, Austrian wines are the wine world's best-kept secret.

THE WINES OF AUSTRIA

PHILIPP BLOM

faber and faber
LONDON · NEW YORK

First published in 2000
by Faber and Faber Limited
3 Queen Square London WC1N 3AU
Published in the United States by Faber and Faber Inc.,
an affiliate of Farrar, Straus and Giroux, New York

Phototypeset by Intype London Ltd
Printed in England by Clays Ltd, St Ives PLC

© Philipp Blom, 2000
Maps © John Flower, 2000

Philipp Blom is hereby identified as author
of this work in accordance with Section 77
of the Copyright, Designs and Patents Act 1988

A CIP record for this book
is available from the British Library

ISBN 0-571-19533-4

2 4 6 8 10 9 7 5 3 1

To my mother,
and to Arnd,
who poured me my first glass of good wine

Contents

CONTENTS

Maps

Acknowledgements

It is a well-used phrase to say that a book could not have been written without the help of so many people, but this project really did depend on the collaboration and kindness of people many of whom were, or have become, good friends.

My first thanks have to go to Constantin Walderdorff, without whose angry insistence on the quality of Austrian wines and his generosity in imparting to me both his knowledge and the contents of his cellar this book would not even have been conceived, far less written. Once I had started my research, Luis Kracher, that indefatigable mover and shaker, *bon viveur* and quite incidentally also star winemaker, put me in touch with the Austrian Wine Marketing Board, who proved the very soul of generosity and helpfulness. Dr Berthold Salomon and Thomas Klinger especially were immensely kind, giving me every possible assistance (financially, logistically and otherwise) while at the same time putting up with my stubborn insistence on independence, and welcoming me not only as a colleague but also as a friend, proving in the process that the spirit of Austrian hospitality and conviviality is as vigorous, and as gracious, as it ever was. Amid her legendary flurry of activity, Dorli Muhr, too, welcomed me warmly and helped me wherever she could, providing invaluable advice, introductions, and wonderful company.

To my immense surprise I did not meet a single Austrian grower who was disagreeable or dislikable; on the contrary, often the rigours of concentrated tasting slid almost imperceptibly into the pleasures of an evening among friends. Their generosity, flexibility and helpfulness are gratefully and fondly remembered, and my only regret is that it is not always possible to translate the appreciation of someone's hospitality into praise for his or her wines. This, I hope, will not be seen as evidence of a mean spirit, but as the outcome of a striving for fairness.

There are many other people who deserve a mention here, as they were always at hand when help was needed. Adi Schmid for his mischief and immense knowledge, Victoria Morrall and Emily Wilkinson for their indefatigable help, Rosemary Hall for making the impossible possible, Hannelore Geyer, Teresa Karl and Manuela Mang for their organizational wizardry, Harald Beck and Romana Haindl for their skill and patience, and Giles MacDonough for his initial advice. On several occasions I was lucky to be able to taste and discuss Austrian wines with Steven Brook, Dagmar Ehrlich, Lucy Faulkner, Lance Foyster and other colleagues, whose comments I valued greatly.

Jancis Robinson proved wonderfully gracious and encouraging, while her own work provided me with an invaluable context for this book. Michael Broadbent and Oz Clarke, too, were very kind. Once the project had become a pile of manuscript pages, Dr Viktor Sigl very kindly read the manuscript, suggested improvements and made himself available despite riding two very demanding jobs. Dr Gerald Schlag kindly answered historical questions for me. Toby Faber and the formidable Julian Jeffs read and edited my efforts with great shrewdness, patience and expertise.

Last but by no means least, I wish to thank my wife Veronica, who put up with my absences in Austria and in front of the computer, and with endless bottles of wine in the house, and who provided me with constant encouragement and love. I have written this book with her in mind: a person who is open-minded but not an expert, willing to find out about something new without being acquainted with the arcane terminology going with wine. If one has to try the patience of a part of one's readership, it is always better to bore the experts (there are fewer of them, after all) than to shut out other interested readers. I hope there will be something worthwhile for both sides.

INTRODUCTION
Singing Lessons

———

When I lived in Vienna in the early 1990s, studying philosophy at the university, I fell in love with the opera. Before long I was hell-bent on becoming a tenor, and so took singing lessons with an eccentric Scot. While I was straining for that elusive C, my eyes drilled into a grotesque caricature of Rossini behind my teacher's piano.

Suffering induces comradeship, and I started talking to another hopeful who was financing part of his studies by working as a chef. 'You realize, of course,' said my fellow student as we trotted down the stairs after a lesson, 'that Austria produces some of the finest wines in the world.' At this I emitted a loud guffaw of derision. I might not be a food expert, but I knew a little about wines, I thought.

I had tasted the local offerings at the *Heurige*, the country inns scattered all around Vienna, and had even bought the two-litre bottles available at every greengrocer's. Nothing to write home about.

The effect of my hilarity was surprising. My otherwise gentle friend took me by the scruff of the neck and dragged me into his cellar. He did not lock me up, as I had feared, but chose instead four bottles from his collection and marched me up to his flat. Several hours and said bottles later, I had to admit defeat. These wines were quite astonishing, and my visit was the beginning of something close to an obsession.

Austrian wines are the best-kept secret of the wine world. They are exciting and immensely innovative, and a small band of top producers regularly wipes the board in blind tastings against the best international competition. What's more, the overwhelming majority of the growers are very pleasant people who are only too glad to welcome visitors on their estate and show them around, much in contrast to their often very much more snobbish French counterparts.

Austria is a small wine-producing country. The average annual yield is 2.5 million hectolitres from 51,000 hectares of vineyards. France, by comparison, makes on average about 65 million hecto-litres and exports five times as much wine as Austria produces in total. The Loire valley alone produces more wine than Austria.

There are good reasons why this book is relatively slim, though I hope there will be later editions that swell in size. First, many of the production methods and styles of wines discussed here have little history in Austria. In most cases they go back no longer than fifteen years and are still evolving as I write.

The second fact is that wines of this quality are still very much in the minority in Austria. Although there are about 30,000 wine-growers who cultivate grapes for wine production, only about 3,000 of these are full-time growers who vinify their own grape material. The majority of wine-growers cultivate small plots of less than a hectare and sell their grapes to other producers. These part-time wine-growers are called *Hauer*. Moreover, of the total amount produced during any year, a quarter is sold either as grapes or as cheap wine by the barrel. Another 10 per cent is produced in the local *Heurige* and *Buschenschanken*. Of the remaining 45 per cent of the vintage, roughly 80 per cent is sold in two-litre or litre bottles which stake no claim to excellence. Only the remaining 20 per cent of this amount – that is, about 9 per cent of the entire vintage – is vinified as wine of high quality. Of the 2.5 million hectolitres which make up the average annual production, this represents only about 200,000 hectolitres, though the proportion of these wines is now rising steadily.

It is these high-quality wines that will be discussed in this book. In selecting the producers, I have chosen not to be comprehensive, discussing every professional winemaker in Austria. Such an approach may be appropriate for more established wine countries, but in this case, with only a fraction of the wines reaching the export market and with other growers still producing fairly unex-citing, old-fashioned wine, I thought it better to guide interested readers to those growers whose wines are representative of the best in Austria, or who promise good things in the near future. The exceptions to this rule are the giant producers who have to be

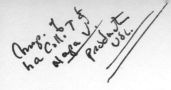

mentioned because their wines are very much in evidence through-out Austria and, partly, abroad.

Established estates producing consistently high qualities are pro-filed in more depth. They are recognizable by the fact that the size of the vineyards (in hectares) and the grape varietals cultivated in them are listed at the head of the entry. Other growers listed are those who are reliably solid or up-and-coming. There are many more, though, which are well worth trying, and the pioneering atmosphere in Austria suggests that in a few years from now (1999) there will be many more who will deserve to be included.

These fine wines are still on the margin of Austrian wine culture, though they are beginning to move towards the centre. Wines of this quality, already discovered by collectors in the USA, will soon be asserting themselves on the international stage. Most journal articles on Austrian wines are full of praise, despite the fact that a note of surprise is still evident in them. Austrian wine can be quite nice after all, they seem to say. Still, wine writers such as Clive Coates, Robert Parker and Jancis Robinson have already expressed their admiration and enthusiasm for some Austrian wines, especially those from the Wachau, Styria, the Kamptal and the Burgenland, while respected journals like the *Wine Spectator* are now regularly reviewing Austrian Rieslings, Grüner Veltliners and nobly sweet wines among others, many of which receive scores well into the nineties according to the hundred-point scoring system used there, placing them among the very best in the world.

Britain, a country otherwise adventurous in its wine tastes, has so far proved curiously reluctant to accept Austrian wines. What is available in the high street is often the simplest, least exciting products – the reliable Grüner Veltliners rather than the great ones, never mind the Rieslings, Sauvignon blancs, Blaufränkisches, St Laurents, Chardonnays, etc.

Among the high-quality wines, it is mostly the sweet wines which have begun to build up an international reputation, and already the USA is far ahead of Britain in appreciating, buying and collecting Austrian wines, as are Germany, the Netherlands and the Scandina-vian countries. The reason for this reluctance vis-à-vis one of the most interesting wine countries in the world is very difficult to comprehend.

Part of the problem is certainly the fact that the best growers usually produce amounts too small to be interesting for most importers. Moreover, many Austrian producers are not even looking for export markets, as they have a very appreciative domestic market. But things are looking up. An increasing number of independent wine merchants are stocking fine Austrian wines – one of them even learning German in order to penetrate the market further.

On the whole, Austrian wines are not cheap. An excellent Wachau Riesling may cost between £10 and £15 a bottle (a price fully justified by the amount of working hours invested in it); other Austrian top growths may command similar prices, with sweet botrytis wines fetching around £20 for a half bottle. This may be a lot of money, but wines of comparable quality from France, Germany, California or Australia are very much more expensive, and wine lovers will find it well worth the open-mindedness required to look for an Austrian equivalent. Simple wines, incidentally, can be very reasonable indeed.

Despite this focus on (costly) quality, Austria's is a fundamentally unsnobbish wine culture. In many ways, the simple wines consumed in country inns on a summer's day can still provide the archetypal Austrian wine experience. The delights of sitting in a *Heurige* in the evening with a few friends, a simple, improbably substantial meal and a jug of white wine on the table are among the most abiding memories one can take from this beautiful country. Such delights are of a very different quality from those experienced in some age-old cellar, precious vintage in hand, with its mystery and immeasurable subtlety, but the two combined now constitute the face of Austrian wine culture.

In retrospect, I am glad that I once laughed at the idea of Austrian wines being good, for otherwise I might never have discovered them. My friend, by the way, did become a singer, though he still enjoys cooking. I have given up my battle with the high C. Perhaps Mr Rossini's grin above the piano was a little discouraging. I blame him, anyway.

PB
London, July 1999

PART ONE
Austrian Wine Past and Present

SLOVAKIA

Weinviertel

Kamptal

Kremstal

Wachau

Donauland

Traisental

Wien

Carnuntum

N

Neusiedlersee

Thermenregion

Neusiedlersee-
Hügelland

Niederösterreich

Mittelburgenland

kilometres
0   25

HUNGARY

Süd-
burgenland

Süd-Oststeiermark

Weststeiermark

Süd-
steiermark

Wien

AUSTRIA

SLOVENIA

Wine-growing areas of Austria

Culture and History

There is a paradox at the heart of Austrian wine culture: it is arguably both one of the oldest in Europe and one of the youngest in the world. The Celts and Illyrians were already making wine in the region, but for most of the twentieth century Austrian wine offered a sorry picture: cheap wines were not only produced here, but were also bought in from Italy and eastern Europe, then bottled and resold as Austrian. The reputation of Austrian wines could hardly have been worse. Only a handful of producers bottled their own wine, and even fewer made wine worth studying.

Today Austria is the most vibrant, most innovative wine-producing country in Europe, and the sheer enthusiasm of the local community of wine lovers and producers is simply staggering. This change began little more than a decade ago. The country has woken up to its potential for producing world-class wines, and there has been an explosion of experimentation, investment, expertise and excitement, and of correspondingly remarkable and often wonderful wines. Austria is abuzz with possibility. No other country has travelled so far in so short a time.

From the Celts to the Romans

The oldest finds of cultivated grape seeds in Austria date back to the ninth or tenth century BC, and were made in the region of Lake Neusiedl, which was then Pannonia. An excavation of a Hallstatt period grave (circa 700 BC) uncovered a clay bowl with grape seeds, which were identified as varietals akin to the modern Chardonnay and Sylvaner, a result of breeding and 'improving' the native Pannonian wild grape. The region was part of the Amber Road, a trade route linking the Baltic coast with the countries by the Mediterranean. Finds from Celtic times also included tools, such as vine knives, and vessels with resin residues that suggest the use of resinated wines in Celtic cults, and possibly the import of such wines from Greece or Rome. Other sources describe the wine culture of the Celts and say that they even drank their wine undiluted with water, at that time an act of considerable culinary daring.

While it is possible that Celtic wine production and consumption have been underestimated until recently, it seems that the Romans brought large-scale wine production to this province of their empire after conquering the region in 15 BC. The Danube marked part of the north-eastern border of the Roman empire, and the new lands therefore had considerable strategic significance both in military terms and as a part of the Amber Road. There were substantial Roman settlements throughout Austria, most notably the city of Carnuntum – capital of the province of Pannonia Superior in the eponymous modern wine-growing area – which had 70,000 inhabitants.

The Romans supplanted the wine culture of the indigenous Celts: they brought with them their own expertise, administration and culture, and tilled the soil of the area in order to guarantee the flow of provisions to their army outposts. This included the planting and tending of vineyards. Wine was grown in areas already cultivated by the Celts, along the Danube in today's Wachau, in Pannonia and in Styria, the latter of which produced wines so good that they were even exported to Rome at the price of one young slave per amphora.

For motives remarkably reminiscent of those of today's European Union, the Roman emperor Domitian in AD 92 upset the wine world of his provinces by ordering the vines to be torn out of the ground. The cause of this was, curiously enough, the eruption of Mount Vesuvius in AD 79. Together with Pompeii, the volcano also buried some of Italy's most important vineyards, and in an effort to compensate for this loss, large amounts of new vineyards had been planted, leading to the market being quickly swamped. The wine imported from the colonies did not improve things.

As the Roman historian Suetonius relates, a poor grain harvest compounded the problem, convincing the emperor that the balance of wine and grain production was askew and needed to be rectified. Some vineyards had to go, and the provinces were the first to

4

suffer. Today, historians question how efficiently this edict was implemented in the far-flung outposts of the realm, and it is probable that a significant number of vineyards remained unscathed in Austria, but Domitian still gets a bad press for this act of economic opportunism.

Two hundred years later Emperor Aurelius Probus (AD 276–282) lifted the edict of his predecessor and even sent soldiers to help with the planting of new vineyards, mainly in Pannonia, today the border region of Hungary and Austria. He seems to have thought highly of Pannonian wine, as he specifically mentioned the Pannonian plains along with Gaul as areas to be replanted: *Probus Gallos et Pannonios vineas habere permisit.*

This really laid the foundation for Austria's wine culture for almost two millennia. According to a time-honoured Roman custom, Probus also gave parcels of land in Pannonia to his veterans for cultivation, thus supporting wine growing and consolidating his hold on one of the border areas of his empire.

Migrations and monks

With the demise of the Roman empire and the great migrations of the early Middle Ages, wine cultivation in the former Roman province came under severe pressure. Pannonia especially was to be overrun by almost every horde or army crossing from east to west, and it changed hands several times in the process. Wine growing, however, requires continuity. The vineyards (and stocks) were vulnerable to the invaders' thirst for destruction, as well as their thirst for alcohol, and continuity was conspicuously absent from the region. During the fifth century AD it was the base of Attila's Huns, and was later taken by the Gepidae, the Ostrogoths, the Langobards and the Avars, until Charlemagne conquered it in 803. From the tenth century onwards it belonged to Hungary.

Styria, historically one of the biggest wine growing areas, suffered an equally turbulent history. It changed hands between the Quadi, the Vandals, the Ostrogoths, Huns, Slovenes, Bavarians, the Franconians under Charlemagne, the Hungarians, the Germans and finally, in 1282, the House of Habsburg.

In the Wachau, wine culture could develop with less severe interruptions. After being ruled by the Langobards and Avars, the region fell to France in 803 and became the Ostmark of Charlemagne's empire, with Salzburg as its administrative and cultural centre.

Charlemagne's conquest of what is today's Austria at the end of the eighth century was to have a great influence on Austrian wine culture. Grapes were classified, and those which were deemed superior were called Fränkisch (Franconian).

Under the title *Capitulare de villis* the emperor (or more probably his son, Louis the Pious) formalized rules for the husbandry of vineyards and vinification methods for the first time. Hygiene was an important issue: the practice of stamping grapes with bare feet was prohibited – tree presses were to be used instead. It is doubtful whether this decree had much practical effect (grapes were stamped with bare feet in Austria, as indeed in France, until well into the twentieth century), but it illustrates the importance accorded to viticulture under Charlemagne.

After military campaigns at the beginning of the tenth century, the eastern parts of modern Austria were again in the hands of the Magyars. When they were defeated at the battle of Lechfeld in 955, the House of Babenberg became Margraves of the Ostmark. The battle also proved to be the last great military adventure of the Magyars, who would now become increasingly settled and Christianized and would themselves turn to wine-growing. In this new atmosphere of stability, Styria and other Austrian regions were planted with vineyards on a much larger scale than had earlier been possible.

The high medieval wine history of Austria is a tale of saints and bishops. After the demise of the Carolingian empire and the establishment of the Duchy of Austria in 1156, most vineyards in the Wachau and Burgenland were in the hands of monasteries. Wine production had distinctly ecclesiastical connotations and a traditional affiliation with the Church that went back to St Severin, who died in Wachau in 482. Today the Nikolaihof in Mauthern, founded as a feoff of the diocese of Passau in Bavaria and still a respected estate, can look back on more than a thousand years of continuous winemaking.

During the high Middle Ages, monastic foundations set the pattern for agricultural practice and land ownership in Austria. Margrave Leopold (1073–1136), the national saint of Austria, founded the monasteries of Heiligenkreuz, Mariazell and Kloster-neuburg, the latter of which still owns a great many vineyards throughout Austria, notably in the hills around (and suburbs of) Vienna: Nußdorf, Weidling, and Grinzing.

The archbishopric of Salzburg had owned extensive vineyards in the Wachau since the days of Charlemagne. These possessions had been managed as one large estate, and historical continuity is guaranteed by the successor of the archbishop of Salzburg, an excellent modern co-operative named the Freie Weingärtner Wachau. The Und monastery in nearby Krems is another survivor from medieval structures.

Krems, the largest town in the Wachau region, was an important centre for wine growing and trade: it was recorded as a wine-producing area in 995, and two hundred years later no fewer than sixteen different monasteries had estates and vineyards in and around the city. The first *crus* of the Wachau, individual vineyards and plots of recognized quality, were recorded during the thirteenth century.

In the region to the west of Vienna, Bavarian monasteries and especially Göttweig Abbey (still standing in all its baroque splendour), dominated wine growing and most other aspects of life in the province.

The history of viticulture in the Burgenland, the eastern part of modern Austria and then still part of Hungary, was dominated by the Cistercians, members of a Burgundian monastic order who in 1203 were given land between the River Leitha and the north bank of Lake Neusiedl by the Hungarian King Imre. His successor, King Andrew II, added to this gift. The Cistercians studied climate and soils, built drainage installations, and imported Burgundian grape varietals such as Pinot gris and, probably, Pinot noir from their home in France.

While the north of the Burgenland was essentially a colony administered by monasteries, the south of the area was under feudal rule, especially the rule of the families of Lutzmannsburg, Seifried and the Counts of Güssing. Even today, the landscapes of the southern Burgenland and neighbouring south-eastern Styria are dominated by large medieval fortifications such as Burg Locken-haus and the Riegersburg, attesting to the violent territorial disputes between neighbouring feudal overlords which were such a prominent feature of life in these parts. Despite the importance of feudal families, however, the proper cultivation of wine here, too, owes more to the Cistercians than to the robber barons.

Medieval wine consumption was robust, partly owing to the scarcity of clean drinking water, and one should spare a thought for the fact that our ancestors were very probably almost constantly inebriated. Even damsels residing in the very basic fortifications of the Burgenland and Styria were personally entitled to about seven litres of good red wine a day, easily enough to make them forget their grim surroundings.

However, wine was not made for domestic consumption alone. By the eleventh and twelfth centuries Austrian wine was being exported all over Europe, especially from Vienna and Krems. Wine from these regions was drunk in Bohemia and Moravia, in north Germany, the Baltic states and even in England, making it a distinct possibility that England imported more Austrian wine during the Middle Ages than it does now.

While expanding their exports, Austrian rulers also saw to the protection of the internal markets. Foreign wines were not allowed into Lower Austria for two centuries after 1364, and much like their French counterparts, the burghers of Vienna were entitled to sell wine within the city limits, just as farmers producing wine could sell their products on the local markets. The Viennese have always loved their wine, and during the Middle Ages they protected it with truly medieval measures: people caught stealing grapes were liable to have a hand cut off. In 1430, a particularly bad vintage, the sale of beer was prohibited in Vienna to boost the sales of wine.

Despite the efforts of the Cistercians and other monastic orders, winemaking techniques and technology were still in their infancy, and the weather was all-important. In 1456, following a bad season, the wine was so sour that the growers decided to pour it all away. The wine was known as *Reifenbeißer*, or hoop biter, as it was said to be so acid that it corroded the steel hoops of the casks it was kept in. The Emperor Frederick III, however, decreed that no divine gift was to be wasted, and so the wine was used for mixing mortar. Some of it stands petrified today between the stones of St Stephen's cathedral.

Sweet wines and bitter wars

During the sixteenth century the area under vines in the region that is now Austria was up to five times larger than it is today.

New laws, new taxes and the rising popularity of beer were to stall and then reverse the expansion of Austrian wines for the next three centuries.

There were exceptions, of course, most notably in the region of the Hungarian (though German-speaking) town of Rust. The town is situated on the western banks of Lake Neusiedl, and the mists rolling across the nearby vineyards make this an ideal area for the production of sweet wines from grapes affected by botrytis, or 'noble rot'. This causes grapes to shrivel and at the same time to maintain their sweetness and produce a distinct aroma.

Even in the Middle Ages the Cistercian monks had experimented with sweet wines of this kind, and by the beginning of the seventeenth century the first Ausbruch wines were being produced by the addition of a small amount of healthy grapes (usually the Austrian Furmint varietal) to grapes affected by botrytis. The Ausbruch wines were similar to that other famous wine of the region, Tokay, which was produced further inside Hungary. (In the production of Tokay, the must of botrytis grapes is added to healthy Tokay wine.)

The first Trockenbeerenauslese, a sweet wine made exclusively from nobly rotten grapes, and a great rarity until the twentieth century, had been made long before, in Donnerskirchen by Lake Neusiedl in 1526. This wine was at that time regarded as a great delicacy, and whenever an amount of it had been taken from a cask, washed pebbles would be added to make up the volume in the cask, and also to keep out air, and with it the danger of oxidation. This technique worked so well that the last of this 1526 wine was not in fact drunk until 1852, 326 years after it had been made. Donnerskirchen being a Protestant enclave in an otherwise Catholic region, the wine came to be known as Lutherwein. To this day it remains a local legend. It is worth noting that it was produced centuries before nobly rotten grapes were vinified in the Sauternes.

The originally small amount of healthy grapes contained in Ausbruch wines later grew to be relatively high, largely because of a court case of 1655, when the peasants rose against their masters over what they regarded as the unreasonable amount of work involved in picking the shrivelled botrytis grapes. The judges ruled that the Ausbruch wines would thenceforth be required to contain a significant quantity of healthy grapes, to ease the workload of the grape pickers.

The burghers of Rust soon found out how to produce these wines, and before long they were doing a roaring trade. Ruster Ausbruch wine was being enjoyed by princes and emperors, and was exported as far as the Baltic states. The wine-growers and merchants of the town grew wealthy, displaying their new riches in the beautiful baroque town houses that still stand in Rust today.

With the rising popularity of the wine came the need to protect it against competitors, and in 1524 the Hungarian Queen Maria granted the town the privilege of branding its casks with the letter R, an early form of trademarking, with the nearby cities of Jois and Neusiedl being given similar privileges at about the same time.

Rust escaped lightly from that scourge of so many seventeenth-century populations, the Thirty Years War. Winemaking in the area was not greatly affected, but by the end of the war in 1648, control over the region was in dispute.

Although the catastrophic war had largely spared the area, the Turkish invasion was a severe threat both to the people of Rust and to their wines. In 1683 the town was laid waste by the Turkish army en route to lay siege to the city of Vienna. During the siege itself, Prince Esterházy, who held his lands in Hungary and Pannonia, appointed the noble beverage of his homelands to a patriotic role: every day, between eleven in the morning and five in the afternoon, casks of wine were distributed *gratis* to the defenders of the city.

The winemakers of Rust were to exact their own peculiar revenge on one Turkish soldier at least: the Purbach Turk, enthusiastically ignoring his religion's requirement to abstain from intoxicating substances, remained blissfully unaware of the retreat of his own troops. The now legendary soldier came to surrounded by his victorious Austrian enemies. The fleeing Turks, meanwhile, had left behind intoxicating substances of their own, as Jan Sobieski, a Polish spy who had aided the Austrian cause, was to find. The curious beans in the Turkish army sacks were to create a legend of their own: the famous Viennese coffee house.

The vineyards of the Burgenland recovered. Tokay was unavailable, as Hungary was still under Turkish influence. However, many wine-growers had fled from Hungary and were now cultivating wine in the Burgenland, bringing Hungarian expertise to the area.

By 1681, Ruster Ausbruch had become so successful and so widely known that the town of Rust was made an Imperial Free City in recognition of its wine production. The price for this distinction, however, was considerable: 500 buckets of the prestigious Ausbruch itself and 60,000 guilders in addition.

The Turks may have been routed, but the winemakers to the south-east were not yet safe. In 1693 a plague of locusts attacked their vineyards, leaving them devastated. Rust and its neighbours were to endure even more. They were repeatedly attacked from the east and pillaged by the Kuruzzes and Haiduks.

Connoisseurs and scholars

The Turks, pushed first back into Hungary, were expelled even further by Prince Eugene of Savoy in a protracted campaign lasting no fewer than twenty-five years. After centuries of invasion and upheaval, the eastern regions of Austria were at last secure. In this time of peace and stability, wine cultivation flourished alongside many other industries.

The Turkish threat neutralized, a new confidence spread through Viennese culture and social life, and the city regained its characteristic *joie de vivre*. Wine production – and consumption – grew markedly. The land under vines increased accordingly, and the wine harvest itself was soon taking as long as forty days, with countless men and women hard at work each year, not to mention some 1,200 horses. Lady Mary Wortley Montagu, who visited Vienna in 1716, remarked in a letter home that dinners for the 'first people of quality' were served on silver or the finest china. She was particularly impressed by the fact that these occasions were accompanied by as many as eighteen different wines, and that a list detailing the names of the wines was laid on the plate of each guest, together with a napkin.

As the eighteenth century progressed, Vienna developed its own hierarchy of crus (in Austrian *Rieden*), with some wines being aged in casks for up to twenty years before being drunk. Considerable rivalry was apparent between the crus of Grinzing, Weidling and Nußdorf, and even comparative tastings were arranged, so that an official decision might be made as to the best wine-producing area of all.

For Pannonia, too, a new era had begun. In many cases, the

ruling families had taken over where the Church's influence had waned, with significant effects on winemaking. The monasteries lost their role as centres of innovation to the cellars of princes in Eisenstadt and Forchtenstein, and to the imperial possessions of Rust, Lutzmannsburg and Purbach.

By now Hungarian Tokay had again eclipsed the Ausbruch wines of Rust, which were also burdened by a special tax. The popularity of Pannonian sweet wines, however, persisted – so much so, in fact, that heavy penalties were introduced to combat the increasing numbers of fraudulent winemakers who aped the sweet Ausbruch wines by mixing other wine with honey, sugar and raisins. The export business, too, was flourishing again, and barrels were shipped not only to the traditional markets of the Baltic region, but even as far as St Petersburg.

The export trade was often carried out by Viennese merchants taking advantage of favourable tax regulations, or by Pannonian wine merchants, many of whom were Jewish. Jews had been forbidden to live in Austria proper from the Middle Ages, and this prohibition remained in force until the passing of the Edict of Tolerance by Emperor Joseph II at the end of the eighteenth century. In the intervening period, the borderland Pannonian cities of Deutschkreutz, Eisenstadt, Frauenkirchen and Mattersburg had developed sizeable Jewish communities.

The reforming Joseph II also harmonized taxes, set limits for wine production and dissolved a third of all monasteries in his empire, thereby changing the pattern of land ownership considerably. Finally, in 1784 the Emperor placed the popular *Buschenschanken* and *Heurige* on a secure legal footing, by allowing his subjects to sell food and wines freely on their own land, provided everything offered had been produced by the vendors themselves.

In the early years of the nineteenth century, Napoleon conquered the Austrians and his armies overran their country, wreaking havoc with its wine production along the way – not least by blowing up the wine cellars of Klosterneuburg Abbey, and in so doing destroying a 'wine library' going back several centuries. The monks of the abbey had used the old wines for medicinal purposes, as they were then regarded as an effective treatment for fatigue. Napoleon's soldiers also drank whatever wine they could find, earning themselves the honorific title of 'thirstiest army in Europe'. Over the ensuing decades, the abbey cellars were restocked, only to be emptied again by Russian soldiers at the end of the Second World War. What they could not guzzle down, they simply machine-gunned to pieces.

There were, however, more encouraging developments during the nineteenth century. Wine nurseries sprang up, and in 1819 a certain Hofrat von Görög founded a nursery containing, according to a contemporary source, an seemingly infinite variety of grapes: no fewer than 565 French varieties, 453 from the Austrian Empire, 257 from Venice, forty-eight from Milan, forty-eight from Dalmatia, forty-five from Sicily, thirty-two from Ragusa, thirty from Florence, twenty from Tripoli, thirteen from Naples and six from Smyrna. The collection seems to have vanished with the good Hofrat's demise in 1833. It is perhaps a significant footnote that he did not seem to have found it necessary to collect German vines, unless of course they were subsumed under the 'imperial' varietals.

During the 1830s the Austro-Hungarian oenologist and writer Franz Schams made a study of the wines grown in the Habsburg Empire which he published in two volumes in 1832 and 1835 under the exhaustive title *Vollständige Beschreibung sämmtlicher berühmter Weingebirge in Österreich, Mähren und Böhmen in statistisch, topographisch-naturhistorischer und ökonomischer Hinsicht* (Complete Description of All Famous Wine Mountains in Austria, Moravia and Bohemia in Terms of Statistics, Natural History and the Economy). Schams compared some Habsburg wines favourably to the wines of Burgundy and also writes that some wines were aged for as long as fifteen or twenty years before being served. Not everyone, though, was so enthusiastic about Austrian, and especially Viennese, wines. Around 1800 one foreign visitor is reported to have written that the wines in the capital were expensive, bad and often 'improved'.

As in the eighteenth century, the most highly regarded wines of the Austro-Hungarian empire, with the possible exception of Tokay and Ruster Ausbruch (which had by now recuperated from its many woes), were those growing around Vienna, particularly in Nußdorf, Weidling, Grinzing and Klosterneuburg. Another wine with a good name was the 'Vöslauer', wines coming from around Vöslau in the Thermenregion. Until the Second World War, Austrian wines were generally referred to not by the grape from which they were made but by their geographical origin. Austrian wine was largely limited to these areas, and to Styria: the Burgenland was still Hungarian, and wine production in the Wachau had declined in favour of orchard plantations.

Franz Schams reported several new developments, such as the experimental planting of red wines in the Thermenregion. He applauded the idea of planting vines in orderly rows, so facilitating work in the vineyard, which he found in the Cistercian monastery of Heiligenkreuz. Elsewhere, as in the Middle Ages, vines were planted at random, with no particular order. Schams also commented on another practice which until very recently appeared to have all but vanished. He found that the growers in Mauer (now part of Vienna) were pricing their wines higher when they had been fermented in new oak barrels. He confessed himself puzzled: 'I am quite unable to clarify', he wrote, 'what beneficial influence the wines might derive from the process of having their alcoholic fermentation take place in new oak barrels,' but he decided nonetheless to try the method in his own winemaking.

In 1880 the first steps were taken to regulate the Austrian wine industry. The first comprehensive Austrian law governing wine was introduced in 1907, and was reviewed four times before being radically recast in 1985. A whole flood of wine literature and oenological tracts from the nineteenth century provides more than enough material to build up a picture of Austrian viticulture during this period. We know about dominant varietals, about the methods of treating vines, grapes and wine in the vineyards and in the cellars, and about the experiments that were conducted.

Many of the wines produced then would be difficult to recognize as Austrian wines today. Furmint and Zierfandler grapes are still cultivated in the Thermenregion today, but the Griechische (Greek) grape, once used widely for wines of lesser quality, has now vanished altogether, along with the Augustrebe and Silberweisse varietals.

Of the grape varietals most common today, only a few were current during the nineteenth century. One exception is the Pinot gris – indeed, this grape has been cultivated in Austria since the Middle Ages. Pinot noir and St Laurent were probably known as well. There was some Grüner Veltliner, but it was then known as Grüner Muskateller and was not as yet widespread. This varietal, today almost the embodiment of Austrian wine and accounting for roughly a third of current production, gained primacy only with Lenz Moser and his method of high training vines in the 1950s.

Muskateller, Riesling and Welschriesling were already grown in Austria, though not on a large scale. There would also have been some Blaufränkisch (probably hiding behind the then current Blauer Zierfandler and/or Schwarzer Muskateller in southern Burgenland, and the Schwarzfränkisch and Mährisch then vinified in Vöslau) and Blauer Portugieser, but the style of Austrian red wines has changed so much since 1985 that, to a current palate, the old grape varieties would taste quite different. Neuburger is an interesting special case, because according to legend it originated from a bunch of vine branches that was fished out of the Danube in the Wachau and planted in that region – a Moses, as it were, among Austrian vines. There is another version of this legend which claims that another grape came floating down the Danube and was planted in, and named after, the vineyard Rizling. This, however, is doubtful.

International varietals which are now very successful, such as Sauvignon blanc and Merlot, had to wait until the late twentieth century, but Chardonnay and Cabernet Sauvignon had come in already during the nineteenth. The structure of the wine landscape, too, was different, as the German system of classifying wines into Prädikat, Spätlese, Auslese, Beerenauslese, etc, was eventually introduced (after an interlude during the Anschluß) in two separate waves of wine-related laws in 1972 and 1985.

In the Wachau, which today produces some of the very finest Austrian wines, the wine landscape was not terribly exciting. The grape favoured here, and incidentally around Vienna, was the Grobe ('rough one') of which the writer Franz Schams wrote that it produced good wines in good years and good vinegar in bad ones. Only after the Second World War did Riesling show how perfectly suited it was to the conditions in the Wachau. During the nineteenth century, however, the locals stuck to their unshakeable faith in the Grobe, dismissing most other varietals as foreign nonsense.

Langenlois, to the east of the Wachau, was even then one of the best wine-producing cities in the Empire, with a huge area under cultivation. The two main varietals here were Roter Muskateller and Grüner Muskateller, that is, Grüner Veltliner. Langenlois was therefore one of the very few places that would have looked much the same to a wine enthusiast one hundred years ago as it does now, with large, extensive vineyards and a great emphasis on the Grüner Veltliner.

By 1860, a school of viticulture had been established in Klosterneuburg in an attempt to breathe new life into local wine production and to spread new knowledge and winemaking technology. The school is still one of the most important centres of learning and research in Austria. Wine was on its way back. Many important new developments have emanated from this school, among them the Klosterneuburger Mostwaage (KMW) – a method, still used, of measuring the sugar content of the must – and important new grape varieties such as Zweigelt and Goldburger.

One further development must be mentioned. During the second half of the nineteenth century, champagne was beginning its triumphal march through Europe, and it was not long before similar wines appeared outside France. Austria has its own tradition of sparkling wine production, particularly in the Viennese district of Döbling, where a great number of sekt (sparkling wine) producers had their headquarters during the nineteenth century. One of these was the house of Schlumberger, founded in 1842 by the German Robert Schlumberger. His main competitor, then as now, was Johann Kattus, whose house even today, in a backward glance at the long-decayed splendours of the Austro-Hungarian Empire, declares itself purveyor to the Imperial Court.

The Universal Exhibition of Vienna in 1873 was an opportunity for the Habsburg Empire to show off its wines to the world. All the wines of the world were invited to present themselves for a universal competition, to be judged by experts.

The British expert at this occasion was one Henry Vizetelly, charged by Her Majesty's Commissioners to draw up a report. In 1875 he published a popular version of his report, drawing on his experiences in Vienna. He was an honest man, a good taster and not given to flattery. About the wines of Austria he wrote:

> The wines of Austria are as diverse as its population. At the extreme south they are so dark and full-bodied that when mixed with an equal quantity of water they are quite as deep in colour and as spirituous as the ordinary wines of Bordeaux ... while in less favourable districts they are excessively poor and so sour as to rasp the tongue like the roughest cider. Many have the

luscious character of Constantia and the Muscat growths of Frontignan and Lunal. Several, on the other hand, are disagreeably bitter, others again so astringent as to contract the windpipe while swallowing them, whereas a few of the lighter varieties possess the delicacy, if not the fragrance, of certain growths of the Rheingau. It must be confessed, however, that although the specimens were remarkably varied and numerous, the better qualities were extremely rare.

The nineteenth century also witnessed two periods of disaster for the vineyards of the Habsburg Empire. One was the temporary drying-out of Lake Neusiedl between 1865 and 1871, which put an end to the production of Ausbruch for a century, the last vintage before our own day being 1894.

The second, much larger disasters were the terrible blights of mildew and phylloxera, the second of which almost completely destroyed wine production throughout Europe. Oidium, mildew, was first observed in France in 1847 and in central Europe soon afterwards. Phylloxera, a plant louse feeding on the roots of vines and destroying them in the process, came hard on its heels and proved far more devastating. It had been imported with shipments of plants from North America. It first surfaced in France during the 1860s, and production of French wine had collapsed from 84.5 million hl in 1875 to 23.4 million hl in 1889. In Austria, phylloxera first came to the attention of wine-growers in 1872, in Klosterneuburg.

During the 1880s phylloxera ravaged the Thermenregion and then went on into other areas. Within twenty years it destroyed 9,029 hectares of vines throughout Lower Austria, a quarter of all the vines. There are no figures for the Burgenland and Styria, but the extent of the destruction was considerable here as well. Recovery was brought about only with the grafting of European vines on to American stocks resistant to the plague, a solution which produced a rather curious viticultural footnote.

Some of the poorer growers, especially in Styria, simply proceeded to make wine from the rootstocks of the American *vitis lambrusca*, which had been imported to replace the destroyed *vitis vinifera* vines, instead of grafting European grapes on to the American rootstocks. Some of the imported grape varieties, however, were reputed to cause imbecility, and the sale of these wines was forbidden by law. The descendants of this wine curiosity still survive in South Styria, where they are known under the collective name of Uhudler, apparently because the growers who had downed this moonshine wine in their own cellars came home drunk as an owl, or *Uhu*. Limited production of Uhudler was legalized only in 1992, and then only in certain districts of South Styria and South Burgenland.

Before phylloxera destroyed the vineyards of the Burgenland, the red wines of this region flourished as well-regarded substitutes for French wines, which had been afflicted by the insects before the plague spread to Austria. After the disaster red grapes were planted again, continuing the newly acquired tradition of making red wines in the area.

The early twentieth century brought the catastrophe of the First World War and the collapse of the Austro-Hungarian Empire. In 1921 the Burgenland, always a region disputed between Austria and Hungary, held a referendum to establish which state its inhabitants wanted to join. The result was, as expected, that German Hungary, as it was still called, finally became the Burgenland, and the wine country of Austria attained the shape familiar to us today.

Before the country settled into its new shape and readied itself for the revolution ahead, however, the wine of Austria became that of the Section Donauland of the Third Reich. Austria was part of the Ostmark, and so the German wine law of 1930 became the basis of Austrian winemaking after 1938.

The glorious revolution of 1985

Despite the efforts of Austria's wine professors and a few growers who strove for the highest quality, throughout much of the twentieth century most of their winemaking colleagues had other ideas. After the Second World War, commercial opportunities for selling cheap, sweet plonk in domestic and German supermarkets meant that the majority of growers went down this road, selling their wines to dealers by the barrel to be marketed under the dealers' names. New technologies and over-optimistic consumption forecasts led to domestic over-production of wine. At this time, an almost universal triumph was enjoyed by the Grüner Veltliner, as a reliable mass-yielding grape, and rather bland staple sorts such as Müller-Thurgau and Blauer Portugieser. Dry, characterful wines were a rarity, though some wines of this kind were produced for domestic consumption by committed wine-growers who were seen widely as lovable but unrealistic dreamers.

Fritz Hallgarten's 1979 book *The Wines and Wine Gardens of Austria* provides an intriguing picture of the country's post-war wine landscape just before the enormously beneficial catastrophe that was to befall it. Hallgarten's Austria is a country in which there are some extraordinary wines, but few international grape varieties or styles. 'Austria does not produce heavy wines full of alcohol,' he declares, a statement very much at odds with the style of modern Austrian winemaking. The 'most lovable, finest and most elegant' Austrian wines, according to him, were grown in the Burgenland.

The wines Hallgarten lists as remarkable (often with tasting notes such as 'we like it') are commonly chaptalized, so much so that he devotes an entire chapter to this practice, which is still legal for some wines in Austria, but is now very much frowned upon. Among the grape varieties used in Austria, international ones feature hardly at all, and grapes such as Müller-Thurgau and Blauer Portugieser were used widely.

Hallgarten describes wines which are often semi-sweet, have German-sounding names such as Loibner Katzensprung, and are made by wine-growers most of whose names have completely vanished from the modern map, while the majority of the growers famous today hardly feature in his lists. The tenor of the Austrian wine culture seems aptly summarized by a quote from the famous wine-grower and oenologist Lenz Moser: 'The grower has the task of supplying good and cheap wine.'

The wines of post-war Austria were overwhelmingly competing at the bottom end of the market, notably, it must be said, with the worst Italian products. It was in the spirit of undercutting the competition at the bottom end of the market that in 1985 some growers in Austria and Italy began adding diethylene glycol, a commonly-used antifreeze agent, to their wines in order to sweeten them artificially.

In Italy (where methyl alcohol had been used in a similar scandal), more than twenty people died as a consequence of this activity, though nobody was hurt as a result of drinking the adulterated Austrian wines. The Italian growers, however, had already begun to push their wines internationally. Tourism helped, and wine-growers such as Angelo Gaia managed to exploit the crisis by publicly denouncing the miscreants.

In Austria the problem had been much smaller, but the fallout was enormous. The export market collapsed almost overnight, and with it great parts of the trading infrastructure. The international media were less interested in reviving the fortunes of Austria as a wine-producing country, and consequently it bore the brunt of the scandal.

In retrospect, nothing better than the 1985 scandal could have happened to Austrian winemaking. New wine laws, the strictest in Europe, were introduced to ensure quality, and with the demise of the old networks for the distribution of poor, sickly-sweet wines and a wave of retirements among the older growers, a new generation, with new ideas, was soon taking over the business. As it had become much more difficult to sell wine in tanks directly to merchants, many of whom had gone bankrupt, increasing numbers of growers began to bottle their own wines and to search for an individual and credible way of promoting their products. Trips abroad also widened the horizons of many young winemakers.

New methods of vinification were tried and new grape varieties planted, some of which, such as Chardonnay (which had, as Morillon and as Pinot blanc, already been grown to some extent) and Sauvignon blanc, proved very successful, though they still represent only a small fraction of the vines in Austrian vineyards. Within a very few years, one of the most backward wine-producing countries in Europe had become one of the most bubblingly exciting.

In 1993, Austrian wine legislation received a further significant amendment. Maximum yields per hectare were set at 9,000 kg (6.75 hl), a high level, set indiscriminately for red and white wines; as already mentioned, producers striving for high quality aim at a level far lower than this.

It is commendable that, on the whole, Austrian growers and legislators seem to have rediscovered their wine history rather than feeling obliged to invent a new one. The 'novelties' which now cause such excitement in the Austrian wine landscape, the emphasis on crus (*Rieden*), the Trockenbeerenauslesen, Ausbruch, oak-fermented and oak-aged wine – all these had already existed at one time or another, later becoming simply victims of changing natural conditions, changing fashions and political upheaval. They are back now and, barring new catastrophes, they give every indication of being here to stay.

The face of Austrian wine culture today

One word above all describes the world of Austrian wines today – excitement. There are now, in a country with considerably fewer inhabitants than London, four journals devoted to discussing and reviewing local (and international) wines: *Vinaria*, *A la Carte*, *GaultMillau* and *Falstaff*. In addition there is a plethora of wine seminars, regional tastings, cellar tours, open days in wineries, blind tastings, wine concerts and other events.

A substantial number of good, very good and excellent restaurants are specializing in Austrian cuisine and wines, and a whole range of books appear every year, assessing the latest vintage, the best wines, the most remarkable young growers and so forth. The energetic Austrian Wine Marketing Board promotes Austrian wines abroad, invites journalists to tasting tours and makes trading connections. At a biannual wine fair in Vienna's Imperial Hofburg, the VieVinum, visitors can taste the very best wines the country produces.

In addition to this, there is the annual Salon Tasting, where wine journalists and other recognized connoisseurs nominate growers, whose wines are then tasted in a series of blind tastings and ranked in a 'hall of fame' of the two hundred best wines and growers in Austria. This invariably produces surprises, as wines from relatively unknown producers appear among the great and the good. It is also a good mechanism to highlight achievement and combat complacency. The Salon sticker is also a reliable guide to interesting wines.

In the thick of this excitement about the changing face of Austrian wines, some wine writers may tend to be a little over-enthusiastic, and the adjective 'great' seems to be on the tip of some tongues whenever a wine shows promise and good structure, but that should not detract from those genuinely great wines that have been produced in Austria in recent years.

Some wine writers have adopted so florid a style when describing Austrian wines that one suspects they may be more of a loss to the literary world than an asset to those simply wanting to know what a wine tastes like. Take, for instance, this (anonymous) extract: 'An elegant play of fruit marches across the palate in the aromatic ring dance of youthfulness, and digs deep furrows of taste which end in fascination.' Happily, in Austria itself there are a number of wine writers whose formidable expertise, knowledge and prowess in tasting is matched at all times by descriptive prose of impeccable elegance.

Among the growers and enthusiasts in Austria itself, wines are frequently celebrated in a very grand manner. For every tasting, whole batteries of fragile Riedel glasses, manufactured in Austria and perfectly suited to wine-tasting, are lined up before the tasters and wines from different varietals, *crus* and vintages are compared and discussed until the conviviality they induce overtakes the purely academic interest of those assembled. This ritual is carried out for all creatures great and small, and I think it is fair to say that Austria's wine lovers generally enjoy the occasion itself as much as the wines they have come to sample.

Formal wine education in Austria is, as might be expected, very thorough. The epicentre of wine knowledge is the Weinbauschule Klosterneuburg, a vocational boarding school and a port of call for most aspiring growers, especially those from winemaking families. There is also a well-regarded school of viticulture in Krems, another one in the Styrian town of Silberberg, and a Wine Academy in Rust, all of which are dedicated to imparting wine-growing expertise. In addition, the Viennese Universität für Bodenkultur (the 'BOKU') carries on work with a stronger emphasis on academic research into soil types, vine clones, climatic factors, vine training methods, etc. Moreover, it has now become accepted practice for young winemakers to spend some time abroad gathering experience, preferably in France, but also in the New World – California, South Africa or New Zealand, a fount of experience exerting a clear influence on recent wine styles.

Amid all this buzzing activity, one thing is certain: Austrian wines are here to stay, and their style and quality are being refined rapidly – so rapidly, in fact, that it seems that, within only a few years, many names and wines from as yet neglected regions will have joined the ranks of those now at the top. Austria, on the whole, is a wine country still awaiting discovery.

What Makes an Austrian Wine?

Fifteen years ago, this question would have been easy to answer. Ignoring the few glaring exceptions of growers who always went their own way, Austrian wine was light, fruity, acidic, often thin and made for consumption within one year – enjoyable on the spot but nothing to write home about.

After Austria's Glorious Revolution of 1985, however (though it would be as simplistic as it would be unrealistic to attribute all change and all production of quality wines simply to the wine scandal), the answer has become more difficult and much more interesting. Austrian wine has most definitely come of age. It is at home with various international and indigenous styles, and it is in the process of defining its own distinctive identity within the context of the wine world at large.

Winemaking begins in the vineyard. It is here that the groundwork is laid for a wine's depth, fruit extract, sugar and alcohol content, and overall quality and character. The weather and microclimate will have to do their part, but much is up to the grower's skill, knowledge and intuition.

Lower yields translate into better wines, as the vines transport the nutrients drawn from the leaves and the soil into fewer grapes. For the grower it is, of course, a gamble, because there will be less wine to sell and the difference in quality may or may not justify his decision to cut back. Usually, however, it does. In Austria, green harvest (cutting down a proportion of the grapes before they are ripe, allowing the others to develop more concentration) is now widespread. The efforts to improve quality are often taken to extremes, leading one top wine-grower, Anton Kollwenz, to compare Austrian viticulture to competitive athletics, where the aim of making small inprovements in performance has long since left thoughts about profitability in the shade.

Although average annual yields have declined overall, indicating that even mass-produced wines are of better quality than they used to be, the top growers have shown the way, in this as in every other respect. The average quantity of wine per hectare between 1967 and 1976 was 58 hectolitres, compared with 48 hectolitres in the period from 1990 to 1998, a calculation which does not take into account the fact that the best wine-growers are often content with yields of around 30 hectolitres per hectare, and significantly less in the Wachau.

The first important Austrian characteristic can be observed by going into the vineyards throughout the country: unlike the practice in many other wine-growing areas throughout the world, the vines here mostly stand in wide rows (about 3.5 m apart), are generously spaced and have trunks which come up above waist height to about 1.3 m, with shoots and leaves extending even higher. This picture results from the Lenz Moser system of training vines, named after its inventor, who propagated it during the 1950s.

Professor Moser found that spacing the vines further apart allowed easier access for machines, while the higher vine plants allowed workers to tend them more easily and without bending down. This system, designed in part as an answer to the problem that increasing numbers of people from rural areas were migrating to the cities, allowed the wine-growers to mechanize the work in the vineyard to a large extent, cutting down working hours per hectare drastically. In addition to this, fewer plants per hectare actually increased yields, as individual stocks were able to carry more grapes. The height of the grapes from the ground also meant that they were less sensitive to frost and rot.

The Lenz Moser training system was swiftly adopted all over the country, in Germany and in many New World vineyards. In Austria it is still dominant. The problem with this system, however, is that it is designed for high yields and low labour intensity, two things almost irreconcilable with the production of top-class wines. The drawbacks of the method are not only the loss of fruit extract owing to the quantity of grapes produced, but also the lower quality of the grapes themselves, which are often hanging in the shadow of the canopy of leaves and therefore cannot mature ideally, leading to lower sugar contents in the must and to thin wines with green aromas.

Nowadays, many ambitious Austrian wine-growers are returning to higher density and lower training of vines, decreasing the yields and improving the quality of the must. These growers view the popularity of the Lenz Moser training method as a post-war interlude. The systems most commonly adopted today in vineyards that are either newly planted or converted are similar to those employed in Alsace and in Burgundy, especially the arched cane method and the *cordon de Royat*, though the Austrian adaptation of these tends to be higher, in recognition of the lower temperatures in the vineyards.

Individual growers also experiment with other methods, notably Willi Bründlmayer, who has trained the vines in some of his best vineyards according to the Lyre system developed by Dr Alain Carbonneau, which increases the leaf canopy (and thus the ability of the wine to photosynthesize) while leaving the grapes with just the right amount of exposure to the sun and protection from the elements. Unlike Lenz Moser, this system is very labour-intensive.

Recent research in Austria has confirmed evidence concerning grape quality by establishing that denser leaf canopies and a fruit zone that is closer to the ground alter the microclimate of the vineyard considerably, with leaf surfaces 1° C warmer than in Lenz Moser vineyards, leading to better ripening of the grape material. The higher temperature, however, also leads to quicker evaporation of water and may necessitate irrigation, adding to the greater workload of the vineyard workers. In some areas of Styria, other more traditional methods persist, with high canopies. Vineyards planted in this traditional way, however, do not occur in significant numbers.

Another fundamental decision is choosing the grape variety suited to the climate, the region, the soil and the microclimate, that indefinable entity which the French call *le terroir*. Here much has changed in the last decade or so, with new, international varietals planted and others taken out almost completely, reversing the post-war trend of going for the most reliable grapes producing the highest quantity. Nowadays growers are both remembering which grape varieties traditionally suited which area and vineyard, and looking beyond their national borders to find other grapes which may work well in Austria.

The chapter dealing with grape varieties will discuss in more detail which variety is suited to which soil type and area. Suffice it to say at this point that different grapes have different degrees of sensitivity to soil types, spring and autumn frosts, sun exposure, etc., and that a perfect marriage of terroir and grape variety is rewarded not only by the high quality of the yield, but also by the fact that the characteristics of the terroir are reflected in the character of the wine. Some classic varieties, such as Grüner Veltliner, Welschriesling, Riesling, Sauvignon blanc, Pinot blanc, Pinot gris and Chardonnay, and Zweigelt, Blaufränkisch, St Laurent and Pinot noir, have emerged already as very successful. There is still, however, a high degree of experimentation.

The question of terroir always brings with it discussion of the merits of individual vineyards (crus), called *Rieden* in Austria. Some areas, notably the Wachau and the Kamptal, have always recognized their best *Rieden* and their individual characteristics. In the Wachau alone, 900 different *Rieden* are recognized, some of them since the Middle Ages. There are also long-established *Rieden* in Styria, Vienna and in parts of the Burgenland. In other areas, good individual *Rieden* (as opposed to larger plots with traditional names) are only now being rediscovered, or discovered for the first time. It will take some time to match them to the ideal grape varieties, a development that is taking place very energetically.

As far as tending the vineyards, harvesting the grapes and pressing them in the winery are concerned, Austria has made gigantic advances since 1985. Gone are the days when pesticides were sprayed liberally, and most growers have now accepted a very careful approach often based on biological principles, such as the introduction of predatory mites to control other mites feeding on leaves and stems. Pesticides and fertilizers are, where necessary, used sparingly.

In the Kamptal and Kremstal it has become common practice not to spray against botrytis, as the relatively dry air discourages the fungus anyway. Throughout all wine-growing areas, grass, sweet peas and rye are often grown between the rows of vines to discourage weeds, usually in every second row, while the remaining rows are kept free of weeds mechanically, allowing the soils to breathe and improving the natural regulation of moisture.

The harvest period is significantly later now than even ten years ago. Depending on the individual year, microclimate, area and grape varieties, the main harvest is now in late October to early November, almost a month later than it used to be, though wines in the Burgenland can ripen much earlier and are often harvested between late September and mid-October.

During the harvest, the grapes for top wines are now almost without exception gathered by hand, often in small containers to prevent squashing of the berries and the onset of oxidation. Several harvesting cycles may be required to pick the ripest grapes only and to eliminate grapes affected by noble rot, which may be used on their own, if sufficient in quantity, for nobly sweet wines such as Beerenauslese or Trockenbeerenauslese. A negative harvest, during which unwanted material is deselected (i.e., cut to the ground), may precede the main harvest.

Red wines require the crushing and possibly destemming of the harvested grapes and maceration, the leaving of the must in contact with the solids in order to extract colour and other matter, such as flavour compounds and tannins. Traditional Austrian red wine growers used only minimal maceration periods, leading to light and often dull wines with little ageing potential. Today, more international methods have been adopted for this as well as for the next step in the process, the separating of must and solids by pressing.

There has been enormous investment in cellar technology throughout Austria. Most top growers, especially in the Burgenland and Styria – which have been heavily involved in the recent boom in building new cellars and wineries – press their grapes in modern, gentle presses to avoid extracting unwanted compounds from the grape skins and stems.

Old-fashioned presses often exerted a high degree of mechanical stress on the grape material, for instance by pushing it along the thread of a screw similar to a gigantic corkscrew inside a cylinder. Modern presses, on the other hand, work more slowly and crush the grapes without bruising stalks and skins more than necessary, with the aim of not releasing unwanted compounds into the must. This technology is expensive, and much of the recent investment has been made possible by grants from the European Union, particularly in the Burgenland, which is recognized as an economically deprived area.

Not all good winemakers have put their money on innovation, though. Cellar practices in the Wachau are very largely traditional, and one grower in the Weinviertel, Roland Minkowitsch, makes very interesting wines using a centuries-old tree press, in which the grapes are crushed in a large open vat by a cylindrical disc weighed down by a massive lever made from a tree trunk. Such presses were the norm throughout Austria, but most of the surviving examples are now used to lend a little rustic atmosphere to modern wineries.

The new technology has made it possible to develop entirely new wine styles. Gentle (often pneumatic) presses and an abstention from pumping the unpressed must, for instance, have enabled wine-growers to vinify late-harvested Grüner Veltliner without the wine being made bitter by unwanted elements in the thick grape skins. This resulted in the discovery of an entire new dimension of this grape variety. Nowadays, late harvest of Grüner Veltliner and full fermentation are very much the done thing, in contrast to the old practice of harvesting early, at times before full ripeness of the grapes and certainly before they reached their maximum sugar content, in order to achieve a higher acidity. The resulting full-bodied (and often very alcoholic) wines are among the finest in Austria.

In order to avoid mechanical stress on the must, and later the wine, by pumping it through long pipes between presses, tanks and barrels, some innovative winemakers have recently built gravitation-driven wineries, which work on the simple principle that the grapes enter the system at the highest point and the finished wine leaves it at the lowest. This gentle approach can have a great influence on the potential quality of the wines.

Fermentation is a process during which yeasts transform sugar into alcohol. The sugar content of the must is critical for this, and it is common practice (and quite legal) throughout Europe to chaptalize or 'improve' must of insufficient sugar content by adding beet sugar or concentrated grape juice. This does not necessarily create sweet wines, as the sugar is usually entirely transformed into alcohol. In Austria chaptalization was, as mentioned earlier, common practice before 1985. Today Austrian wine law prohibits it for wine qualities from Kabinett upwards, though the country's better winemakers overwhelmingly reject chaptalization altogether for all their wines, attempting instead to achieve the necessary sugar content by limiting yields and thus working with musts of better quality.

The choice of yeast for fermentation determines the speed and temperature of the fermentation and has a great influence on the aromas of the wines. Grape must contains its own yeast cultures, which will start the process off naturally, but some growers prefer to rely on industrially produced yeasts which give them a predictable pattern of fermentation. A third way is to freeze yeasts from the previous harvest and to use these to start the fermentation with a small quantity of must from grapes picked a few days before the main harvest. This 'ambience yeast' method allows control while using a yeast sympathetic to the local conditions and the must.

Some winemakers will control the temperature of the fermentation closely until they believe they have achieved their goal; others (especially in the Wachau and the Kamptal) feel that the wine must be allowed to find its own equilibrium between alcohol content and residual sugar and should only be heated or cooled during fermentation if the fermenting must is in danger of overheating (and killing the yeast) or cooling down too far and interrupting the process. In the Wachau especially, fermentation is allowed to stop naturally, which can in years such as 1995 lead to wines with a sugar content that is strictly speaking too high for the style of wine pursued there. In Styria, where the acidity of the wines is generally higher, the fashion at the moment is to interrupt fermentation in order to maintain a residual sugar level of three to five grams. The fermentation will stop naturally when the sugar content of the wine is too low or the alcohol content too high for the yeasts to be effective.

After fermentation, the clear wine is drained off from the solids and matured. The wine may or may not be filtered as well, and this process is subject to endless debate, as filtration removes not only unwanted particles but also some elements of flavour. Whether or not a wine is filtered and which method is used differs not only from estate to estate, but often from wine to wine. The wine can also be clarified, using various substances which sink down in the barrel or tank, settling at the bottom together with the unwanted particles. A traditional method which has gained renewed currency is clarification with egg white.

Traditionally, Austrian wines were fermented and matured in

large wooden barrels, which do not impart any flavour to the wine but allow for some air contact through the 'breathing' of the wood. Today, after the usual interlude with concrete tanks, many of which still clutter Austrian cellars, temperature-controlled stainless steel tanks have been installed by most growers, though some use large wooden casks, either as an alternative to steel or for all their wines. Fermentation in steel keeps the wine entirely away from contact with air. This 'reductive' style of winemaking, which prevents the oxidation of the wine, keeps the fresh fruit flavours of the grapes, often at the expense of the complexity and ageing potential of the wine.

In Austria, vinification in steel tanks and large barrels is used for the majority of the simpler wines, as well as for some high-quality wines, notably in Styria and in Lower Austria. This style of wine is often called 'classical' in Austria, as it produces the kind of wines which have always been popular here and which are characterized by good primary fruit and high acidity. Many Austrian wine-growers have a 'classical' line and an 'international' one, which involves fermentation and/or maturation in small oak barrels, though this varies from area to area. In the Wachau, for instance, the overwhelming majority of wines are made without small barrels, though some winemakers prefer using large oak barrels rather than steel tanks.

Small barrels have become very important for the new style of powerful wines that are designed to age, as the wood imparts tannins, lactones and phenolic aldehydes such as vanillin to the wine, adding to its flavour and complexity while allowing a small amount of oxidation through the wood, and stabilizing it for better ageing. These wood characteristics can easily overwhelm the wine, and it is part of the winemaker's craft to attune the use of wood to the individual requirements of different grape varieties, terroirs and vintages. New barrels give off more wood characteristics, and judging the percentage of new to one or two-year-old barrels in order to balance the wine is a delicate matter of choice for the winemaker.

Most of these small casks, in Austria invariably called barriques, are imported from France and made from Allier oak, though Austrian, American, Russian and Slovenian oak are also used, as well as other woods such as acacia. Various degrees of toasting (the exposure of the interior of the barrel to heat, thus altering its chemical qualities) are used, according to the judgement of the individual growers. Wooden barrels are expensive, both because of the wood itself and because of the cooperage, and oak ageing invariably increases the price of a wine.

It was not until recently that Austrian growers discovered the possibility of malolactic fermentation of their wines: that is, a secondary fermentation during which bacteria transform the astringent malic (apple) acid into the mellower and more buttery lactic (milk) acid. This is another arrow in the winemaker's quiver and is used mainly for red wines and big white wines, typically Chardonnays, but also others, such as Pinot blanc and, recently, Grüner Veltliner.

Finally a wine is, if appropriate, aged in casks and then in bottles and released. The process of maturing a wine by ageing it in steel or large or small casks until it has reached a certain point of maturity (*élévation* in French) is called *Ausbau* in German. It, too, is a matter of judgement for the winemaker. While most Austrian wines are drunk young, there is now a trend, especially among red wine-growers, to allow their wines more time to mature before putting them on the market. This is not least a financial issue, but the customers, too, sometimes have to be convinced that a three-year-old wine is not too old to enjoy. Here, as with everything else, some outstanding growers are leading the way. While it is not yet possible to taste the best Austrian wines at the peak of their maturity, one can only hope that this will become more common in the future.

The style of Austrian wines today is very distinctive, though often with a strong international orientation. International or not, Austrian wine now has little to do with that of neighbouring Germany. It is unfortunately true that Austria has adopted the German wine classification system, and it is also true that, like Germany, Austria produces mainly white wines, but the styles and traditions of both countries are very different indeed. The difference, in fact, is increasing, as the majority of young Austrian growers are going their own ways in the search for more individual and often decidedly modern styles. Tempting as it may be to compare the Rieslings of the Wachau with those of the Mosel, I find that, if anything, Austria's Rieslings are more similar to those of Alsace, while the latest wines emerging in Austria are often very modern in style – New World wines, somehow, from the Old World.

Austrians do speak (Austrian) German and their country does border Germany, but it is also worth remembering that it shares the majority of its borders with the Czech Republic, Slovakia, Hungary, Slovenia, Italy and Switzerland. This is central Europe. Road signs in the centre of Vienna point to Prague, Budapest and Brno, not to Munich or Berlin. There is still a considerable pride in the country's Habsburg heritage, and the frontiers of the Habsburg Empire are, understandably, still important for wine traditions in areas with historically fluid borders, such as the Burgenland and Styria.

As already indicated, the sophistication of winemaking during the last ten years has improved astonishingly quickly. On the margins of this metamorphosis, there has also been a record chase for the highest alcohol content in dry wines and residual sugar in sweet ones. Some veritable monsters have been produced in this class: dry wines reaching astronomical alcohol contents of up to 17 per cent through natural fermentation, and concoctions so sweet and so treacly thick that they are almost undrinkable. These, it seems, are phenomena that the winemakers – not to mention the journalists – simply had to get out of their system, and the chase is now practically over, though there is still a certain gleam in the eyes of some growers when they recite their wines' 'technical data'.

Regional styles in brief

Amid all this development, stylistic trends are clearly discernible in the individual regions, and it is worth remembering that some of these wine styles have pedigrees going back centuries.

The Wachau has always had – and indeed claims – a special status. The wines here are almost exclusively white and overwhelmingly made from Grüner Veltliner and Riesling, with a certain amount of Pinot blanc, Pinot gris, and Muskateller.

The Wachau is almost predestined to produce sophisticated and powerful dry wines, with great ageing potential. These belong without doubt to the best produced in Austria, and indeed anywhere in the world. Ageing in small oak casks is almost unknown here, and attitudes are conventional, with technical innovations being adopted sparingly. Some of the best growers still rely on traditional methods, and the general policy is to allow fermentation to cease naturally, which can, as mentioned above, result in relatively high levels of residual sugar in exceptional years.

The best modern Wachau wines emphasize the mineral character of the terroir, and strive to bring out the hallmarks of the individual *Rieden*, which can be very pronounced here. As many of the vineyards are on steep, terraced hills, yields tend to be very low and the wines correspondingly expensive.

There are three kinds of Wachau wine, classified by alcohol content. The most powerful, and usually the best, called Smaragd, have about 12 to 14 per cent alcohol and are very dry. They are generally made to be drinkable straightaway, but some may be somewhat overwhelming initially, and they almost all benefit from ageing for between two and eight years, though some of them can age very much longer, with forty-year-old Rieslings and Grüner Veltliners still showing very well. The two lower designations are Steinfeder and Federspiel.

In nearby Kremstal and Kamptal, attitudes are similar, and so are the wines, if perhaps a little broader, owing to the change in soil. The scope of grapes and winemaking here is a little wider as well, and there are very good Chardonnays, good sparkling wines and some very interesting reds. Pinot noir especially seems to find here everything it needs. Until now these reds have been a sideline, but some growers are beginning to recognize their considerable potential. The growers in this region often use more modern vinification methods, and display more openness to such innovations as new oak. Kremstal and Kamptal wines can be beautifully luscious.

In the other regions of Lower Austria (Carnuntum, the Thermenregion, the Donauland, the Weinviertel and the Traisental) the wine quality tends to depend very much more on the individual grower, though there are pockets with specific soil characteristics that are recognized for their potential. In these regions most wines are still overwhelmingly simple in style, though there can also be excellent individual results.

In the Thermenregion, the more ambitious wines now tend to be made from international grape varieties such as Chardonnay or Pinot noir, but so far success is still limited to a handful of producers. The majority of the wines made here, though, are the local white wine varietals Zierfandler and Rotgipfler, vinified as a cuvée or individually, which can be powerful, but often are quite simple.

In Carnuntum, more than half the wines are red, made from Austrian varieties such as Zweigelt and Blaufränkisch. The chief white varieties are Welschriesling and Pinot blanc. The Donauland is a relatively small area producing mainly Grüner Veltliner, Riesling and Pinot blanc. It is beginning to acquire a distinctive profile in terms of style and quality.

The Weinviertel is the largest wine producing area in Austria. It produces mainly Grüner Veltliners, which the growers like to describe as 'crisp and fruity' and pleasant for easy drinking. Among those cultivating its 18,000 hectares of vineyards, though, are some who are extraordinarily innovative, and this region will repay closer investigation.

Vienna, or the hills surrounding it – historically some of the best crus – mainly supplies the local *Heurige* industry with Grüner Veltliner and Welschriesling. However, there is also some fine Pinot blanc, Pinot gris and Chardonnay.

The Burgenland is a law unto itself, or rather several laws. The eastern shore of Lake Neusiedl mainly produces sweet wines of great distinction, for which the region has become justly famous. A little north of the lake and around its upper half, some of the best Austrian red wines are produced, a few of them of truly international calibre.

There is a clear trend in this region to find an Austrian idiom for these wines, while integrating the potential of oak ageing and other modern winemaking methods. The regional style is achieved mainly by using indigenous grapes in the cuvées, not by going for easy, primary fruit. The white wines, too, can be excellent, especially Chardonnay, which can be cultivated here to produce a complexity that leaves many a good Burgundian in its shadow. This region, called Neusiedlersee-Hügelland, also has a strong culture of vinifying wines by crus. The town of Rust on the western side of the lake occupies a special position with its Ausbruch sweet wines, as well as very good dry wines.

Further south in the Burgenland, we come into Austria's main red wine producing area. The style here tends to be Austrian traditional, with an emphasis on good, immediate fruit aromas and, by now, oak tones. These are not wines for long ageing, although there are exceptions. South Burgenland is one of the hot spots of new building activity and experimentation, and many growers pride themselves on their computer-controlled wineries. If used too enthusiastically, these 'computer wines' can be a little uniform in character, and it is a standing joke that the young winemakers of this region go to California to gather experience, while those of the Wachau prefer to travel to Burgundy. The main grape varieties currently are Blaufränkisch and Zweigelt, with a small but increasing quota of international varieties, such as Cabernet Sauvignon, Pinot noir and Merlot.

Styria, only a few kilometres away, is very different indeed. These are perhaps the most internationally-styled wines produced in Austria: Chardonnay and Sauvignon blanc, vinified both in New World fashion and *à l'autrichienne*. At their best, these are as good as anything produced in the world. The excellent Pinot blanc and Pinot gris from this region tend to be very much underestimated.

South-East Styria is the largest of the three wine-growing regions within Styria. Nine out of ten of the wines made here are white: mainly Welschriesling, Traminer, Sauvignon blanc, Pinot blanc, Müller-Thurgau and Riesling. The only red grape to be found here frequently is Zweigelt, which incidentally was tested here originally. Despite the size of the region, the overall quality of the wines here still has great room for improvement.

The smallest of the Styrian regions, South Styria, still has the largest area under vines and a great number of the state's finest producers. The wines here, Welschriesling, excellent Sauvignon blanc and Chardonnay, Pinot gris and Pinot blanc, are almost exclusively white. This region has demonstrated its enormous promise, which is exploited by a few producers who have made great names for themselves. It is very possible that others will follow soon.

West Styria is known for a single wine, a rarity, the Schilcher, a very acidic rosé, made as a refreshing summer wine from the Blauer Wildbacher grape. The landscape here can be very beautiful, as indeed in all of Styria.

There are some vineyards outside these official wine-growing regions, in Vorarlberg especially, but most of these are smaller than one hectare and have neither economic nor culinary significance.

This, then, is a bird's-eye view of Austrian wine and its regions. If any generalization is possible, it might be fair to say that Austria is now producing, apart from simple, fruity white wines, a range of wines staking a strong claim on the international stage. What makes them distinctively Austrian, apart from indigenous grape varieties, is perhaps their emphasis on early drinkability, an attractive primary fruit and good acidity. The best wines are usually high in alcohol, too.

Beyond this, it is simply too early to tell. Despite a wine-growing tradition of more than two thousand years, Austria in its present incarnation is still a very young wine country, full of innovation and experimentation, and in many regions still in the process of defining the identity of what are and what will be her very best wines.

Legal framework

Austrian wine legislation is among the strictest in Europe, partly a response to the 1985 scandal. With Austria's entry into the European Union in 1995, Austrian wine laws were brought into line with EU legislation. In some respects, however, they remain even stricter than those of other countries within the EU.

The legal framework is drawn essentially from the German system of classification, which is regarded by many commentators as a misfortune for Austrian wines. There are moves afoot to change this. German wine law classifies wine largely according to the sugar content of the grapes when harvested (the so-called 'sugar pyramid'). The French system, by contrast, is based on the geographical origin and typicality of the wines. The major disadvantage of the German system is its underlying assumption that high sugar contents and alcohol gradations are equivalent to a higher quality of wine. This clearly does not always hold true, and in any case says little about the character of the wine. German-style classification also means that labels can be difficult to understand for non-specialists and for those who do not read German.

To make things even more difficult, the sugar content of the grape must is not measured in Beaumé or Öchsle, but in KMW (Klosterneuburger Mostwaage), a system measuring the must weight of the grape material, which in itself is very coherent and practical, but does nothing to make for easier understanding by foreigners. The following small conversion table may be of some help in this respect:

Öchsle	Beaumé	KMW
73	9.8	15
84	11.2	17.1
94	12.4	19
105	21	21
127	25	25

The quality categories according to Austrian wine law are as follows:

TAFELWEIN: the simplest wines, with a minimum 10.6° KMW.

LANDWEIN: minimum 14° KMW. Treated as Tafelwein, but must originate from a specific wine-growing area and must be made from legally sanctioned grape varietals. Maximum yield per hectare 9,000 kg.

QUALITÄTSWEIN: minimum 15° KMW. The must may be chaptalized by up to 4.25 kg of sugar per 100 litres, up to a maximum 19° KMW for white wines, 20° KMW for reds. Alcohol content must be a maximum of 9 per cent for whites and 8.5 per cent for reds.

KABINETT: minimum 17° KMW. Regarded as a Qualitätswein, but must not be chaptalized. Maximum alcohol content 12.7 per cent. Residual sugar must not be higher than 9 gm per litre.

PRÄDIKATSWEIN: must not be chaptalized; residual sugar must be the result of either interruption of fermentation or natural ending of the fermentation process. No concentrated grape juice may be added. Grape material must come from a designated wine-growing area. Export is only in bottles, not in tanks. May not be sold before 1 May, with the exception of Spätlese, which may be sold after 1 March.

SPÄTLESE: minimum 19° KMW. Grapes must be fully ripe. May not be sold before 1 March.

AUSLESE: minimum 21° KMW. All faulty or unripe grapes must be excluded.

BEERENAUSLESE (BA): minimum 25° KMW. Produced from over-ripe grapes or grapes affected by noble rot (botrytis).

AUSBRUCH (produced only in the Neusiedlersee region): minimum 27° KMW. Produced from nobly rotten, overripe grapes or naturally shrivelled grapes. Fresh grape must, Auslese or Beerenauslese from the same cru may be added for harmony.

TROCKENBEERENAUSLESE (TBA): minimum 30° KMW. Produced from overripe grapes, naturally shrivelled grapes and those affected by noble rot.

EISWEIN: minimum 25° KMW. Grapes must be frozen when harvested and pressed.

STROHWEIN: minimum 25° KMW. Produced from overripe grapes which are stored and air-dried on straw or reeds for at least three months.

BERGWEIN: wine made from grapes grown on slopes or terraces with a steepness of over 26 per cent.

There is a special regulation for Wachau wines, containing three quality steps:

STEINFEDER: maximum alcohol content 10.7 per cent.

FEDERSPIEL: minimum of 17° KMW, maximum alcohol content 11.9 per cent.

SMARAGD: minimum 18° KMW. Minimum alcohol content 12 per cent (no maximum).

The members of the Wachau association Vinea Wachau Nobilis Districtus follow a strict policy of not chaptalizing their wines and of taking sugar and alcohol contents as ripeness and natural fermentation dictate.

Sugar content of the wines:

TROCKEN (dry): up to 9 gm residual sugar, if the total acidity is less than the residual sugar by a maximum of 2 gm per litre.

HALBTROCKEN (semi-dry): up to 12 gm per litre residual sugar.

LIEBLICH (sweet): up to 45 gm per litre residual sugar.

süß (sweet): over 45 gm per litre residual sugar.

Wines harvested before 1995, apart from Landwein, must have a paper banderole or cap in the Austrian national colours: red-white-red. After 1995, this banderole was supplanted by a conventional plastic or paper bottle cap with the national colours on top of it.

Wines of a higher category than Landwein and Tafelwein must have a Staatliche Prüfnummer (official analysis number), which is allocated after chemical analysis of the wine.

Labels must list the ABFÜLLER, the estate or firm filling the wine into bottles or other containers. Erzeugerabfüllung is a designation allowed where the wine has been filled into bottles by the producer.

Recently, Austria's sixteen wine regions have been 'expanded' to eighteen by the invention of the regions of Weinland Österreich (comprising Lower Austria and Burgenland, but not Vienna) and Bergland Österreich (the remainder of Austria without Styria). These are two purely administrative terms allowing wine producers in the areas Lower Austria, Burgenland and in other Austrian regions to produce and label their wines as the higher Qualitäts-wein and not, as previously declared by law, only as Landwein, even if the wine comes from the general region and not from an already recognized area. A bureaucratic feat in the best tradition of the administrative casuistry of the Habsburg empire, this change allows especially smaller wine producers to simplify their range (which is much needed) by making one Qualitätswein which reflects the region instead of several ones from individual denomi-nations.

There is currently a potentially very important debate going on in Austria, namely whether to adopt the French appellation system for Austrian wines and to move away from the German system completely. The German system is based on the very contestable assumption that the sugar content of a wine is in some way indica-tive of quality. In addition, the German-language labelling system makes the wines less approachable for foreigners.

Many progressive growers with an eye to export markets now argue for a French-style wine law, especially since the idea of crus (particular vineyards with particular characteristics) has gained currency recently, a concept that had indeed existed since the

Middle Ages. Moreover, the grape varietals best suited to each area are now much better understood.

A good proportion of the top growers are *de facto* already abandoning the German system by writing on the labels of their wines not the German-style gradations of wine, but adopting a (confusing) variety of systems for naming their steel and oak fermented wines or their lighter and their more substantial (and often better) wines. In the Wachau this is done with Steinfeder, Federspiel and Smaragd, while many others use terms like 'classic' for a lighter style of wine fermented in steel. As a result of this, it is anything but easy for a casual wine lover to find his or her way through this maze.

It would therefore seem a good idea to adopt a French-style system in which an *appellation contrôlée* gives an indication of a wine typicality, with a limited number of grape varietals allowed to be sold under the name of this appellation (while wines made from other grape varietals could still be sold under the area name without the appellation). It also seems reasonable to tie wine quality to particularly good plots of land, instead of to the sugar content reached by the must at the time of harvest.

This combination of appellation, cru and producer would be a far simpler indication of quality and character than the present system, and would have the great additional advantage of being familiar to wine lovers all over the world, most of whom cannot be expected to take the trouble to learn the Austrian system (or, by now, systems) solely in order to understand Austrian wines. A scheme of this kind would of course be far from foolproof – no system is perfect, but I believe it to have a potential far greater than the current one. However, many growers, especially the smaller, less well-known growers who may not produce the 'typical' grape varietals of one area, are opposed to this idea, decrying it as bureaucratic and inflexible. It may yet be possible to win them over.

Grape Varieties

Percentages in brackets indicate the share of a grape of the entire area under vines.

White grapes

BOUVIER (<1 per cent)
A soft, fat grape variety named after Clothar Bouvier, who culti-vated it on his estate in Bad Radkersburg in Styria at the end of the nineteenth century. It was probably brought into Austria from Slovenia, and to there from Switzerland. Today it is mainly used for botrytis wines, where it can achieve good quality, and for the popular Sturm, i.e. wine drunk during fermentation in country inns, and produced almost exclusively in the Burgenland, with some additional vineyards in Vienna and Styria. Bouvier needs fertile soils and ripens early. On its own it tends to lack acidity and character, and is therefore often blended with Welschriesling in order to soften the wine. It is golden in colour and has an aroma reminiscent of Muscat. There is also some Bouvier grown in Hungary.

CHARDONNAY (Styria: MORILLON, Wachau: FEINBURGUNDER) (1 per cent)
Officially, Austria did not have any Chardonnay until 1986, when suddenly 300 hectares appeared on the map. The reason for this miraculous transformation was that nobody had realized that the Styrian Morillon and some of the supposed Pinot blanc in Lower Austria and the Burgenland were in fact Chardonnay. It was legally recognized as Chardonnay and sanctioned as a Qualitätswein only in 1986. Chardonnay can therefore be regarded as a traditional

Austrian variety, certainly at least as much as other, more recent arrivals which are thought of as typically Austrian, such as Zweigelt and Blauburger.

Chardonnay's recent popularity is based on the fact that it can produce big, buttery wines with a strong oak background as well as leaner, fruity wines in most parts of the wine producing world. Because of this facility in adapting to most soils, climates and wine styles, Chardonnay has become an international runaway hit and brand name, the wine everybody loves to drink and wine buffs love to hate. The origins of this grape variety lie in Burgundy, where Chardonnay is used to make most white wines. From there, it has been exported to all parts of the new wine world, and many parts of the old world.

In Austria, Chardonnay has more than a century of history, and can therefore not be said simply to be a 'fashionable' variety. After the phylloxera catastrophe, Chardonnay shoots were imported into Styria from the village of Morion in Champagne where it established itself as Morillon, a name it has retained in Styria until today. Chardonnay produced here is among the best in Austria, surpassed only, perhaps, by those of the Neusiedlersee-Hügelland, where Chardonnays of truly international calibre are made, perhaps softer than their Styrian cousins, which tend to be more broadly structured and with more pronounced varietal fruit. The Chardonnays of the Wachau are more of a sideline compared with Grüner Veltliner and Riesling; they are often dense and lean, and usually fermented in steel or in large barrels.

In general there are both international, oaked Chardonnays and a leaner, more traditional 'classical' line in Austria. The latter is vinified reductively in steel tanks (and occasionally in large barrels) and without malolactic fermentation to emphasize the finesse of the fruit and the acidity. Most growers will vinify some of each. After initial over-enthusiasm for new oak, there are some beautifully balanced Chardonnays now being made, especially in Styria and the Burgenland, where the variety finds the gentle slopes and poor, limey soils it prefers without being subjected to frosts too frequently.

FURMINT (GELBER FURMINT, MOSLER, ZAPFNER) (<1 per cent)
In Hungary, Furmint is the main ingredient of Tokay wines. Just across the border, in the Burgenland, it is now making a slow

comeback for Ausbruch and other sweet wines. Furmint is thought to have been brought to Austria by Italian immigrants who were admitted to Hungary during the thirteenth century. It is high in acidity and has a reputation for being difficult to grow, requiring the warm, dry soils found only in the best vineyards and producing yields of widely varying quantities. Some growers, especially in Rust, have good successes with it, though, and are often rewarded with its finely tuned aromas and high alcohol and acidity. As the variety ripens late and has relatively thin skins, it is particularly sensitive to noble rot, which makes it an ideal candidate for producing Ausbruch.

FRÜHROTER VELTLINER (MALVASIER) (1 per cent)
No relative of the Grüner Veltliner, despite its name, the Frühroter Veltliner is related to Malvoisie grapes and is thought to have originated in Greece, being imported to Austria via northern Italy. Originally used in the Gemischter Satz, it is now also planted as an individual variety, especially in Lower Austria, and traditionally also extensively in the Thermenregion. It is not easy to master, being very sensitive to frost and yielding often neutral wines with little acidity and high alcohol. It is tolerant of lime and thrives on dry soils, where it belongs to the early-ripening varieties. Although Malvoisie grapes are planted around the world, especially in Italy, the Frührote Veltliner is cultivated almost exclusively in Austria. The wines produced from this grape variety are hardly ever of very high quality. At their best, they have a pleasant, earthy aroma reminiscent of bitter almond, but their low acidity and high alcohol often make them unbalanced.

GOLDBURGER (<1 per cent)
A new variety (1922), a crossing of Welschriesling and Orangentraube made by the Austrian wine pioneer F. Zweigelt. It has gold-coloured skins and ripens well on poor soils, mainly around the Neusiedlersee, in the Weinviertel and in South-East Styria. As dry wine it tends to lack character, but as it tends to reach high must weights it can be be used for sweet wines up to TBA.

GRÜNER VELTLINER (37 per cent)
The most common grape in Austria by far, but also found in other east European countries. Only in recent years has it been discovered to be extraordinarily versatile as well as reliable. It began its

unstoppable conquest of more than a third of all Austrian vineyards only after the Second World War, when the ethos of cheap and efficient production of white wines made it an ideal candidate for the newly developed Lenz Moser training system of vines. Before that it had been known in Austria as Grüner Muskateller, and is thought to have been grown in Austria even in Roman times, though the first reliable documentation dates from the eighteenth century.

While Austria's *Heurige* culture would be inconceivable without the grape, growers in the Wachau, the Kamptal, Kremstal and also in the Weinviertel, the Donauland and the Traisental have begun to vinify it as a high-quality wine. In its most simple incarnation it is pleasantly fruity, with notes of pepper and grapefruit, but it can evolve into extraordinarily complex wines with aromas reminding one of tropical fruit, pineapple and even walnuts, backed up by high acidity and alcohol, the latter of which is sometimes overdone in Austria.

Although eminently drinkable in their youth, the best wines have an extraordinary ageing potential and will have lost nothing of their power and structure after thirty years. The grape is often compared to Riesling but, growing in the same areas, especially the Wachau, great Grüner Veltliners often age better than Riesling. Those grown on primary rock miraculously take on a buttery depth and complexity otherwise only found in white Burgundian grands crus (i.e. Chardonnays) – with which they are sometimes confused in blind tastings – while Grüner Veltliners from the loess and loam soils in the Kamptal and Kremstal can acquire an ageing note reminiscent of Riesling. As the revolution in Austrian winemaking took place relatively recently, it is not yet possible to gauge the full ageing potential of Grüner Veltliners produced with all the benefits of modern vinification knowledge and techniques, but some Veltliners from the 1960s and even the 1950s still retain their youthfulness and structure and are wonderfully enjoyable.

As already mentioned, Grüner Veltliners often display tones of honey, citrus and grapefruit with a distinctive peppery note during their youth. Wines from riper grape material tend to have pronounced tropical fruit aromas, while the Veltliners of the Wachau also display a remarkable mineral backbone. Depending on vinification, the wines can be light and fragrant or powerful battleships, often weighing in at 14 to 15 per cent alcohol, a strength only the best winemakers are able to control. It is, however, also high in acidity and often manages to balance out its sheer power.

A supremely adaptable variety, Grüner Veltliner takes well to poor and to fat soils, to loess and to lime, and can yield up to a hundred hectolitres per hectare. For high-quality wines, however, the yields have to be limited severely, at times down to around twenty hectolitres per hectare on the steep terraces of the Wachau, where it finds its most reliably excellent expression. The best and most characteristic results are achieved on primary rock soils, such as those in the Wachau and the Kamptal, where it can produce wines which are a beautiful expression of their terroir. On loam and loess, if not treated with the greatest care, the wines can become too fat and lose character.

Grüner Veltliner is planted throughout Austria, overwhelmingly in the Weinviertel, where it produces spicy and quaffable wines. In the Kamptal, Grüner Veltliners can be excellent, if not quite as lean as in the Wachau. In the other wine growing areas of Austria, it is mainly used for simple wines without great distinction.

Grüner Veltliner can be found throughout eastern Europe, and is cultivated in the Sopron district of Hungary, where it is known as Zöldveltelini, in the Czech Republic and in Slovakia as Veltlin Zelene or Veltlinske Zelené, in Yugoslavia, and in Germany. Experiments with the variety in New York State did not prove successful, but Grüner Veltliner seems an ideal candidate for export to New World countries.

MÜLLER-THURGAU (RIESLING/SYLVANER, RIVANER) (8 per cent)
Described by Jancis Robinson as 'the bane of German wine production', this varietal was developed in Geisenheim, Germany, in 1882 as a crossing of Riesling and Sylvaner, though it is now thought to be a crossing of two Riesling grapes, or possibly Riesling and Chasselas. Whatever it was, it was not a success in qualitative terms, and there is little or no Müller-Thurgau of true interest around.

The grape can be grown in most conditions and on most soils, ripens early and produces bountifully, especially on fertile soils and in cool climates: 150 hl/ha (more in some years), almost twice what can be expected from Riesling. In Germany, it is synonymous with the dreaded Liebfraumilch. In Austria, it is also responsible for mass-produced wines, especially in the Burgenland. If treated with great care, Müller-Thurgau can produce wines similar to Riesling in fruit, though not in depth and structure. It can also have a pronounced Muscat aroma. Low alcohol and acid content do not help to give it great character. It is still very common, especially at the lower end of the market, but is now progressively being abandoned by more ambitious growers in favour of grapes of higher quality. The demise of this variety is no great loss.

MUSKATELLER (GELBER MUSKATELLER, MUSCAT-LUNEL) (<1 per cent)
Cultivated since the fifteenth century, Muskateller (a gold-skinned variation of the French Muscat blanc) is still one of the most consistent grape varieties in Austria. A late-ripening variety with a preference for sandy or gravelly soils, Austrian Muskatellers are produced mainly in the Wachau, in South-Eastern Styria and in the Burgenland, especially around Rust, where they are used for Ausbruch wines, turning their sensitivity to rot into an advantage. There are beautiful dry Muskatellers made in the Wachau, where it is light and aromatic, with a characteristic aroma of roses and nutmeg. In Styria, a more muscular version has evolved during the last ten years.

MUSKAT-OTTONEL (1 per cent)
A variety held in great affection by some growers despite its often low yields, Muskat-Ottonel produces mild wines with low alcohol and acidity. Its name probably derives from confusing it with the French Muscat-Lunel, which is in fact another name for Muskateller. Like the latter, Muskat-Ottonel ripens late and is sensitive to diseases, noble rot among them. It was popular in Austria in the 1960s and 1970s, but there is little Muskat-Ottonel cultivated now, mainly in the Burgenland. With its intensive Muscat aroma and light fruit it can be vinified dry as an aperitif wine. Nowadays, however, it is more commonly used in nobly sweet wines, especially in the Neusiedlersee region, where it can often be found in cuvées.

NEUBURGER (GRÜNER BURGUNDER) (3 per cent)
This is the Moses of the Austrian varieties; according to legend it was fished out of the Danube in the 1860s and planted in the Wachau. An Austrian variety by origin, it may be a chance offspring of Pinot blanc and Sylvaner, but is treated as a Burgundian grape and often vinified in casks, where it can produce wines with good

ageing potential, a nutty, fleshy character and very pleasant acidity. The dual heritage of this grape can still be guessed at: the grapes look similar to Sylvaner, but the aroma of its wines is definitely Burgundian and akin to Pinot blanc. Neuburger is a relatively early ripener and prefers crystalline, dry to heavy soils. It is grown throughout the Austrian wine producing areas with the exception of Styria. It also makes good botrytis wines. After the war it was used for unremarkable, sweetish wines and this reputation is still dogging it. Today, however, it has been recognized that Neuburger can make wines of considerable complexity and interest.

PINOT BLANC (WEISSER BURGUNDER, WEISSBURGUNDER, KLEVNER) (4 per cent)

A relatively late arrival in the world of grape varieties, Pinot blanc is a mutation of Pinot gris that was first observed in Burgundy at the end of the nineteenth century and was long confused with Chardonnay, which it resembles very closely. Popular in Alsace, in Germany and in Italy, it is known in Austria as Weißburgunder or Klevner. Pinot blanc is a demanding variety and needs very good conditions in order to ripen well. It prefers deep, chalky soils with plenty of nutrients and good sun exposure and will not yield high quantities. If and when these requirements are met, especially in the Burgenland, in Styria, the Wachau, the Kamptal and other parts of Lower Austria, Pinot blanc can achieve good must weight and can be made into beautifully full-bodied wines, which are characteristically fat, round and almond-scented, high in alcohol and often very powerful, with plenty of ageing potential.

PINOT GRIS (GRAUER BURGUNDER, GRAUBURGUNDER, RULÄNDER) (<1 per cent)

A white mutation of Pinot noir, *the* red grape in Burgundy, this grape was probably brought to Austria in the thirteenth century by Cistercian monks. In Alsace it is widely grown and for some mysterious reason known as Tokay. Now that the world has been flooded with cheap versions of the Italian incarnation of the grape, Pinot Grigio, it has a bad press. In the appropriate conditions and on the right soil, however, it can produce soft and gracious wines with lovely fruit and full body. Styria seems to offer ideal conditions for this variety. Here it develops the acidity necessary to give it bite and can be made into truly remarkable wines, though it tends to be underestimated even in Styria – obviously a case of the prophet not being recognized in his own land.

RIESLING (RHEINRIESLING) (3 per cent)

Sometimes called the queen of white grapes, Riesling is not important in quantitative terms in Austria but hugely important in terms of quality. Long regarded as the German grape *par excellence*, Riesling is one of the few white varieties to age well for many decades, and it can produce great wines which may be very dry, high in residual sugar, or affected by noble rot. Famous for its combination of acidity and fruit extract, the typical taste of Riesling is often described as flowery yet tart, with petrol overtones in maturity, and always strongly determined by its terroir.

Riesling is thought to have originated in the Pfalz region of Germany, though some authors still believe that a vineyard by the name of Rizling in the Wachau may in fact be the oldest recorded place of Riesling cultivation.

The grape is famously wedded to its terroir and is often thought to provide the most perfect expression of the conditions it finds in soil, microclimate and weather conditions. While Riesling will grow on most soil types, it is sensitive to high chalk content and will not develop into wines of great character on loess or loam. The wood of Riesling vines is harder than that of many others, and the grape is consequently not very sensitive to frost, although it does need sheltered, south-facing vineyards with good sun exposure to ripen fully and yield the best quality grape material.

In view of its sensitivity to terroir, it is not surprising that in Austria Riesling is very much associated not only with particular areas – the Wachau and the Kamptal – but with particular vineyards that have long been known to offer ideal conditions for its cultivation: dry, deep soils of primary rock, able to retain the warmth of the sun and to release it gradually for the benefit of the vines. In the Kamptal, Zöbinger Heiligenstein, Lamm and Gaisberg are famous for Rieslings, while in the Wachau there are various renowned Riesling crus, among them Singerriedel, Steinborz, Achspoint and Tausend-Eimer-Berg in Spitz; Hochrain and Kollmitz in Wösendorf; Pichlpoint in Joching; Achleiten in Weißenkirchen; Kellerberg in Dürnstein; and Loibenberg in Loiben – all of which, incidentally, are also great crus for Grüner Veltliner.

While the Rieslings of the Wachau are justly famous for their vigour, complexity and their strong mineral note, those of the Kamptal and the nearby Kremstal tend to be a little fuller, while the Rieslings around Vienna are much broader and less concentrated. The Austrian Riesling idiom is closer to that of Alsace than to that of Germany: often high in alcohol and extract with clear mineral character and usually vinified dry, though there are some nobly rotten Rieslings in years which lend themselves to this vinification.

ROTER VELTLINER (ROTER MUSKATELLER) (<1 per cent)

A mutation of Grüner Veltliner. If the yield is kept down, this grape variety can show very good fruit and finesse. It is, however, sensitive to frost, rain and rot, and needs fat loam and loess soils to mature fully. It can produce high yields, but tends to be unreliable and achieves good qualities only when yields are restricted radically. Most of this wine is made in the Weinviertel, in Wagram, in the Kamptal, and around Krems and Gedersdorf. Both the dry and sweet varieties can be successful. Nowadays a rarity, it is by no means negligible and can produce quite beautiful wines, especially in the Kamptal.

ROTGIPFLER (<1 per cent)

Probably originating in Styria, the Rotgipfler has now firmly established itself in the Thermenregion, where it is often used in cuvée with its twin brother Zierfandler. Rotgipfler is certainly the lesser of the brothers: late ripening, very demanding in terms of soil and location, and sensitive to wind chill and botrytis, it can produce some full-bodied wines that are capable of ageing. At its best, Rotgipfler is expressive with marked acidity and golden colour. Often, though, it produces light and fresh wines that are not remarkable for sophistication and complexity. Often used in a cuvée with Zierfandler which is called Spätrot-Rotgipfler.

SAUVIGNON BLANC (MUSKAT-SYLVANER) (<1 per cent)

The global Sauvignon blanc boom has produced its fair share of techno wines in Austria as in everywhere else. Traditionally, this grape variety is used for Sancerre and Pouilly-Fumé in France, but its easily recognizable fruit reminiscent of gooseberries, capsicum, grass and what is at times described as 'tomcat' has helped to make it one of the most popular grape varieties in the world.

There are producers in Austria who have made this variety their passion, and especially in Southern Styria it is capable of great things. Sauvignon blanc ripens late and needs fertile, not too dry soils to flourish, which it gets in Styria as well as in parts of the northern Burgenland. There is also some Sauvignon blanc in the Kamptal and in Vienna. Styrian growers are convinced they are producing some of the best Sauvignon blanc in the world, and recent vintages have borne out this enthusiasm. Some of these wines have wonderful fruit and a complexity equal to the very best produced in the New World. In other parts of Austria, Sauvignon blancs can be a valuable added string to the wine-grower's bow, without reaching the dizzying heights of their Styrian counterparts.

SCHEUREBE (SÄMLING 88) (<1 per cent)
Originating in Alzey in 1916 from a crossing of Riesling and Sylvaner (unlike Müller-Thurgau, which is often called Riesling × Sylvaner but is not), the Scheurebe, named after its inventor Dr Georg Scheu – and sometimes after its greenhouse name Sämling ('seedling') 88 – produces good yields, regularly reaches a high must weight and is popular in Germany, where it can produce some interesting wines. It places few demands on the soil, but needs good vineyards in order to mature fully. It is also sensitive to frost. In Austria, Scheurebe wines are often quite bland when vinified dry. Prone to botrytis, it is, however, a good varietal for the production of nobly rotten wines, both on its own and in cuvées. In this incarnation it is quite common around the Neusiedlersee, especially in Illmitz.

SYLVANER (<1 per cent)
Probably originating in Austria (in Germany it used to be called Österreicher) and still common in Alsace and in Franken in Germany, this variety used to be more common before the introduction of the high training of grapes in Austria. Copious in yield and high in acid, this early ripener is a typical workhorse varietal that rarely produces exciting wines. It used to be widely planted in the Burgenland and after its almost total demise it is now occasionally planted again as a light aperitif wine. Nevertheless, its earthy and often bland aromas have not made it many friends in Austria.

TRAMINER (GEWÜRZTRAMINER, GELBER TRAMINER, ROTER TRAMINER, WEISSER TRAMINER) (<1 per cent)
A pink-skinned grape, Gewürztraminer – as its most common clone

is called in Germany and Alsace – is one of the oldest known grapes, and is documented as having been grown in Austria, in Tyrol, around the year 1000. In Alsace, Gewürztraminer belongs to the 'triumvirate' of white grapes, together with Riesling and Pinot gris.

Traminer mutates easily between the varietals Gewürztraminer, Roter Traminer and Weißer Traminer, and there is a certain amount of confusion between them. According to the ampelographer Pierre Galet, Gewürztraminer is a varietal of Traminer, which is also called Roter Traminer in Austria, Savagnin Rosé in France and Klevner d'Heiligenstein in Alsace (not to be confused, of course, with Pinot noir, which is sometimes called Klevner in Austria). Gewürztraminer, the most popular mutation of the Roter Traminer, is also called Gelber Traminer in Austria and Savagnin Rosé Aromatique in some areas of France.

The last Traminer grape, Weißer Traminer, is called Savagnin blanc in France, and, just to compound the chaos, Gelber Traminer in some parts of Styria. Traminer grapes are also grown under different names in eastern Europe.

In Austria, different cousins of the Traminer family are often planted together in one vineyard and can be distinguished in autumn by the different colour of their berries, especially in the case of the Roter Traminer and Gewürztraminer. Ripening late, Traminer prefers warm and deep soils. Occasionally there are quite exceptional Traminers in Austria, Muscat-like and full-bodied with rose and lychee notes on the nose. They typically have a deep golden colour and can have a very high alcohol content. Traminer is scattered all over Austria, with the notable exception of the Wachau. There are fine exponents of this variety in the Burgenland and in Styria, but there are also very good Traminers in the Weinviertel.

Traminer grapes are grown in small quantities throughout the wine growing world, but Alsace is still its spiritual and qualitative home.

WELSCHRIESLING (10 per cent)

Welschriesling is the second most commonly grown grape variety in Austria after its almighty cousin, Grüner Veltliner. As indicated by its name, which translates as 'foreign Riesling', it is not related to the Riesling. Its origins are lost in the mists of time, though the name points to an origin outside Austria, possibly in Romania.

High in acidity, Welschriesling is most commonly used for simple, light wines for summer drinking. It needs deep, warm and nutrient-rich soils and ripens late, best in sheltered, south-facing vineyards. Most Welschriesling is grown in the Burgenland, in Lower Austria and in Styria. It is mostly vinified as a classic *Heurige* wine for drinking in country inns and on a hot summer's day. It is usually distinguished by good acidity and an appealing green apple fruit. In the hands of good growers it can be made into wines with fine, lemony acidity, and is an ideal cuvée partner for sweet wines up to TBA, especially around Lake Neusiedl, where, according to Jancis Robinson, it reaches its apogee.

ZIERFANDLER (Spätrot-Rotgipfler) (<1 per cent)
Usually planted in tandem with Rotgipfler in the Thermenregion, Zierfandler makes lean, spicy wines up to the higher reaches of the Prädikat range and is distinguished by an aroma reminiscent of quinces. Botanically it is a relation of the Grüner Veltliner, without having either the latter's potential for depth or its adaptability. It is certainly superior to its brother Rotgipfler in this region; it can be full-bodied, high in alcohol (up to 15 per cent) and have good ageing potential. A cuvée of Zierfandler and Rotgipfler is called Spätrot-Rotgipfler.

Despite its name, Zierfandler is no relation to the Zinfandel which has made such an impact on Californian winemaking. Zierfandler is very much a local speciality, though some is also produced in Hungary, where it is called Cirfandli. Many international wine experts feel, though, that the beautiful slopes and chalk-rich, gravelly soils around Gumpoldskirchen which it needs to ripen have potential that is not exhausted by this variety and could be better realized by others, perhaps even Burgundian ones.

Red grapes

BLAUBURGER (<1 per cent)
Created in 1922 by the legendary Professor Zweigelt from Blauer Portugieser × Blaufränkisch, two other Austrian varieties, Blauburger's main claim to fame seems to be that it can lend colour to pallid reds without, however, being capable of being made into

great wines itself. Undemanding, the variety is nevertheless sensitive to frost, mildew and rot. It can still be found throughout Austria, in the Weinviertel, the Kamptal, Carnuntum, Thermenregion, around Lake Neusiedl, and, in small quantities, in Styria and in Vienna.

BLAUFRÄNKISCH (5 per cent)

Documented first in Austria in the second half of the eighteenth century, Blaufränkisch is, after Zweigelt, the most important red grape variety in the country. Its name suggests that its origins are probably medieval, when by Charlemagne's decree the superior grape varieties were called *fränkisch*, or 'Franconian'. This would mean that Blaufränkisch was already well established in the eighth century. In the nineteenth century the variety was called Blauer Frankentaler, and a great many legends are in circulation, both about this name and about the origin of the variety.

The best wines from this grape are made in the middle and south Burgenland, where it can create powerful, tannic wines with characteristic pepper and bramble fruit. Here, where the grape has swept to victory over the last thirty years and now represents the majority stock, the wine-growers even call their part of the world 'Blaufränkischland'. Here it finds the deep, nutrient-rich soils it needs to flourish. It is tolerant of chalky soils, but needs good exposure to sun and shelter against strong winds, all of which are provided by the gentle hills of the middle and south Burgenland. There is a small-berried and a large-berried variety, the latter of which produces more rustic wines.

Blaufränkisch wines have a characteristic midnight-blue colouring, the darkest of all red wines made in Austria. If the vines are cut back and the yields kept limited, Blaufränkisch can have an overwhelming, deep bouquet of cassis, bramble and pepper, and very characteristic notes of liquorice and dark berry fruits, with notably high acid. In smaller years green aromas can dominate, but recently, notably in 1997, the grape has realized its potential. The most ambitious growers treat it very much like Syrah and vinify Blaufränkisch in small, new oak. The result can be very impressive wines with good ageing potential, sometimes reminiscent of Rhône wines. It is also often used in cuvées, either with Zweigelt or with Cabernet Sauvignon or Pinot noir.

Blaufränkisch is also grown in Germany, where it is called Limberger or Lemberger, and throughout central Europe. As it was long thought to be identical with the Beaujolais grape Gamay, it is still called Gamé in Bulgaria, while in Hungary it is known by its translated Austrian name as Kékfrankos, or as Nagyburgundi. In Slovakia it is called Frankovka, while in the north-east of Italy, in Friuli, it is called Franconia. Wine-growers in Washington State in the USA know it as Lemberger.

BLAUER PORTUGIESER (5 per cent)
'Common in both senses of the word' according to Jancis Robinson, this grape is grown in Germany and in Austria, to where it was imported in 1770 from Portugal by the Austrian Count Fries. From Austria, a Johann Philipp Bronner brought it to Germany in 1840. A high yielder (up to 160 hl/ha) that ripens early, makes few demands on the soil and is resistant to illnesses and frost, Blauer Portugieser is popular for mass wines that are almost invariably cheap and cheerless – thin and low in acid, colour and character – though some producers do their best to elevate it into a wine with more individuality. I have not yet been convinced that it has this potential – it seems to take up a great amount of perfectly good vineyard that could be put to better use planted with more promising varieties.

Blauer Portugieser is also grown in Hungary and Romania as Kékoporto and in Croatia as Portugizac Crni or Portugaljka. It was also known widely as Portugais Bleu in south-west France, but many growers there are sensibly ripping it out.

BLAUER WILDBACHER (SCHILCHER, KRACHER, KRÄTZER) (<1 per cent)
Blauer Wildbacher is a variety that was already planted in Styria in the fourth century. A local speciality, this grape is traditionally vinified as a light rosé, a process that seems to involve doing everything one would otherwise try to avoid: planting it where it will not have much too sun and harvesting it early in order to make a wine high in acidity and low in sugar. Its name is derived from *schilchern* or *schillern*, the interplay of colours between white and red, indicating that this wine is hardly ever vinified red. Another name, however, displays a different dimension of the wine: Heckenklescher. After downing a few glasses of this innocuous thirst-quencher on a pleasant summer's day, it was apparently by no means unusual for revellers to go outside to answer the call of nature. Here the combination of standing up and the heat of the

day would quite commonly result in a sudden fall into the hedge, hence the epithet 'hedge crasher'.

Sensitive to spring frosts and rot, Blauer Wildbacher needs airy sites to ripen well. The yields are typically no higher than 60 hl/ha, and the acidity of the must, the hallmark of Schilcher wines, is very high at 10 to 15 per cent. In Styria, it has been used for rosé wine for at least two hundred years. Some Schilcher is also used for the production of sparkling wine.

CABERNET FRANC (<1 per cent)

This French grape exists in Austria mainly because when its vines were planted they were thought to be Merlot. In France, it is mainly used as an alternative for or supplement to Cabernet Sauvignon in cuvées with Merlot, though it can produce some very fine varietal wines, especially in the Loire. Usually lighter in colour and tannins than Cabernet Sauvignon, it can nevertheless be made into great wines, notably in the famous Château Cheval Blanc. In Austria, it has little impact, and is planted on less than half a per cent of the total area under vines, mainly in the Burgenland. It was sanctioned in Austrian wine law as a Qualitätswein grape in 1986.

CABERNET SAUVIGNON (<1 per cent)

One of the most popular red grapes worldwide, Cabernet Sauvignon originates in France, where it is used especially in the Bordeaux, typically blended with Merlot and sometimes Cabernet Franc. A classical variety for cuvées, it lends power, tannic backbone and structure to varieties that show a more mellow, softer profile. Cabernet Sauvignon was introduced to Austria experimentally in 1860, in Vöslau, where it was made into a Bordeaux-style cuvée with Merlot. After becoming fashionable in Austria more recently, it has turned out disappointingly in most regions apart from the Burgenland, where some very interesting wines are made from the grape, both on its own and in Bordeaux-style cuvées. Part of the problem is that it rarely ever achieves full ripeness in Austria and ripens very late, though it poses little demands on the soil and has good frost resistance. Like some other international grape varieties, it was recognized by the Austrian wine law only in 1986. Some good successes have been achieved by blending it with Blaufränkisch.

MERLOT (<1 per cent)

As already mentioned, much of what was thought to be Merlot in Austria is actually Cabernet Franc. The soft, velvety cuvée partner in many Bordeaux wines, Merlot has not had the success in Austria it has had in the New World. Merlot was one of the first of the international varieties to be planted in Austria, but has not yet produced wines of great quality and has not established a firm footing here, partly because it rarely ever reaches full ripeness and is extremely sensitive to frost and rot. Merlot is made into some soft and mellow wines, especially in the Neusiedlersee-Hügelland and in Mailberg in the Weinviertel, where it is commonly blended with Cabernet Sauvignon, but hardly ever reaches anything approaching the complexity for which it is justly famous.

ST LAURENT (PINOT ST LAURENT, SANKT LAURENT) (<1 per cent)

St Laurent hails from France and is probably a descendent of Pinot noir, which it resembles in many ways with its low tannins, pale colour and often smoky morello cherry note. Its name is derived from the fact that it usually begins to ripen on St Lawrence's Day, 10 August. If the yields are limited, it can make fine, elegant and sophisticated wines with floral Pinot noir aromas. It was probably imported into Austria via Germany in 1870, though Joseph Umathum, one of the best St Laurent growers in Austria, believes that it might have come to the country with the Cistercian monks who colonized the Lake Neusiedl region during the thirteenth century and who introduced Pinot gris to the area.

If vinified in the traditional way, in large barrels, it reaches its full maturity after two to five years. Recently, however, it has been given the full barrique treatment and has demonstrated that it benefits from new oak and can develop into a much more complex wine with greater ageing potential. The best St Laurent is grown on the northern shores of Lake Neusiedl, where it occasionally reaches truly international stature and where it finds the light and chalky soils it prefers. Late frosts, rain during the flowering period and mildew present considerable hazards for growers, though its thick grape skins protect it from rot. It is also used in cuvées with Blaufränkisch, Cabernet Sauvignon, Pinot noir and Zweigelt.

St Laurent is a capricious and difficult grape variety, and most growers think it is not worth their while, particularly because of its dangerously early flowering, which makes it sensitive to late frosts and causes it to be unreliable in quantitative terms. It does, though, tend to ripen much earlier than Pinot noir and can therefore reach full ripeness also in less warm years.

Some Austrian growers feel, with some reason, that it may yet prove to be one the best Austrian red wine grapes, together with the two other indigenous varieties, Blaufränkisch and Zweigelt.

St Laurent is also grown as Vavrinecké or Svatovavrinecke in Slovakia and the Czech Republic, as Sentlovrenka in Croatia and Slovenia, and to a lesser extent in the German Pfalz region.

PINOT NOIR (BLAUER BURGUNDER, BLAUBURGUNDER, BLAUER SPÄTBURGUNDER, KLEVNER) (<1 per cent)
The most successful red import from France, Pinot noir – the main red grape variety of Burgundy – has been grown in Austria for almost two hundred years. It is now grown all over the world. Its characteristic low tannin, transparency and morello cherry aromas are highly prized. Pinot noir is difficult both in the vineyard and in the cellar: it demands good, light and fertile soils that are not too dry, and good sun exposure. In addition to this, it is sensitive to late frosts, rot and viral diseases. Pinot noir usually ripens late and does not achieve high yields, which effectively rules it out for mass production. There are, however, few other red grape varieties that so successfully express the characteristics of their terroir, which makes it highly interesting for ambitious growers.

Pinot noir can yield pleasant wines in the Thermenregion. The best results, however, are achieved around the northern shores of Lake Neusiedl, where some finely balanced and dense, distinctively Burgundian Pinot noirs have been made in recent years. There are indications that other growers are now realizing the considerable potential of this grape in Austria.

UHUDLER (<1 per cent)
A Styrian speciality, Uhudler is hardly grown any more. It originated from American varieties used as rootstock after the phylloxera catastrophe in the late nineteenth century. Some Styrian growers did not go to the trouble of grafting European vines on to the American ones and grew wines from the rootstocks instead. Uhudler is therefore not a single variety but the collective name for wines grown directly from the descendants of American root grafts. The resulting wine was not allowed to be sold in Austria until 1992. There are about 23 hectares of Uhudler remaining in

Southern Styria and in Heiligenbrunn in South Burgenland. It has a curious, foxy taste, reminiscent of strawberry wine.

ZWEIGELT (BLAUER ZWEIGELT, ROTBURGER) (8 per cent)
A cross between St Laurent and Blaufränkisch, Fritz Zweigelt's 1922 creation can probably be regarded as the red Austrian grape *par excellence*. It is the most common red variety, can be found in all wine-growing regions of Austria, grows well on all but the most chalky soil types, and is not sensitive to frost or illnesses. The grape yields reliably and plentifully, in good years up to 100 hl/ha. Zweigelt ripens quite early, typically in the second half of September or in early October.

Zweigelt wines are dense and dark, with characteristically mellow cherry fruit. They are usually elevated in large wooden barrels, but can also be vinified in small barriques to add backbone to their otherwise round structure. If restricted to low yields, this variety can make beautifully concentrated wines that have a distinctive liquorice note in good years such as 1997. The ageing potential of high-class Zweigelt is not yet clear, as such wines have been produced only recently. Another factor in the continuing increase in quality of this grape variety is that many vineyards are only now coming of age, yielding more concentrated and more interesting wines. Zweigelt is grown in all red wine areas of Austria: in Lower Austria, the entire Burgenland, and in Styria.

Another popular method of elevation is a cuvée of Zweigelt and Blaufränkisch, an Austrian equivalent to the magic worked in Bordeaux with Cabernet Sauvignon and Merlot, the Zweigelt being the softer and more mellow Merlot stand-in. This can work superbly well and produce some wines that marry fruit and tannic backbone. These wines, though, are still in their infancy, and we may expect more yet.

Some Zweigelt is grown in Saxony in eastern Germany.

OTHER VARIETALS
There are experiments with international varieties such as Nebbiolo, Syrah, Sangiovese, Gamay and Zinfandel, but these are as yet of little consequence. Other native grape varieties, such as Grüner Hainer, Kardarka and Trollinger, are being pushed out of the game altogether, which is not necessarily a bad thing, as their names tend to be their most interesting characteristic.

PART TWO

Austrian Wine-Growing Areas
and Growers

Burgenland

Area profile

With a little under 20,000 hectares, the Burgenland is Austria's second largest wine region. It is also a region with a very unquiet history and a long pedigree of making wines. The Celts were already making wine here, and it is possible that grapes were cultivated here in the Bronze Age. Far from being Austria's oldest wine producing region, though, it is one of the youngest, as the Burgenland did not become part of Austria until 1921.

The history of the area has been marked by migrations and by migrating peoples. Everyone who was anyone in European history came through this area at one time or another, more often than not looting and pillaging what was there. There is an Illyrian ring fortress here, pointing to invasions even before Roman times. In Roman times, the Burgenland was significant mainly because it formed part of the Amber Road from the Baltic to the Mediterranean, and because it was an outpost towards the east.

It is difficult to tell exactly how far the wine history of the area reaches back. The find of a cauldron containing grape pips dating back to 700 BC indicates the value of wines to the ancient inhabitants of the area, though it cannot be said for sure that they did indeed make wine. Both the Celts and the Romans made wine here, though, as the remains of a Celtic vine knife from the late Iron Age, and those of a Roman wine press excavated near Mörbisch, bear out.

The area was fought over by, among others, the Ostrogoths and the Magyars until Charlemagne pacified it for a while and brought with him Franconian settlers and vines. In 1157, the Cistercians received land on the northern shore of Lake Neusiedl and founded a monastery in Güssing, in the southern Burgenland, bringing with them Burgundian Pinot grapes (Pinot gris) from their base on the Côte d'Or. Parts of the lands have been owned by Cistercians ever since and are still, or again, used as vineyards.

During the Habsburg era, the area was, administratively speaking, a part of the Hungarian Kingdom, whose king was, of course, the Emperor. For a few centuries, the Burgenland did not suffer catastrophic change – give or take the Turkish war in 1683 and numerous raids by Turks and Kuruzzes on towns such as Mörbisch and Rust. The Turkish occupation of the wine growing regions around Lake Balaton in Hungary was a boost for the wines of the Burgenland, as Tokay was unobtainable during this period.

With relative stability came prosperity, and the Habsburg emperors were quick to acquire estates in the Burgenland in order to profit from the popularity of its wines, which were sold as far afield as the Baltic. A key role in this development was played by the town of Rust, as outlined already in the general historical chapter.

Hungarian nobles also settled in the Burgenland, notably the Esterházy family, whose palace at Eisenstadt is still standing. Today, after several ambitious redecoration projects throughout the centuries to bring it into line with the fashion of the times, the building looks something of an architectural mess, with its classical features plastered awkwardly over a baroque façade. The inside of the palace and the Arcadian park behind it, though, are still very beautiful – though the portraits are not much to look at. It seems as if they had all been painted by republicans. It is also possible, however, that the Esterházys themselves were no oil paintings, especially as they showed a robust disregard for biblical injunctions against inbreeding. In order to preserve the integrity of his estate, one of the Esterházy princes even married his own brother's daughter, and had eighteen children by her.

It was in this Eisenstadt palace that Joseph Haydn spent much of his life – glad, no doubt, to have escaped the stiflingly hot and unhealthy climate of his prince's summer palace at Esterháza in Fertöd, which the ambitious nobleman had built right in the swamps of Hungary.

The Burgenland was, in many ways, a historical limbo, inhabited by communities who were not tolerated in Austria proper: Protestants, Jews and Gypsies settled here. The village of Gols is an example of this historical state of anomaly. It is a very close-knit community, overwhelmingly Protestant even today, with only a handful of surnames to go round, and surrounded entirely by Catholic villages.

The wine trade in the area was dominated by Jewish merchants, notably the Wolf family of Eisenstadt, a dynasty of wine merchants from the seventeenth century until their demise during the Nazi Era. The Esterházys were tolerant towards the Jews, valuing their trading connections over their own faith, and Eisenstadt still holds a special position in central European Jewish history. Apart from Eistenstadt, there were other Jewish communities in the Burgenland, some of which had been established in the fourteenth century.

Swept along by the cataclysmic civil unrest of the revolutions of 1848, the Hungarian parliament, led by Lajos Kossuth, achieved a degree of independence for the country. Together with the rest of the kingdom, the Burgenland became much more 'Hungarian'. While up to this point the majority of its inhabitants had been German-speaking, Hungarian was now the official language, the language taught at school. Many people adopted Hungarian names, though their main language remained German. Others emigrated to the United States.

While people were leaving, pests were arriving. In most of Burgenland, as in the rest of Europe, first oidium (mildew) and then the dreaded root louse phylloxera destroyed vineyards during the latter half of the nineteenth century. Only the vineyards of the See-winkel, whose sandy soils did not allow the lice to survive, were spared.

The catastrophe, however, had other results. As the vineyards of France had been routed by phylloxera almost three decades before those of Burgenland, the wine growers of the area had started to plant and make red wines and to sell them to wine merchants desperate for alternatives to the unobtainable red wines of Burgundy. This was the introduction of Pinot noir to the area. This reaction to the misfortunes of France also brought a degree of prosperity to the Burgenland which enabled it to recover from the destruction of its vineyards.

Even after the phylloxera catastrophe, the majority of the wines planted in the Burgenland were red, now especially Blaufränkisch. Sixty per cent of the wines made in Rust during this period were red, very much in contrast to the previous centuries, when the town had made its name with its sweet white wines.

After the collapse of the Austro-Hungarian Empire at the end of the First World War, the people of the Burgenland decided in a referendum to stay with Austria. 'Burgenland', the name adopted for the region, has its roots in the thirteenth and fourteenth centuries, when the region reached its greatest extent and included the districts of Eisenburg, Ödenburg, Weiselburg and Pressburg (now Bratislava). After these cities – not after any imaginary castles – it was called the Vier-Burgen-Land (the land of four *burgen*), and then simply the Burgenland, though this name was not adopted officially until a new designation had to be found for the former German West Hungary when it became part of Austria in 1921. After an interlude during the Third Reich when the region was split up, Burgenland regained its autonomy in the Second Austrian Republic.

It was not until after the Second World War that a small area on the eastern side of Lake Neusiedl began to make wine in earnest: the region around Illmitz and Apetlon. Vineyards had already been recorded here in the late sixteenth century, but even by the end of the nineteenth century there were little more than sixty hectares under vines. Today, the 1,500 hectares planted here produce some of the finest nobly sweet wines in the world.

The Burgenland is still a very rural district. It is, as already mentioned, recognized as an area worthy of special funding by the European Community, which has enabled great investments to be made in wine cellars and technology. It is a small and traditional community, whose old men on benches in village squares and old women dressed in black and wearing headscarves remind one of neighbouring Hungary. This kind of observation, however, is not likely to endear a visitor to the locals, who pride themselves on their Austrian identity. Hungarians are mainly used as cheap labour in this region, and the majority of harvest workers make the short journey across the border in order to work in the vineyards of the Burgenland.

Especially on the eastern side of the lake, the architecture bears out this unquiet history, the fact that there is no natural stone here in sufficient quantity to use as building material, and the recent wealth of the area. The traditional farmhouses of the area, whitewashed cottages with reed roofs, were built from soft mud bricks and had to be rebuilt regularly, if indeed they were not burnt down first. Today, most of the old farming villages have disappeared, supplanted by squat, practical, new bungalows in cheery colours. Driving through these villages, it is hard to remember that they were once very beautiful in a romantic, impractical sort of way.

In terms of scenic beauty, the eastern shores of Lake Neusiedl with their villages of Gols and Illmitz have little to offer (though this is more than made up for by the wines). Aesthetic requirements of this kind are satisfied on the other bank, in Rust, a beautiful Baroque town.

The Burgenland lies on the cusp of two climatic zones, broadly speaking Pannonian and western European – an important factor for its wines. Moreover, it also divides into four distinct wine growing areas: Seewinkel or Neusiedlersee, Neusiedlersee-Hügelland, Middle Burgenland and South Burgenland.

NEUSIEDLERSEE

Vineyards: 10,387 ha
Soils: mainly loess, black earth, gravel and sand
White (85 per cent): Welschriesling, Pinot blanc, Bouvier, Scheurebe, Muskat-Ottonel, Traminer, Chardonnay, Neuburger
Red (15 per cent): Zweigelt, St Laurent, Blaufränkisch, Cabernet Sauvignon

The soils on the north-eastern shores of Lake Neusiedl, right around the northern tip of the lake and down to the winemaking villages of Weiden, Gols, Mönchhof and Halbturn, are made up of loess, loam and black earth. Red wines dominate here. Going south along the lake, we come to the Seewinkel, the eastern shore with its numerous small and shallow salty ponds. Here loam and sand dominate on a gravelly subsoil.

The wine villages of Podersdorf, Illmitz and Apetlon are directly by the lake, while Frauenkirchen, Andau, St Andrä, Wallern and Pamhagen lie some kilometres inland. It is here, and on the western shore around Rust, that the lake has its greatest effect on wine production. Strictly speaking, Lake Neusiedl is more of a giant puddle than a lake: it is only two metres deep at the deepest point, though it is thirty-six kilometres long. The mists rolling inland from the lake provide ideal conditions for the development of

Neusiedlersee and Neusiedlersee-Hügelland

botrytis, or noble rot, on the grapes. Meanwhile, the lake itself weakens climatic extremes and temperature changes, allowing late harvesting.

In terms of climate, this region is part of the Puszta, the great central European steppe stetching across Hungary and further east. The climate here is Pannonian, a continental climate, characterized by hot summers and cold winters. There is less annual rainfall (500 mm) and more sun here than on the other, western shore of the lake. Partly owing to the lake's regulating influence on temperature, the vegetation period here is 250 days, up to two weeks longer than in the rest of the Burgenland. The influence of the lake is very beneficial, too, as the summer highs can reach up to 40° C, with minimum winter temperatures of −25° C.

About 4,900 growers around Lake Neusiedl are cultivating 10,400 ha under vines, 80 per cent of which are white. The proportion of red wines is rising steadily, with more and more producers switching from cheapish white wines to the more up-market red (and white) varieties. Austria's own Grüner Veltliner has the lion's share of the ground, followed by Welschriesling, Pinot blanc, Chardonnay and Müller-Thurgau. Among the reds, Zweigelt, Blaufränkisch, St Laurent, Cabernet Sauvignon and Pinot noir are the dominant varieties.

In an attempt to capitalize on the reputation of this region for sweet wine, other methods are used for making these wines. Eiswein is very popular here, made by leaving the grapes until the first frosts and then immediately pressing the frozen grapes so that only the sugary concentrate is pressed off. These wines are often more powerfully sweet and sometimes less sophisticated than the botrytis wines and can be made only in years when the frosts come early enough, i.e. at the beginning of November.

Other methods of making sweet wines used here are Strohwein and Schilfwein, or *vin de paille*. Grapes are dried in the wind on mats of straw or reed, taking in some of the aromas of the matting while doing so. This, however, is little more than a local speciality, even if some growers are fiercely proud of their straw or reed wines.

Apart from excellent sweet wines, this region also produces some of Austria's best red wines, especially in the centre, around Gols, Mönchhof and Frauenkirchen. Here, conditions are very good indeed for the harmonious ripening of grape varieties like Pinot noir, St Laurent and Zweigelt, and the growers able to exploit this are producing excellent reds.

In contrast to the growers of Illmitz and environs, who rely mainly on sweet wines, the dry wine producers of Gols and Frauen-kirchen often vinify their wines as single crus or *Rieden*. Important crus are Altenberg and Gabarinza in Gols; Kreuzjoch, Kurzberg, Pohnbühel and Waldacker in Mönchhof; and Hallebühl in Frauen-kirchen.

Top growers by the Neusiedlersee

Paul Achs

18 ha

Welschriesling, Chardonnay, Blaufränkisch, Zweigelt, Cabernet Sauvignon, St Laurent, Pinot noir, Pinot blanc, Traminer, Muskat Ottonel

'Before I had worked in California for some months and had gathered experience in 1990,' says Paul Achs, 'we did not make red wines worthy of the name.' Things have certainly changed, for today Paul Achs is one of Austria's foremost red wine producers. His flagship is a Pannobile cuvée built around that most capricious of Austrian red grapes, St Laurent, together with varying parts of Cabernet Sauvignon and Pinot noir. This wine and his Pinot noir and Blaufränkisch all nod towards Burgundy, and there are worse places to nod towards.

Achs Paul (as he is known in local parlance, which just as in Hungary, a few miles down the road, mentions the family name first) manages to make full bodied wines with not too much primary fruit and with good complexity and ageing potential. Vines are cut back to one bunch per shoot, and weeds are largely combated by mechanical means. The yields per hectare are limited to 35 hectolitres and the wines are harvested with the utmost care. The wines ripen in small and large oak, and in large acacia barrels, and Achs is also experimenting with producing unfiltered and unclarified wines. He also makes interesting oak-aged Chardonnay and Pinot blanc.

Paul Achs, Neubaugasse 13, 7122 Gols (phone 02173-2367, fax 02173-3478).

Beck

One of the growers in the Pannobile association, known for his good Neuburger, Matthias Beck has one advantage over many of his colleagues: experience. He has led the family estate since 1974. Also makes fine Pinot blanc and Pannobile cuvée.

Christine and Matthias Beck, Untere Hauptstraße 108, 7122 Gols (phone 02173-2755, fax 02173-27554).

Alois Gangl

Some good Beerenauslesen and very clean white wines.
Alois Gangl, Obere Hauptstraße 32, 7142 Illmitz (phone 02175-2402, fax 02175-3335).

Josef Gangl (Weingut Zum Nationalpark)

A traditional estate producing white wines up to TBA and Blaufränkisch Eiswein. Unlike many other growers in the area, Mr Gangl still has a good deal of Grüner Veltliner.
Josef Gangl, Schrändlgasse 50, 7142 Illmitz (phone and fax 02175-3207).

Gsellmann & Gsellmann

These two brothers have found an interesting way of dividing up the work: one looks after white wines, the other after red. The style of the estate is very much a search for big, powerful wines, and the Gsellmann brothers produce very good Pinot blanc Auslese, interesting Zweigelt, and Blaufränkisch.
Obere Hauptstraße 28 & 38, 7122 Gols (phone 0173-2214, fax 02173-3414).

Haider

10 ha
Welschriesling, Bouvier, Traminer, Neuburger, Scheurebe, Sauvignon blanc, Cabernet Sauvignon, Zweigelt, Blaufränkisch
Martin Haider is a quiet and unassuming man, very much in contrast to his sweet wines, expressive beasts which keep winning national and international prizes. His small estate, which looks little different from the private houses around it, is only a few hundred metres from Lake Neusiedl. He makes a surprising variety of fine botrytis and other sweet wines and is especially proud of the Welschriesling Trockenbeerenauslese, a perfect example of its kind. Haider's style is determined by fruit extract, not alcohol. He has much more to offer, though, and is very willing to let others taste the subtle differences between grapes and vintages, tastings that can become marathon sessions of contemplation and comparison.

Welschriesling especially is a variety that still keeps him under its spell. In his hands this grape – otherwise mostly made into the simplest of everyday wines – displays great finesse and complexity, with sufficient acidity to balance the high sugar content. His

Bouvier TBA is another speciality: softer and more rounded, but still backed up by enough acidity to make it truly memorable. *Martin Haider, Seegasse 16, 7142 Illmitz (phone 02175-2358, fax 02175-23584).*

Heinrich
12 ha
Zweigelt, St Laurent, Cabernet Sauvignon, Blaufränkisch, Merlot, Syrah, Chardonnay, Pinot blanc, Pinot gris, Neuburger

Coming to Gernot Heinrich's estate is something of a shock. Here, surrounded by rather drab bungalows and folksy private houses, a seemingly alien building has alighted on the hill, a postmodernist palazzo with large, stylish rooms decorated with contemporary art, a place Gernot Heinrich himself calls his house for living, working and dreaming.

Like his house, Gernot Heinrich's wines seek to go new ways. In the basement of the house, backing up his ambition to marry traditional grapes and innovative vinification, is a state-of-the art winery with plenty of gleaming steel. The results of Heinrich's striving for perfection are exceptionally dense and often complex wines that may well be as much guests from the future as the building they are made in. They should see that future, for they have good ageing potential. The Pannobile cuvée (Heinrich is a founding member of the Pannobile Association) is particularly fine and illustrates his concern with finding a specific Austrian character of red wine by concentrating on indigenous grape varietals such as Blaufränkisch, St Laurent and Zweigelt. There is also a very good white Pannobile, made from Pinot blanc, Neuburger, Chardonnay and Pinot gris. As with all Pannobile wines, the balance of grape varieties in these cuvées varies from year to year. Heinrich also takes especial care with his cuvée of Zweigelt and Blaufränkisch from his vineyard Gabarinza, a cru in which he sees great potential. It is aged in (largely) new oak for eighteen months and left in bottles for another six months before being sold. Another interesting prospect is Heinrich's new plantings of Merlot and Syrah, the former of which has not so far done very well in Austria.

Gernot Heinrich is still a young man, but he is already one of the best red wine growers in Austria and may well be one of those leading the way to a style of red Austrian wine that is both distinctive and of international stature.

Gernot Heinrich, Baumgarten 60, 7122 Gols (phone 02173-31760, fax 02173-31764).

Hillinger

Leo Hillinger had spent several stints in California before he took over the family estate, and he has brought a decidedly modern outlook to the banks of Lake Neusiedl. Both Hillinger and his bottles appear very much *à la mode* and he is at times described as a 'designer winemaker', an unjust epithet as his wines are, in fact, very much rooted in local tradition, with the possible exception of his French-orientated Chardonnay. Apart from this, there is a range of clean and well-made wines, all of which are polished without, however, having great individuality and depth.

Leo Hillinger, Untere Hauptstraße 35, 7093 Jois (phone 02160-8317, fax 02160-8129).

Juris (G Stiegelmar)

11 ha
Welschriesling, Pinot blanc, Chardonnay
Pinot noir, Zweigelt, St Laurent, Cabernet Sauvignon
Like almost everybody else, Georg Stiegelmar and his son Axel were building a new cellar and winery when I visited them in 1998. 'Juris' is local dialect for George, and as there are only a very few family names to go around in this part of the world, it was felt that the estate would be more distinctive with this name. Not that its wines would not already lift it above the crowd. Axel, who has spent time working and learning in Germany, California and Bordeaux, has strengthened the estate's hand of red varieties, especially Pinot noir and St Laurent, and he achieves beautifully balanced wines that strike a happy equilibrium between being Austrian and international, with a specifically French, Burgundian, direction.

His white wines, too, bear out this direction: the 1997 Cuvée Juris, made from Chardonnay and Neuburger, which manages comfortably to tuck away a stately 16 per cent alcohol, and the Chardonnay, of which there is an Austrian 'classical', steel-ripened line and also a harmonious barrique-aged variety. More than by this Chardonnay, I was impressed by his 1997 Pinot noir, which is perhaps more international than Austrian, but fine nonetheless, and aged in barriques, in large barrels and in bottles before reaching the market. With a Robert Mondavi World Wine Trophy, a Winemaker

THE WINES OF AUSTRIA

of the Year at the London Wine Challenge and high praise from the Institute of Masters of Wine, Axel Stiegelmar has a standard to uphold and shows every sign of doing just that.

Georg and Axel Stiegelmar, Untere Hauptstraße 60, 7122 Gols (phone 02173-2203, fax 02173-3323).

Kracher (Weinlaubenhof)

7.5 ha
Welschriesling, Chardonnay, Scheurebe, Traminer, Muskateller, Bouvier
Zweigelt, Blaufränkisch

'I am just a simple farmer,' Alois Kracher likes to remark, one of the most disingenuous things any grower could say. Not only is 'Luis' an international star and one of the few Austrian growers to export the greater part of his production, he is also an inveterate campaigner behind the scenes who combines a voracious appetite for discussion and fine wine with a taste for French films and, last but not really least, with the ability to create miraculous sweet wines.

Kracher recently annoyed colleagues by making minute quantities of dry red wine, which proved that in this field he would excel as well if only he wanted to. His speciality, however, is the sweet wines, which have earned him the London Wine Challenge title of Winemaker of the Year no fewer than three times (most recently in 1998) and other international awards by the bucketload. Having said this, Alois Kracher had never planned to take over his father's estate. He started his professional life as a chemical engineer. When he did decide to come home, however, he decided to make no compromises and to produce top wines. This he has achieved.

Kracher's botrytis wines manage that rare miracle: they are sweet wines without seeming to be sweet, producing on the palate a revelation of complex fruit notes which linger in the mouth for a very long time indeed. All this happens on an estate which is curiously unprepossessing and easily missed. Kracher's vineyards are a stone's throw away from the banks of Lake Neusiedl, where the soils are mainly a mixture of sand and black earth. He works with natural yeasts and vinifies several distinct styles of wine, most noticeably the two lines Zwischen den Seen, a more Austrian wine without prominent oak aged in large barrels for up to fifteen months, and the internationally orientated Nouvelle Vague (the name is an *hommage* to French cinema), which is elevated in new oak.

Being a true Neusiedlersee grower, Kracher produces a dazzling variety of different cuvées each year, though he himself professes a preference for the Welschriesling/Chardonnay wines such as his excellent No 14 Nouvelle Vague, which combines the acidity of Welschriesling with the lusciousness of Chardonnay and is aged in new barriques for eight months. The Austrian 'miracle year' of 1995 worked many of its wonders in his cellars, and some of his older wines are traded like rare gems.

Alois Kracher, Apetloner Straße 27, 7142 Illmitz (phone 02175-3377, fax 02175-33774).

Lang
12 ha
Chardonnay, Welschriesling, Pinot blanc, Scheurebe, Grüner Veltliner, Sauvignon blanc, Gewürztraminer
Zweigelt, Blaufränkisch, Pinot noir

Helmut Lang is one of Lake Neusiedl's finest and largest sweet wine producers. Unlike his illustrious neighbour Alois Kracher, he puts his faith not in powerful cuvées but in delicate single variety wines, of which he, typically for the region, offers a great diversity, even if they may be available only in minuscule quantities. This is almost an exercise in gratuitous variety, and every conceivable vinification of Austrian sweet wines is sure to have a fine exponent in Lang's cellar.

Lang's Scheurebe and Welschriesling TBAs are perhaps the most consistently convincing wines, though his Gewürztraminer TBA can be superb, too. There is also fine Pinot blanc and oaked Chardonnay Ausbruch, a rarity on this side of the river.

Helmut Lang, Quergasse 5, 7142 Illmitz (phone and fax 02175-2923).

Leitner
Young and interesting winemakers belonging to the Pannobile group. Good red and white cuvées, as well as a Syrah as yet more notable for its rarity than for sheer quality.

Melitta and Matthias Leitner, Quellengasse 33, 7122 Gols (phone and fax 02173-2593).

Lentsch (Zur Dankbarkeit)

Lentsch's winery is attached to his restaurant Zur Dankbarkeit, which is famous throughout the area. Here he makes very good Pinot gris, both as a botrytis wine and as a dry variety seemingly built for eternity. His cask aged Pinot noir *vieille vigne* is also interesting, but needs some ageing.

Josef Lentsch, Hauptstraße 39, 7141 Podersdorf/See (phone and fax 02177-2223).

Münzenrieder (Pannonia Weingut)

Johann Münzenrieder began to bottle his own wine only in 1990, twelve years after founding the estate. While the overall quality of his wines does not make him one of the giants of the area, he has a knack of producing very remarkable individual wines, such as his barrique aged 1997 Zweigelt, which was a fine example. Also good Scheurebe, Welschriesling and Bouvier TBA.

Johann Münzenrieder, Wallenerstraße 27, 7143 Apetlon (phone 02175-2259, fax 02175-3179).

Nekowitsch

4 ha
Welschriesling, Scheurebe, Traminer, Grüner Veltliner, Müller-Thurgau
Zweigelt, Blaufränkisch

Gerhard Nekowitsch is not only a maker of fine sweet wines but also a civil servant who commutes to Vienna every day. It is all the more astonishing that he finds the time to produce a dazzling variety of very complex sweet wines, including botrytis, Eiswein and Schilfwein, which is his particular favourite, usually a cuvée of Welschriesling, Grüner Veltliner and Scheurebe. He also makes rare red Schilfwein from Zweigelt and Blaufränkisch. It seems that every possible combination of grape varietals is employed to make his wines, understandably in very small quantities. Still, these wines are very much worth looking out for.

Gerhard Nekowitsch, Schrändlgasse 2, 7142 Illmitz (phone and fax 02175-2039).

Hans and Anita Nittnaus

10 ha
Cabernet Sauvignon, Blaufränkisch, St Laurent, Merlot
Welschriesling, Sauvignon blanc, Chardonnay

Not to be confused with another Hans Nittnaus down the road (or with six others in the same village for that matter), Hans Nittnaus made headlines with his 1993 and 1994 Comondor, a dense and powerful red cuvée from Cabernet Sauvignon and Blaufränkisch. Nittnaus had initially intended to become a concert pianist, but he now puts his hands to good use in the vineyard. His approach to winemaking is both traditional and innovative. He has forsworn the Lenz Moser training method and adopted lower vines planted with higher density. Despite strong filtration and clarification, the wines retain good fruit. Nittnaus has set out to strengthen his red wines, and is currently experimenting with grapes that are new to the region, such as Syrah and Nebbiolo.

Hans and Anita Nittnaus, Untere Hauptstraße 49, 7122 Gols (phone and fax 02173-2248).

Hans and Christine Nittnaus
Self-taught grower. Good Chardonnay and Traminer Spätlese.
Untere Hauptstraße 105, 7122 Gols (phone and fax 02173-2186).

Opitz
5 ha
Welschriesling, Weißburgunder, Scheurebe, Grüner Veltliner, Gewürztraminer, Muskat Ottonel
Blauburger, St Laurent, Zweigelt
If there is any name in Austrian wine that is known internationally, it is Willi Opitz's, a fact which is only partly due to the quality of his wines. Mr Opitz is a tireless self-promoter, forever coming up with new marketing ploys, partly in collaboration with Formula One racing. He even produced a wine which he called Mr President and presented at the White House in Washington. There seems to be little he will not try to make his wines better known, and part of his approach to publicity may stem from his previous incarnation as a manager in an American-owned firm.

Fortunately, his wines can stand the exposure, as he also happens to be one of the best growers around. He is especially proud of his Schilfwein, which he claims to have invented, though not everybody else agrees. His botrytis wines are fine examples of their kind, too, *primus inter pares* perhaps being the Goldackerl, a cuvée from Welschriesling and Scheurebe. Much as other growers in the area, he produces a wide variety of wines, though. Always determined

to go his own way, Opitz still uses an old hand-operated grape press.
Willi Opitz, Quergasse 11, 7142 Illmitz (phone and fax 02175-2084).

Pöckl
11 ha
Zweigelt, Cabernet Sauvignon, Pinot noir, Merlot, St Laurent, Blaufränkisch, Neuburger, Cabernet Franc
Welschriesling, Chardonnay
Josef Pöckl has never been very interested in white wines, but his reds have been enormously transformed. He started making 'serious' reds only in 1985, did not use malolactic fermentation or new oak until 1989, and was considered to have reached the peak of his profession by the middle of the 1990s. His best cuvée is called Admiral (Zweigelt/Cabernet/Merlot), and this is also one of the most successful in the country, a wine with a real possibility of development with age that already reconciles fruit with structure and length. During the last few years Pöckl has become a little disillusioned with the St Laurent grape, another grower to abandon this difficult but richly endowed varietal. He does, though, experiment with several other grape varietals, such as Syrah, Sangiovese, Nebbiolo and Zinfandel.
Josef and Theresa Pöckl, Baumschulgasse 12, 7123 Mönchhof (phone 02173-80258, fax 02173-802584).

Renner
One of the Pannobile growers; increasingly good Chardonnay and red cuvées.
Helmut and Birgit Renner, Obere Hauptstraße 97, 7122 Gols (phone and fax 02173-2259).

Schuster
Good red wines, especially the cuvée CMB.
Rosi Schuster, Prangergasse 2, 7062 St Margarethen (phone and fax 02680-2624).

Tschida (Angerhof)
6 ha
Pinot blanc, Scheurebe, Welschriesling, Grüner Veltliner, Muskat-Ottonel
Zweigelt

Johann Tschida is one of those Illmitz growers who seem to have gold medals growing on their vines: he harvests a whole armful every year, and deservedly so. His botrytis wines (the great majority of his production) are complex and finely judged, their sweetness unlocking the aromas without overwhelming them. His Welschriesling, Muskat-Ottonel and Scheurebe are particularly outstanding examples. He also produces very good Eiswein and Schilfwein. *Johann Tschida, Angergasse 5, 7142 Illmitz (phone and fax 02175-3150).*

Umathum

12.5 ha
Zweigelt, St Laurent, Pinot noir, Blaufränkisch, Cabernet Sauvignon
Welschriesling, Pinot gris, Chardonnay, Sauvignon blanc
It is always a great pleasure to visit Josef 'Pepi' Umathum on his estate just outside the little town of Frauenkirchen. An apprenticeship in France gave him the confidence to turn a farm with a sideline in mainly white wines into one of Austria's foremost and largest red wine estates. Umathum is quietly passionate not only about the quality of his wines but also about the surrounding countryside, and at the slightest provocation goes to great lengths to explain its geology, architecture and history. His wines reflect this single-minded devotion to the land. Although not surprisingly he takes his stylistic leads mainly from France, he wants to create – or help to create – a red wine style that is distinctly Austrian, and he is happy to speculate about this at length in his beautiful newly built cellar, taking and discussing barrel samples with friends and interested visitors.

Indigenous grape varietals such as Zweigelt and Blaufränkisch understandably play an important role in the production, but Josef Umathum is also one of the few growers to tame the difficult St Laurent and make it into wines of considerable, almost Burgundian complexity. Perhaps it is this which leads him to think that St Laurent is a clone of Pinot noir developed here by monks in the Middle Ages. His Pinot noir and Blaufränkisch are also fine. Very much in the French style, his best wines come from separate vineyards, with St Laurent Vom Stein, aged in new barriques for twenty months, and the cuvée Hallebühl (Zweigelt/Blaufränkisch/Cabernet

Sauvignon), aged in 70 per cent new wood for twenty months, among the finest.

Umathum is an inveterate experimenter with large and small barrels, French and Austrian oak, and different fermentation times, which leads one to think that he is still polishing his idiom. Generally his wines are less chunky than other reds made here, but with more emphasis on length and earthy flavours. In good years these wines can be truly exceptional, even if weaker vintages tend to be a little blunt and lacking in profile – but that is a problem felt in the whole region.

Josef Umathum, St Andräer Straße 7, 7132 Frauenkirchen (phone 02172-2173, fax 02172-21734).

Velich

3 ha

Welschriesling, Chardonnay, Neuburger

If Roland Velich gambles on Chardonnay this is surely a good thing, because he knows all about gambling: at night he works as a croupier in a Vienna casino, though now he would like to concentrate entirely on his vineyards. Before turning to gambling and wine, he studied philosophy and psychology in Vienna. In his daytime incarnation, however, he and his brother Heinz (currently a student at the Agricultural University in Vienna, and oenologist-in-chief) make one of Austria's very finest Chardonnays.

Their cautious use of small oak barrels especially seems to be ten years ahead of what some of their more trigger-happy colleagues are still doing. These wines may seem less spectacular initially, but they release a beautiful range of secondary aromas which have secured them a place at the very top of Austria's Chardonnays. The Chardonnay Tiglat is a wine to contemplate. The oak often takes some time to be integrated into the structure of the wine, but the 1993 vintage, a great and much sought-after rarity in Austria, is wonderfully stylish, full-bodied and complex. The cuvée of Welschriesling and Neuburger is very good, too.

Heinz and Roland Velich, Seeufergasse 12, 7143 Apetlon (phone 02175-3187).

NEUSIEDLERSEE-HÜGELLAND

Vineyards: 6,264 ha
Soils: loess, black earth, sand, loam
White (75 per cent): Welschriesling, Pinot blanc, Neuburger, Chardonnay
Red (25 per cent): Zweigelt, Blaufränkisch, Cabernet Sauvignon, St Laurent

The western shore of Lake Neusiedl, less than fifteen kilometres away, comes under the influence of the Leitha-Gebirge, a small mountain range, technically the last ripple of the Alps, which lies towards the south-west of the area. There are three bands of soil type here, with intensely varied soils throughout. By the lake shore, sand, loam and black earth predominate. Further up the slopes, there is chalky loam and marl with loess layers, while the vineyards on the higher parts of the soft hills have soils of crystalline slate with chalk deposits.

The vineyards on the hills of the western shore of Lake Neusiedl open themselves up to the Pannonian climate while being protected from cold northerly and westerly winds. The proximity of the hills, however, increases the annual precipitation to 800 mm per year, while the increase in height also lowers the average temperature and the degree to which grapes are affected by botrytis. Needless to say, the closeness of the lake is a tempering influence here, too. While the vineyards near to the lake, around Rust, Oggau, Mörbisch, Donnerskirchen and Purbach, are used overwhelmingly for white wines, many of them sweet, those in the hills, especially around Großhöflein and to the west of Rust, are being increasingly utilized for powerful dry white and red wines of great potential.

The largest town of the region is Eisenstadt, seat of the Esterházy family and unloved domicile of Joseph Haydn. Eisenstadt can look back on a long history as a wine trading centre on the route between Hungary and Germany, but the wine produced in the town is not to be recommended, with a few laudable exceptions. Growers in nearby Großhöflein, however, produce very interesting red wines indeed, and Rust offers a full complement of excellent sweet and dry wines, both white and red. It is also a town of very considerable beauty.

The most famous wine produced here is the Ruster Ausbruch, a speciality sweet botrytis wine which is not quite high enough in sugar for classifying as a TBA and different in style, with the alcohol more pronounced than the sugar content.

During recent decades, the old cru system has come back in force for dry wines. The *Rieden* of Großhöflein and Rust especially have produced excellent wines. Some of the best *Rieden* are Bartsatz, Point, Steinzeiler and especially Tatschler in Großhöflein; and Hoher Baumgarten, Marienthal, Pandkräftn, Rieglband and Turner in Rust. These are excellent vineyards, suitable especially for red varietals (Blaufränkisch, Cabernet Sauvignon, Zweigelt) and big Chardonnays of truly Burgundian proportions. Other good crus in the area are the Goldberg near St Margarethen, Eisner and Rosenberg in Purbach and Lehmgrube in Kleinhöflein.

Top growers in Neusiedlersee-Hügelland

Feiler-Artinger
23 ha (19 ha in use)
Welschriesling, Pinot blanc, Sauvignon blanc, Chardonnay, Traminer
Blaufränkisch, Zweigelt, Cabernet Sauvignon, Merlot
This is one of the most famous names in the Burgenland, renowned both for its wines and for the wonderful baroque house in the middle of the equally beautiful town of Rust that is the heart of the Feiler estate. The sweet wines, especially the Ausbruch, are among the very best in Austria, and the lady of the house is quick to show the international medals and blind tasting results which frequently rate these botrytis wines (and those of some of her husband's colleagues) far above more famous French names. Hans Feiler is a silent, thoughtful man who keeps a watchful eye on his son Kurt, heir to a considerable tradition. The production now includes a brand-new cellar lined with Allier oak casks, which are used to ripen the top range of wines.

Feiler-Artinger also produce well-known dry red and white wines, especially the red Solitaire (Blaufränkisch/Zweigelt/Cabernet Sauvignon), but these I found less remarkable and less complex than others made in the region. With the changeover from one generation to the next, it is possible, and desirable, that they will begin to fulfil their potential – the benchmark is set pretty high by the Ausbruch.

Hans and Inge Feiler, Hauptstraße 3, 7071 Rust (phone 02685-237, fax 02685-6552).

Kollwentz (Römerhof)
22.5 ha
Blaufränkisch, Cabernet Sauvignon, Zweigelt
Welschriesling, Chardonnay, Sauvignon blanc, Pinot blanc

The Römerhof is one of the great Neusiedlersee estates, not only because of its size – it has more than twice the area under vines than many other growers around here – but also because of the consistently superb quality of the wines produced here. For about thirty years now, Anton Kollwentz has been a great innovator. He was among the very first to plant international grape varietals like Cabernet Sauvignon and Chardonnay, to produce international, oak-fermented wines to standards that were quite frankly in a different league from those of many of his colleagues. Son Andreas was sent to Bordeaux (Château Palmer, Château La Tour Blanche, Château Bonnet) and on study trips to various destinations in the New World. He came back full of ideas, which he is now implementing, much to his father's delight. 'I am glad that Andi is so intensively busy with things we didn't know about back then,' he says. Some of the new practices introduced by the son include careful harvesting and pressing, while in the cellar, great attention is given to balancing out new and old oak.

In keeping with his then revolutionary orientation, Anton Kollwentz was one of the first in his area to pay close attention to the terroir and to vinify his wines by vineyard. The results are absolutely convincing. The cuvée Steinzeiler (Blaufränkisch/Cabernet Sauvignon/Zweigelt), aged in 50 per cent new oak for one year, is the flagship wine, and what a flag it flies! Great density and complexity combine with length to make a wine with considerable ageing potential and character. I also tasted wines from as far back as 1969 (which for Austria is ancient) that showed an intact structure, even if they had lost much of their size and punch – but as Mr Kollwentz said, 'We didn't know a tenth back then of what we know now.' The Zweigelt is equally powerful and well structured, while the Chardonnay Tatschler, aged in 80 per cent new oak for one year, proved wonderfully complex and harmonious in finely judged Burgundian style, well ahead of some premiers crus from Burgundy and certainly one of the best Austrian Chardonnays. The simpler wines set an impressive starting level. *Anton and Andi Kollwentz, Hauptstraße 120, 7051 Großhöflein (phone 02682-65158, fax 02682-6515813).*

Landauer

A small, traditional producer who can produce some remarkable wines. Good Welschriesling Ausbruch and Pinot noir Spätlese. *Haydngasse 5, 7071 Rust (phone 02685-278, fax 02685-2784).*

Leberl

Very ambitious red wines, built to last, also fine Sauvignon blanc BA. One to watch. *Hauptstraße 91, 7051 Großhöflein (phone and fax 02682-67800).*

Mühlgassner

Thomas Mühlgassner teaches mathematics at a local high school and makes wine part-time only. In his 1.2 ha of vineyards near Zagersdorf, some of the oldest vineyards in Austria, he makes exclusively Blaufränkisch. The results can be spectacular and show very distinctive, deep cherry fruit. Also Blaufränkisch rosé. *Thomas Mühlgasser, Dreifaltigkeitsstraße 72, 7000 Eisenstadt (phone 02682-64473).*

Prieler

Engelbert Prieler's estate is marked by a meeting of traditionalism and openness to innovation. Not one of the mighty generation of young wine growers, Mr Prieler has led the estate since 1972 and produces consistently interesting wines, especially Blaufränkisch, aged in barriques for two years, and Chardonnay, but also Pinot blanc and Cabernet Sauvignon. Prieler is not a producer in the limelight, but his wines are still consistently among the good or the very good of the region. *Irmgard and Engelbert Prieler, Hauptstraße 181, 7081 Schützen am Gebirge (phone 02684-2229, fax 02684-22294).*

Schandl

Good, typical wines, especially Pinot blanc and Blaufränkisch and Pinot gris Ausbruch. *Peter Schandl, Haydngasse 3, 7071 Rust (phone 02685-265, fax 02685-2654).*

Schröck

A former 'Austrian Wine Queen', Heidi Schröck is one of the most promising young wine growers in Rust. After serving an apprenticeship in Germany, the Bordeaux and South Africa, she went on to make herself a name with her Muskateller/Welschriesling Ausbruch, as well as with dry Muskateller and Pinot blanc. Ms Schröck has also replanted the traditional Rust grape Furmint. Her red wines have undergone a metamorphosis towards a more international line, and she now makes barrique-aged Zweigelt and Blaufränkisch.

Heidi Schröck, Rathausplatz 8, 7071 Rust (phone 02685-229, fax 02685-2294).

Ernst Triebaumer

11 ha
Blaufränkisch, Cabernet Sauvignon, Merlot
Chardonnay, Welschriesling, Pinot blanc, Sauvignon blanc, Furmint

Ernst Triebaumer may be commonly known by his initials, but there is nothing alien about him. On the contrary, he seems as firmly rooted in this part of the earth as his wines, which are quite simply among the very finest in the country. It was not always clear that this would be so. A younger son of a small grower, he was supposed to become a carpenter, but according to him, he neither liked getting up at four nor climbing around on roofs. After coming to an agreement with his brother Paul about the inheritance and expanding his share of the vineyards by buying up other plots, he set about producing wines with an emphasis on biological methods, which at the time was as untypical as it was unfashionable. His 1986 Blaufränkisch, though, silenced his critics and made Austrian wine history, being one of the first indigenous reds of international calibre.

Since that time the winery has gone from strength to strength. Like many of the best growers in the region, Triebaumer vinifies his better wines by vineyard. His Blaufränkisch Mariental, aged in mainly new barriques for fourteen to eighteen months, tops the bill: a beautifully structured and dense wine which combines the black fruit notes of the grape with an unobtrusive but firm oak backbone, earthy tones and enormous potential. These are wines to collect and lay down for a long time. He also makes an excellent

Cabernet/Merlot. Ernst Triebaumer is also a great friend of sweet wines, and his botrytis cuvées are very well regarded indeed, particularly his Ausbruch, which is elevated in large barrels for six months. Among his white wines the Chardonnay is particularly fine: well balanced and aged in oak for about a year. Triebaumer's son Herbert is also working in the winery and follows his own ideas, especially with oak-aged sweet wines.

Margarethe and Ernst Triebaumer, Raiffeisenstraße 9, 7071 Rust (phone and fax 02685-528).

Paul Triebaumer

8 ha
Blaufränkisch, Pinot noir, Cabernet Sauvignon, Merlot, Syrah, Zweigelt, Nebbiolo
Welschriesling, Chardonnay, Furmint, Gelber Muskateller, Grüner Veltliner, Traminer

Paul Triebaumer is somewhat eclipsed by the fame of his younger brother, but this should not distract from the fine wines he produces. More given to experimenting than Ernst, Paul has planted several 'exotic' varieties and has had some good successes with them, especially his Nebbiolo. His cask-aged Chardonnay Ried Gertberg and his Pinot noir are very good, though he himself prefers cuvées, such as his Blaufränkisch/Nebbiolo Erster Nebel. Owing to the extreme diversity of his vines, he does not concentrate on any one wine.

Waltraud and Paul Triebaumer, Neue Gasse 18, 7071 Rust (phone and fax 02685-6135).

Wenzel

7 ha
Blaufränkisch, Cabernet Sauvignon, Pinot noir
Muskateller, Sauvignon blanc, Welschriesling, Pinot blanc, Pinot gris, Furmint, Gemischter Satz

Michael Wenzel's family have been making wine in Rust since the seventeenth century, and he clearly feels this tradition keenly. Michael's father Robert, who has handed over the running of the estate, was especially concerned with championing the Furmint and Muskateller grapes, as well as Pinot blanc. His subtle and well-balanced Ausbruch wines have made a great name for themselves, and he also produced some very interesting sweet Sauvignon blanc. Michael Wenzel has taken the estate gently one step further.

His 1997 Pinot noir was a great surprise: an elegant, sophisticated wine of great distinction. Another grower making very interesting wines away from the limelight.

Familie Wenzel, Hauptstraße 29, 7071 Rust (phone 02685-287, fax 02685-2874).

MIDDLE BURGENLAND

Vineyards: 2,107 ha
Soils: gravel, sand, loam, crystalline deposits
White (30 per cent): Welschriesling, Pinot blanc
Red (70 per cent): Blaufränkisch, Zweigelt, Cabernet Sauvignon

The Middle Burgenland, southwards along the Hungarian border, is 'Blaufränkischland': the country of the Blaufränkisch vine. Geologically speaking, this stretch of countryside was conditioned by prehistoric rivers that brought gravel with chalky and crystalline deposits, together with sandy and marly layers. There is some basalt around Oberpullendorf, but sand, loam and an occasional area of gravel predominate. The area is protected from winds by the Ödenburg mountains and opens towards the Pannonian plains, allowing access to the warm air of the central European winter. Though Lake Neusiedl is twenty kilometres away, its influence is still noticeable.

The distinctive, peppery Blaufränkisch-based wines are beginning to open up to international influences, with more Cabernet being planted and more complex wines being produced, some of which are very good indeed. There are traditional crus here (Hochäcker and Gfanger in Horitschon, Hochberg in Deutschkreuz), but wines are often blended or labelled by variety, giving the crus less significance than in the northern area of the Burgenland.

Top growers in Middle Burgenland

Gager
Very committed to high-quality reds, with very interesting results. His Cuvée Quatro is especially worth tasting.

Karrnergasse 8, 7301 Deutschkreutz (phone 02613-385, fax 02610-321516).

THERMENREGION

Neckenmarkt

Ritzing
Horitschon   Deutsch-
Kreutz
Lackendorf

MITTEL-   Nikitsch
BURGENLAND

Oberpullendorf

Lutzmannsburg

Lockenhaus

Pinkafeld

Rechnitz

HUNGARY

Großpetersdorf

Eisenberg
Deutsch-
Schützen

SÜD-BURGENLAND

Güssing

SÜDOST-
STEIERMARK

N

Heiligenkreuz

Jennersdorf

kilometres
0   10   20

Middle and South Burgenland

Gesellmann
17 ha
Blaufränkisch, Cabernet Sauvignon, Merlot, Zweigelt, St Laurent,
Pinot noir
Chardonnay

If the names on the bottles from this estate seem nothing short of eccentric, the wines themselves can certainly stand up in the face of international competition. Engelbert Gesellmann is in the process of handing over the reins of winemaking to his son Albert, who spent a crucial apprenticeship at Stellenbosch in South Africa and Cuvaison in California. Being in the middle of the Burgenland, the Gesellmanns concentrate on red wines, especially Blaufränkisch, which, together with Cabernet Sauvignon, represents 50 per cent of their area under vines.

The red wines are very well made indeed. The Opus Eximium is a cuvée similar to the Pannobiles of the Neusiedlersee area, with Cabernet Sauvignon, St Laurent and Pinot noir, aged partly in new oak for twelve to fourteen months. Its quality seems to improve year by year, producing a red wine of a complexity and length that is rarely found in a country so preoccupied with primary fruit and that testifies to Albert's international orientation. Other notable wines from this stable (indeed, they sound a little like racehorses) are Bela Rex (Cabernet Sauvignon/Merlot), Hochacker, Creitzer and the Steinriegel Chardonnay, which is very pleasant but perhaps still oaked a little too strongly.

Engelbert and Albert Gesellmann, Langegasse 65, 7301 Deutsch-kreutz (phone 02613-80360, fax 02613-89544).

Heinrich

Johann Heinrich is on his way to becoming one of the better red wine producers in the region. His Blaufränkisch Goldberg is his best wine and illustrates his attempt to find a round, soft style with emphasis on fruit, not the high-tannin creatures often made here. I was less taken by the Pinot noir and Cabernet Sauvignon.

Johann Heinrich, Karrnergasse 59, 7301 Deutschkreutz (phone and fax 02613-89615).

Iby
10 ha
Blaufränkisch, Zweigelt, Pinot noir, Cabernet Sauvignon, Merlot

Anton Iby is forever enthusiastically improving his wine cellar, and

has just built a high-tech affair made to his exact specifications. He strongly believes in being in control, and has made the very modest estate he took over from his father into one of the most famous in the Middle Burgenland. Mr Iby has a second passion apart from winemaking: the local church choir, of which he is an enthusiastic member. His wines bespeak the tight direction of their genesis, for nothing escapes Mr Iby's eagle eye: he uses industrial yeasts, the fermentation is computer-controlled to within an inch of its life, and the big wines are aged in barriques for twelve months. Too often, a strong reliance on technology can be at the cost of a wine's individuality. Still, he produces good Blaufränkisch, the main variety of his estate and of the area, with typical fruit.
Anton and Johanna Iby, Kirchengasse 4a, 7312 Horitschon (phone 02610-2292, fax 02610-2292).

Igler
10 ha
Blaufränkisch, Cabernet Sauvignon, Pinot noir, St Laurent
Hans Igler, the father of the current owner, was one of the red wine pioneers in this area. Today the estate is led by his daughter Waltraut together with her husband, Wolfgang Reisner, who rather bizarrely also has a day job as director of the local bank. The wines produced here, almost exclusively red, stand at the forefront of Austrian reds, managing to balance fruit and structure. The cuvée Vulcano (Blaufränkisch/Cabernet Sauvignon), aged in barrique and large oak barrels for one year, is especially convincing and also ages well, though the Blaufränkisch and Cabernet Sauvignon wines also show the great care with which they have been made and have considerable potential.
Waltraut Reisner-Igler and Wolfgang Reisner, Langegasse 49, 7301 Deutschkreutz (phone 02613-365, fax 02613-8683).

Kerschbaum
10 ha
Blaufränkisch, Zweigelt, Cabernet Sauvignon
Pinot blanc
Paul Kerschbaum's winery is right in the middle of Austria's 'red wine country' and it therefore comes as little surprise that he concentrates on those two warhorses of the Austrian red wine production, Blaufränkisch and Zweigelt, though his Cabernet Sauvignon has also received high praise. Never has a Zweigelt been

darker than those that he produces, and never more classically in the Austrian tradition, with great emphasis on primary fruit. He does have the advantage of being able to work with old vineyards and he makes full use of it. His cellar (expanding, like all around him) sports many a cask from Allier as well as some Austrian oak, and all his wines are elevated in wood. Kerschbaum is a retiring man whose passion for dark, densely structured red wines shines out only when he is in his cellar, where he delights in trying samples from various casks. I found a little too much emphasis on primary fruit in these wines, at the cost of their length and complexity. His Blaufränkisch wines, though, are very highly thought of by others. *Paul Kerschbaum, Hauptstraße 37, 7312 Horitschon (phone 02610-2392, fax 02610-2392).*

Lehrner
Interesting red wines, especially Zweigelt and Cuvée Paulus. *Paul Lehrner, Hauptstraße 56, 7312 Horitschon (phone 02610-42171, fax 02610-421718)*

Strehn
Monika Pfneisl-Strehn is a new kid on the block, now managing a large estate (43 ha) with a helping hand from the Australian flying winemaker Michael Gadd. *Familie Strehn, Mittelgasse 9, 7301 Deutschkreuz (phone 02613-80246, fax 02613-80706).*

Wellanschitz (Donatus-Weingut)
Fine red wines from a very stylish winery. The Blaufränkisch Barrique, Pinot noir and Cabernet Sauvignon are especially worth looking out for, and have been well received. *Stefan and Georg Wellanschitz, Lange Zeile 28, 7311 Neckenmarkt (phone 02610-42302, fax 02610-423024).*

Weninger
Only red wines; very good results with traditional cellar techniques. *Familie Weninger, Florianigasse 11, 7312 Horitschon (phone and fax 02610-2165).*

SOUTH BURGENLAND

Vineyards: 457 ha
Soil: slate, clay, loam

White (60 per cent): Welschriesling, Grüner Veltliner, Pinot blanc, Muscat Ottonel

Red (40 per cent): Blaufränkisch, Zweigelt, Cabernet Sauvignon, Uhudler

Sandwiched between Styria in the west and Hungary in the east, the South Burgenland is treated as a separate area. There are only a few pockets of wine growing here, spread over some twenty kilometres, mainly around the villages of Rechnitz, Eisenberg, Deutsch Schützen, Eberau and Heiligenbrunn in the very south. It is the smallest wine producing region of the Burgenland, at least in terms of area under vine. This is a landscape of gently rolling hills, with climatic and geological conditions quite different from those of the other parts of the Burgenland. The hills here rise up to almost 900 metres above sea level and on their slopes weathered blue slate makes up the majority of the soil, while deep clay and loam dominate in the valleys.

The Eisenberg, a centre for wine growing, was used as a mine for iron ore in Roman times. It protects the vines from northerly winds while exposing them to the warmth streaming up from the Pannonian plains, and the wooded hills let the air cool down during the night, adding to the difference in temperature between day and night. With around 600 mm annual precipitation, the South Burgenland lies between the figures for other parts of the Burgenland.

South Burgenland seems far away from everything, a remote region of idyllic rolling hills, dark woods and medieval castles – among which, incidentally, is Lockenhaus, the forbidding fortress where the violinist Gidon Kremer holds his legendary music festivals.

A local rarity is the Uhudler, a rosé made directly from American rootstocks (see Grape Varieties) in the village of Heiligenbrunn. The only other Uhudler is made in neighbouring West Styria.

Top growers in South Burgenland

Krutzler
6.5 ha
Blaufränkisch, Zweigelt, Blauburger, Cabernet Sauvignon
The Krutzler winery, beautifully located in the rolling hills of South Burgenland, is one of the most highly rated red wine producers,

not only locally but throughout Austria. Led mainly by Krutzler's sons Erich and Reinhold, it has been at the very front of the pack for more than ten years. As usual in this area, the main grape is Blaufränkisch, at times rounded off with a little Zweigelt. Krutzler's best wine, the Perwolff, grown on heavy loam soils, is a cuvée of Blaufränkisch, Zweigelt and Cabernet Sauvignon which is aged in up to 50 per cent new oak for eighteen months. This is a very fine wine indeed: dense and full-bodied with good tannic structure, typically Austrian fruit and plenty of depth and complexity, possibly a style leading the way for red wines in this part of the world with its peppery spice and surprisingly good length.

The last Alter Weingarten (old vineyard) that I tasted was extraordinarily good, a smooth but assertive cuvéc that seemed to combine the best in Austrian reds. It was a 1996 vintage, which is usually difficult for red wines here. The greater 1997 vintage led to some wines with immense potential which will need to age for a few years. They already show a beautiful interplay between fruit and structure, as well as impressive length, though the primary bramble tones still dominate.

Krutzler's wines are widely acknowledged to be as close to the ideal of what a red wine from Middle Burgenland should be as anyone has achieved yet. They are also among the best produced in the country.

Erich and Reinhold Krutzler, Hauptstraße 84, 7474 Deutsch-Schützen (phone and fax 03365-2242).

Szemes
Blaufränkisch, Cabernet Sauvignon (all bought in)
Tibor Szemes is an immediately engaging, genial man, but does not actually possess vineyards, nor are there any around his estate. As if this were not peculiar enough already, he is originally Hungarian, as his name suggests, and is a fervent monarchist. The Szemes family settled here as wine dealers, and only Tibor has begun to buy grapes and to make wines out of them in his own cellar filled with Allier barrels. He makes only two wines, called (appropriately for his convictions) Tradition and Imperial. He also makes a red cuvée called Arachon, together with F. X. Pichler and Manfred Tement.

Tibor and Illa Szemes, Weinhoferplatz 7, 7423 Pinkafeld (phone 03357-42367, fax 03357-42157).

Weinviertel

Area profile

Vineyards: 18,004 ha
Soil: loess, loam, primary rock, black earth
White (85 per cent): Grüner Veltliner, Neuburger, Müller-Thurgau, Pinot blanc, Ruländer, Traminer, Welschriesling, Roter Veltliner, Frühroter Veltliner
Red (15 per cent): Blauer Portugieser, Zweigelt

With more than 16,000 ha of vineyards, a third of the country's entire area under vines, this is the largest wine producing region

Weinviertel

of Austria. The landscape here can be very pleasant: softly rolling hills stretching in all directions, vineyards and woodland punctuated by small towns and villages with lovely baroque architecture. Small wonder, then, that it has become a favourite retreat for writers and artists.

The Weinviertel ('wine region') stretches over most of northeastern Austria, right up to the Slovak border. Being Austria's chief provider of wine, it contains a great number of good, reliable producers. The best are often distinguished from their rivals by their ability and diligence, not by their terroir, though there are some pockets with distinctive soils and microclimates that have been recognized as being particularly suited to certain grape varietals and styles.

The geology of the Weinviertel is diverse. There is loess and black soil, mainly planted with Grüner Veltliner and Müller-Thurgau, pure loess for a variety of white and red varietals, and loam, thought to be particularly suited to Pinot blanc and Traminer. Sandy soils are less popular with the growers here, while chalky soils are planted with Pinot blanc, Neuburger and Zweigelt, especially in the Mailberg region. There are some primary rock soils as well, which are planted mainly with Grüner Veltliner, Welschriesling and, alas, Blauer Portugieser.

The climate in the Weinviertel is moderate. With an average precipitation of about 500 mm per annum (only 400 mm around Retz and Wolkersdorf), it is one of the driest wine-producing areas in Europe. The mean temperature, however, is lower than in the Kamptal, Kremstal and Wachau to the west: 6–7° C. Unlike Carnuntum and the Burgenland to the south, the climate of the Weinviertel is not dominated by the Pannonian plains, whose influence is broken by the hills of Slovakia. In this area, western European weather systems dominate, and at 180 days the vegetation period can be considerably shorter than that of other areas. The sheer extent of the region, however, means that various microclimates create conditions under which very different wines can ripen.

One such microclimate distinguishes the Mailberg area, a small pocket situated in the north centre of the Weinviertel. This cauldron-shaped valley with sand and loess soils allows some interesting red wines to ripen on the south-east facing hillsides. Owing to the enclosed nature of the valley, daytime temperatures are higher than those of the surrounding areas, while at night cool air comes streaming down from the wooded top of the Buchberg in the west. The growers of this area, incidentally, market their wines under the English designation 'Mailberg Valley', a very New World approach.

A notable feature of the Weinviertel are its Kellergassen (cellar streets), streets lined with the façades of wine cellars, looking very much like stuccoed baroque houses built into the hills. These little towns, all of whose inhabitants live in bottles, can be enormously atmospheric places, conjuring up images of a lost world.

Retz, which has proper live inhabitants, is the most important centre: a charming seven-hundred-year-old town with some quite beautiful buildings and a labyrinthine system of cellars and vaults crisscrossing under the foundations of the houses to a total length of twenty-six kilometres.

These cellars are not only an ideal storage space for wines, but also provided a network of escape routes for some of the town's inhabitants during its numerous periods of occupation: by the Swedes during the Thirty Years War, the Prussians in the eighteenth century, Napoleon's army during the nineteenth and the Germans and Russians in the twentieth century.

The soils around Retz, mainly weathered gneiss and granite, and one of the lowest annual precipitation rates in Austria make this fertile ground for light, aromatic wines, 70 per cent of which are white.

Apart from these specific districts, the wines produced in the Weinviertel can broadly be divided into east and west. The west (around the towns of Retz, Horn, Hollabrunn and Korneuburg) is mainly planted with indigenous varietals such as Grüner Veltliner, Gemischter Satz, Müller-Thurgau, Welschriesling and Frühroter Veltliner, and smaller amounts of Pinot blanc, Chardonnay and Riesling. Among the red wines, which are very much in the minority here, there is Blauer Portugieser, Zweigelt and Blauburger, and more recently Cabernet Sauvignon.

The eastern Weinviertel (around Mistelbach and Gänserndorf) produces mainly light, fresh and acidic wines, vinified predominantly from Grüner Veltliner, but also Welschriesling, Müller-Thurgau, Pinot blanc, Frühroter Veltliner and Riesling. There are some 'red islands' in which Blauer Portugieser and Zweigelt are grown. Welschriesling is also used as a basic wine for sekt, especially by the renowned Viennese firms Schlumberger and Kattus.

Top growers

Diem
Good, long-lived Pinot blanc and Zweigelt are made on this well-known estate. His 1998 Grüner Veltliner shows beautifully clean fruit, while his Müller-Thurgau shows some real (and rare) character.
2223 Hohenruppersdorf 118 (phone 02574-8292).

Fidesser
These are surprisingly well defined wines with pleasantly articulated fruit. The Grüner Veltliner and Sauvignon blanc are especially worth looking out for. The 1998 vintage was a great step forward for the estate, with rose-scented Frühroter Veltliner and a beautiful Roter Veltliner Höhweingarten with good extract and plenty of fruit. His Muskateller was voted one of the best of the entire vintage.
Rudolf Fidesser, 2051 Platt 6 (phone and fax 02945-2592).

Friedberger
An undramatic, classic Weinviertel estate which produces good solid Grüner Veltliner, Riesling and Pinot blanc. His 1998 Riesling Spätlese Isperinnen, however, was something out of the ordinary.
Leopold Friedberger, Hauptstraße 17, 2102 Bisamberg (phone 02262-62446).

Schlossweingut Graf Hardegg
43 ha
Grüner Veltliner, Riesling, Pinot blanc
Merlot, Zweigelt, Cabernet Sauvignon, Viognier
Being a count who has the largest agricultural estate in Austria, which also produces wine, has the agreeable side effect of enabling one to produce barriques from one's very own oak. Ripening in these barrels are the best Hardegg wines, especially the first growths, which are called MAX like the first sons of the family. Apart from wines, the Hardegg estate, set in a Habsburg yellow baroque castle surrounded by water, offers beauty in plenty. The wines themselves, though, merit at least as much attention as the

splendid paintings in the family chapel. The Merlot/Cabernet MAX is without doubt the best red wine in the area, while the Riesling and the highly regarded Pinot blanc are mighty, meaty wines which manage to combine power and elegant aromas. As a concession to modern times, their easy-drinking Grüner Veltliner is called Veltlinsky. Hardegg also makes Austria's first, and so far only, fortified Port-style wine.

Maximilian Hardegg and Peter Veyder-Malberg, 2062 Seefeld-Kadolz (phone 02943-2203, fax 02943-220310).

Malteser Ritterorden (*see* Lenz Moser, Kremstal)

Minkowitsch
Roland Minkowitsch is one of the few Austrian growers still to use an old tree press. He also ripens all his wines in barrels, both large and, in the case of his Chardonnay, small new oak. Resulting from this are beautifully dense and fruity wines with considerable individuality. I was especially taken by a marvellously rich Gewürztraminer Auslese. His Riesling 'de vite' and Welschriesling Ausbruch are also fine, with good and harmonious interplay between fruit and acidity.

Roland Minkowitsch, 2261 Mannersdorf an der March 64 (phone and fax 02283-2583).

Nebenführ
Erich Nebenführ's wines are quite rustic in style and often lack refinement. He is, however, a consistent producer of Grüner Veltliner, Sauvignon blanc and Gewürztraminer.

Erich Nebenführ, 2070 Mitterretzbach 64 (phone 02942-2186).

Pfaffl
25 ha
Grüner Veltliner, Riesling, Chardonnay, Sauvignon blanc, Welschriesling
Cabernet Sauvignon, Zweigelt
Though known as 'Mr Veltliner', Roman Pfaffl is making an effort to increase his red wine production. It was hard graft for him to get to this position, and nobody would have predicted it when he took over a farm with a little under one hectare under vines in 1979. He increased the vineyards and improved his wines steadily year by year, and slowly began to be recognized as one of the better wine growers of the area. With the 1997 vintage, he managed

to break through into the top ranks of the white wine growers with Veltliners that not only had the distinctive pepper note (the 'Pfaffl-Pfefferl') so much associated with his wine, but also some breadth to back it up. These Grüne Veltliners are unashamedly Austrian, not looking to emulate foreign styles.

On 25 hectares of terraced loess vineyards, Mr Pfaffl also cultivates other grapes, all with good success. In 1997 his Riesling, technically *lieblich* (semi-sweet), turned out elegant and long. His red cuvée of Zweigelt and Cabernet Sauvignon is also interesting. Recent investments in cellar technology and work in the vineyard according to organic principles produce a happy marriage between nature and culture of which his wines give eloquent testimony. A fine grower.

Roman Pfaffl, Hauptstraße 24, 2100 Stetten (phone 02262-673423, fax 02262-673661).

Pleil

Josef Pleil may not be a large grower, but he is a decidedly big cheese. As president of the Federation of Austrian Wine Growers, he exchanges the vineyard for a Vienna office to represent his fellow producers. His own estate is still evolving, with a good deal of new plantings yet to come into their own. Best for Grüner Veltliner, Welschriesling and Riesling.

Josef and Christian Pleil, Adlergasse 32, 2120 Wolkersdorf (phone 02245-2407, fax 02245-24074).

Salomon

An old estate producing consistently good Grüner Veltliner, Riesling and Sylvaner. His estate benefits from the distinctive microclimate around Falkenstein, a valley surrounded by forests that shield the vineyards from cold winds. Not to be confused with the Undhof Salomon, or with Fritz Salomon of Gut Oberstockstall.

Josef Salomon, 2162 Falkenstein 24 (phone and fax 02554-437).

Schuckert

Rainer Schuckert is a creative grower, constantly engaged in driving forward the character and possibilities of his wine, especially his Grüner Veltliner and Chardonnay – which demonstrate that he is very much on the right track.

Rainer Schuckert, Wilhelmsdorferstraße 40, 2170 Poysdorf (phone and fax 02552-2389).

Schwarzböck

A small producer with very good Riesling and fine Zweigelt.
Rudolf Schwarzböck, Schloßgasse 21, 2102 Hagenbrunn (phone and fax 02262-672784).

Setzer

Well off the beaten track, Hans and Ulrike Setzer are producing some very remarkable Grüner Veltliner, Sauvignon blanc and a mighty oak-aged Chardonnay, demonstrating that both grower and region have considerable potential.
Hans and Ulrike Setzer, 3472 Hohenwarth 28 (phone 02957-228, fax 02957-205).

Strell

A consistent producer in a corner of the Weinviertel not otherwise known for wine production. The quality is going up steadily, and the Grüner Veltliner, Pinot blanc and Sauvignon blanc are interesting wines already. There is also an improving production of Cabernet Sauvignon and Pinot noir.
Josef and Juliana Strell, 3710 Radbrunn 138 (phone 02956-2466).

Taubenschuß

Among the most consistent performers of the Weinviertel, the Taubenschuß wines are always competent, though never spectacular. There is a good, straight Chardonnay Classic, vinified in steel, and a meaty Pinot blanc Selection. The majority of the wine produced is Grüner Veltliner.
Helmut and Monika Taubenschuß, Körnergasse 2, 2170 Poysdorf (phone 02552-2589, fax 02552-2589-4).

Weinrieder

Friedrich Rieder concentrates his efforts on sweet wines, a rarity in this region. Apart from his remarkable Eiswein, however, he also makes dense Grüner Veltliner and Riesling.
Friedrich Rieder, 2170 Kleinhadersdorf 44 (phone 02252-2241, fax 02252-3708).

Wöber

At times very good, clean Grüner Veltliner, especially Alte Reben.
Anton Wöber, Hollabrunner Straße 3, 3710 Ziersdorf (phone 02956-2261).

Zens

Good, peppery Grüner Veltliner, also Riesling and a very respectable Chardonnay Spätlese are made on this estate.

Josef Zens, Holzgasse 66, 2024 Mailberg (phone 02943-3557, fax 02943-2803).

Zull

In addition to good Grüner Veltliner and Riesling, Werner Zull makes a red cuvée from Cabernet Sauvignon, Merlot and Zweigelt, which has made him well known beyond the Weinviertel.

Werner Zull, 2073 Schrattenthal 9 (phone and fax 02946-8217).

Thermenregion

Area profile

Vineyards: 2,814 ha
Soils: chalky loam in the north-west, gravel, clay, sand
White (70 per cent): Pinot blanc, Neuburger, Zierfandler, Rotgipfler
Red (30 per cent): Blauer Portugieser, Zweigelt, Pinot noir, Cabernet Sauvignon

Just south of Vienna, the Thermenregion got its name from the many health spas (*Thermen*) which could be found here, though the Viennese still call it, less ceremoniously, Südbahn ('southern railway'), as the tracks for the old southern railway run through the area and its vineyards. The Viennese often take the Thermenregion as a natural extension of their city and go to a *Heurige* in, say, Baden or Gumpoldskirchen instead of choosing the nearer ones in the suburbs.

This charming landscape was traditionally known for its remarkable wines, and ambitious writers have compared its soils to those of the Côte d'Or. Such flights of fancy aside, the Thermenregion offers excellent conditions for making wine and has long been known for its consistent and good production. As already mentioned, these wines especially were often referred to by their town of origin, e.g. Vöslauer or Gumpoldskirchner. Red grapes were already planted here experimentally during the second half of the nineteenth century.

The Vienna Woods protect the entire region from the cold northerly winds and leave it in the Pannonian sphere of influence: hot summers, cold winters and an annual mean temperature of 10° C. In warm years grapes can suffer heat damage, especially in the southern Thermenregion, and wine growers have to be careful not

Thermenregion and Carnuntum

to produce wines with low acidity. The annual precipitation is around 650 mm, and the vegetation period is about 230 days.

The southern, drier part of the region, also called Steinfeld, has soils dominated by layers of sand and clay on chalk with large deposits of gravel, a constellation especially suitable for red wines. This region is extremely vulnerable to spring frosts.

In the north of the Thermenregion there is a higher groundwater level. Porous loam soils in the lower parts give way to the weathered volcanic rock that marks the soils of the Vienna Woods. The maritime origins of the low-lying soils are demonstrated by the frequent finds of petrified coral, seashells, etc., especially in the area around Sooß.

To the south-east, the region is dominated by a chain of hills of which the Anninger, 674 metres, is the highest. The heavy and rich slopes in the north-west of the Thermenregion are good ground for more demanding white varietals such as Pinot blanc, Chardonnay and Traminer, as well as the more traditional Zierfandler, Rotgipfler and Neuburger, the latter of which can be both powerful and complex. There are also red wine 'islands' in the south of the area, around the towns of Sooß, Bad Vöslau and Tattendorf. Zweigelt, Blauer Portugieser, St Laurent and Pinot noir dominate here.

Some very enthusiastic producers in the Thermenregion are making remarkable wines. Still, the potential of soils and climate here does not seem to have been fully explored yet. Perhaps this region is due for a renaissance.

Top growers

Alphart
Karl Alphart is concerned to conserve some of the indigenous grape varietals, such as the Zierfandler and Rotgipfler, for which this region is particularly well known. He makes them into very interesting wines, especially cuvées. He also makes good sweet wines from Riesling and Rotgipfler.
Karl Alphart, Wiener Straße 46, 2514 Traiskirchen (phone 02252-52328, fax 02252-523284).

Aumann

Leopold Aumann is a young grower whose wines have started to attract some attention. Red varieties such as Zweigelt and Cabernet Sauvignon seem to flourish especially well under his care.

Leopold Aumann, Oberwaltersdorfer Straße 105, 2512 Tribuswinkel (phone 02252-80502).

Biegler

Manfred Biegler has one of the best *Heurige* in the area, beautifully situated in a Renaissance house in Gumpoldskirchen. Among his wines there are, apart from the local heroes Zierfandler and Rotgipfler, some good Rieslings and Chardonnay.

Manfred Biegler, Wiener Straße, 2352 Gumpoldskirchen (phone 02252-62196, fax 02252-621964).

Chorherren Klosterneuburg

With 103 ha, this is the largest estate around, though only about a third of the vineyards, those for red wines and Spätrot-Rotgipfler, are in the Thermenregion. The Chorherren, a religious order, also have possessions in the Donauland and Vienna. The Stift Klosterneuburg in which the winery is located is worth a visit for the museum and the ancient, sprawling cellars alone. The wines are not often very exciting, but there is good, clean Pinot blanc, Chardonnay and Traminer, and a very solid St Laurent.

Franz Kaufmann, Am Renninger 2, 3400 Klosterneuburg (phone 02243-36375-0, fax 02243-37555).

Fischer

Christian Fischer produces both red and white wines, but it is the reds that steal the show. There is a good Pinot noir with moderate new oak. The Cabernet Sauvignon and Zweigelt are also clean and powerful.

Christian Fischer, Hauptstraße 33, 2500 Sooß (phone 0225-87130).

Richard Fischer

Good Pinot noir and Zweigelt, also a very respectable Scheurebe Auslese.

Richard Fischer, Enzensfelder Straße 16, 2544 Leobersdorf (phone 02256-62287).

Grabner-Schierer

Those invited to the Vienna Hofburg in an official capacity are likely to encounter the consistent and well-produced red wines from the Grabner-Schierer estate, though for my taste they are too traditionally Austrian and somewhat one-dimensional with little to excite an internationally oriented palate.

Karl Grabner and Sepp Schierer, Hauptstraße 55, 2500 Sooß (phone 02252-87392).

Reinisch (Johanneshof)

25 ha
Chardonnay, Pinot blanc, Riesling, Sauvignon blanc
Cabernet Sauvignon, Merlot, Pinot noir, St Laurent, Zweigelt

As he was trained in California, it is hardly surprising that Johannes Reinisch should strive to replicate his American experience, not only in terms of cellar technology, but also by building a state-of-the-art winery right in the middle of the Thermenregion. From the belfry and the large brick cellars with 350 barriques, inbuilt romanticism and indirect lighting, to the modern winery itself, the filling and packaging rooms and the reception area and *Heurige*, this is about as perfect as an architect can design it, and the Californian inspiration is unmissable. All this was not anticipated when Johannes Reinisch senior had to take over his father's orchards and vineyards at the age of twenty, but together with his son he has pioneered this new approach to winemaking in Austria.

The wines produced in this impressive high-tech family dream are nothing if not innovative along a New World line. There is powerful oak-aged Chardonnay with full, ripe aromas (which often does not quite manage to integrate the amount of new oak thrown at it), as well as dense Pinot noir and a cuvée of Cabernet Sauvignon-Merlot, the latter two aged in barriques for eighteen months. Perhaps better than these and closer to home is Reinisch's meaty barrique-aged St Laurent Reserve. Recently, the Reinischs have also begun to produce interesting dessert wines.

Johannes Reinisch, Im Weingarten 1, 2523 Tattendorf (phone 02253-81423, fax 02253-81924).

Schafler (Schaflerhof)

From the whole palette of wines offered by Andreas Schafler, the Chardonnay 'Großer Wein' and the Spätrot-Rotgipfler BA are especially remarkable.

Andreas Schafler, Wiener Straße 9-11, 2541 Traiskirchen (phone 02252-523780, fax 02252-523788).

Schellmann
A pioneer of dry wines in his area, Gottfried Schellmann produces a very good Chardonnay and a fine Traminer, as well as wines typical for the area, such as a good Zierfandler and Zierfandler BA.
Gottfried Schellmann, Wiener Straße 41, 2352 Gumpoldskirchen (phone 02252-62218, fax 02252-622184).

Stadlmann
An estate particularly strong on indigenous grape varietals, such as Zierfandler and Rotgipfler, but also known for interesting Rieslings. Stadlmann's Zierfandler can be quite complex and interesting, with good depth and fruit notes.
Johann Stadlmann, Wiener Straße 41, 2514 Traiskirchen (phone 02252-52343, fax 02252-56332).

Thiel (Kremsmünsterhof)
It is rare for a grower in this region to produce a truly exceptional Riesling, but in 1997 Richard Thiel managed to do just that. Amid an enormous range of wines, the Chardonnay and the Zierfandler-Rotgipfler TBA are very good, too.
Richard Thiel, Badener Straße 11, 2352 Gumpoldskirchen (phone and fax 02252-62372).

Zierer
Harald Zierer is something of a specialist when it comes to sweet wines. Wines like his Rotgipfler-Chardonnay TBA 1995 and Rotgipfler BA are widely respected, lean and dense, with plenty of promise.
Harald Zierer, Badener Straße 36, 2352 Gumpoldskirchen (phone and fax 02252-62169)

Carnuntum

Area profile

Vineyards: 995 ha
Soil: sand, loam, gravel, loess
White (80 per cent): Grüner Veltliner, Welschriesling, Pinot blanc, Chardonnay
Red (20 per cent): Blaufränkisch, Zweigelt, Cabernet Sauvignon, St Laurent

Carnuntum is a somewhat synthetic administrative entity, named after the eponymous capital of the Roman province that existed here 2,000 years ago. Situated on the banks of the Danube, Carnuntum was the largest city in the Roman border colony, an important trading point on the Amber Road. Seventy thousand people lived there, compared to 1,200 today. Relics such as a triumphal arch and an amphitheatre still testify to this part of the region's past. The modern Carnuntum is a wedge between the Weinviertel to the north, delineated by the river Danube, and the Neusiedlersee region to the south, reaching some fifty kilometres from Vienna to the Slovak border.

In terms of wine production, the most important area of Carnuntum is the four-kilometre stretch between Göttlesbrunn and Höflein which contains the majority of forward-looking winemakers. The vineyards in the second area, to the east near Prellenkirchen, are mainly cultivated by part-time growers and *Heurige* producers. Wine of distinction is a rarity there.

The geology of the area is dominated by the changing course of a prehistoric river, which deposited gravel throughout. This was partly overlaid by loess during the Ice Age. The soils of the vineyards of Carnuntum are deep and fertile, with some loam and sand.

Climatically, the Leitha mountains and the Vienna Woods to the north-west shield the area from the influence of western European weather systems. Pannonian influences prevail here, leading to hot summers and cold winters. During summer nights, cool air from the Vienna Woods increases the temperature variation between day and night. The barrier of the Vienna Woods, however, can lead to a shortage of rain, as the clouds reaching the area from the west have often shed their load over the hills. Another problematic aspect of the climate of the area is the northerly winds, which push down winter temperatures as low as −20° C, leading to frost damage to the vines. Only the vineyards around Göttlesbrunn are protected from this to some degree by the Alstenberg and Schüttenberg, two hills shielding the vineyards on their southerly slopes from the influence of the wind.

The wines produced here are often meaty reds and substantial white wines, the former usually made from Blaufränkisch and Zweigelt, the latter from Grüner Veltliner, Gemischter Satz (i.e. a mixture of varietals on one plot), Müller-Thurgau, Welschriesling, Pinot blanc and Riesling.

Top growers

Glatzer
Walter Glatzer can surprise with wines one would not think possible in this area. In some years his Pinot blanc is of almost Burgundian proportions, while his cuvée Gotisprun (Zweigelt/Blaufränkisch/Cabernet Sauvignon) can be very compact and well structured. He also produces a powerful Zweigelt.
Walter Glatzer, 2464 Göttlesbrunn 76 (phone 02162-8486, fax 02162-8901).

Grassl
Good Chardonnay and Zweigelt.
Hans Grassl, Am Graben 4 and 6, 2464 Göttlesbrunn (phone and fax 02162-8483).

Markowitsch

12 ha

Chardonnay, Grüner Veltliner, Sauvignon blanc

Blaufränkisch, Cabernet Sauvignon, Merlot, Pinot noir, Zweigelt

Gerhard Markowitsch is a rising star in the Austrian red wine world and has produced some very remarkable wines. His declared aim is to produce wines that will mature for many years but which are ready to drink even when young (he is certainly not alone in trying to achieve this). His Pinot noir Reserve takes its inspiration from Burgundy, while his Redmont (Zweigelt/Cabernet Sauvignon) is aged in American oak and is a real New World wine from central of Europe. In 1997, his Zweigelt Rubin was hailed by Austrian tasters as the best Zweigelt of the year. Next to these very considerable red wines, there is also a broadly structured Chardonnay and an intense Grüner Veltliner.

Gerhard Markowitsch, Pfarrgasse 6–8, 2464 Göttlesbrunn (phone and fax 02162-8222).

Pitnauer

Hans Pitnauer is a grower in step with his time; he even sells his wines over the Internet. No surprise, then, that he uses not only Cabernet Sauvignon but also Syrah for his best red wines. His cuvée Pegasus is made with 80 per cent Syrah and equal parts of Zweigelt and Cabernet Sauvignon, and promises to be a beautiful wine: intense, with rounded tannins and good length. The St Laurent and Zweigelt are also good and well structured. Among the white wines, the cask-aged Pinot blanc shows especially good potential and density.

Hans Pitnauer, Weinbergstraße 4–6, 2464 Göttlesbrunn (phone and fax 02162-8249, e-mail pitnauer@austrian-wines.com).

Donauland

═══════

Area profile

Vineyards: 2,814 ha
Soil: loess, gravel, loam
White (85 per cent): Grüner Veltliner, Riesling, Pinot blanc, Roter Veltliner
Red (15 per cent): Zweigelt, Blauer Portugieser, Blauburger

Named almost by default, and a successor to various other administrative districts, the Donauland is the stretch of land separating Vienna from the Kamptal and Kremstal on the north side of the Danube and the Traisental on the south side. The vineyards of the Donauland amount to about 2,800 hectares.

There are two reasons why Klosterneuburg is the most important town in this region: the splendid monastery, which was founded in the twelfth century and still owns many of the vineyards throughout Austria, and the Klosterneuburg School of Viticulture – or, to give its full name, the *Höhere Bundeslehranstalt und Bundesamt für Wein- und Obstbau* – the centre of Austrian research and teaching on vines and wines for more than a hundred years.

The influence of the Klosterneuburg school is difficult to overestimate. Not only was Austria's most popular red grape, the Zweigelt, developed here, but the know-how acquired here by young growers travels into every corner of the country and has only recently been rivalled and complemented by the expertise brought back from all over the wine world by those curious enough to venture abroad. A large proportion of aspiring young wine growers still spend the last few years of their schooling boarding at Klosterneuburg.

There are three areas in this region: the Wagram on the north

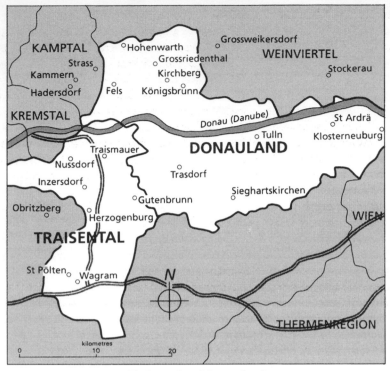

Traisental and Donauland

bank of the Danube has soils which are almost pure loess on gravel, with some pockets of loam and gravel near the surface. It is possible to carve long and deep cellars out of this soil without any need for reinforcements, and wine growers take advantage of this fact. Near Klosterneuburg, lying on the other side of the Danube, almost an island as far as wine growing is concerned, weathered sandstone, loess and loam determine the soil, with more chalk than on the north bank.

The Wagram hills in the east of the Donauland and the foothills of the Manhartsberg open up the region to the influence of the Pannonian climate, tempered by the proximity of the Danube, which acts as a regulating influence on the temperature and moisture levels. Klosterneuburg benefits both from more varied soils and from its nearness to the river and to the Vienna Woods, creating a specific microclimate.

Grüner Veltliner and Roter Veltliner especially take to these conditions very well. Most growers here cultivate vineyards as a part of mixed agriculture, and there is a particularly strong tendency here to make wine *naturnah*, i.e. without chaptalization and with as few chemicals in the vineyard as possible. Riesling and Pinot blanc are also growing well here. The Großriedental, towards the Kamptal in the north-west, is famous for its Eiswein.

The Tulbingerkogel, the third area, produces Grüner Veltliner, Neuburger, Riesling, Sylvaner and Welschriesling, and red wines such as Zweigelt, Blauer Portugieser and Blauburger. This is also an area recognized for its Eiswein.

Top growers

Bauer
Good cuvée from Chardonnay and Pinot blanc with good citrus fruit, and dense Sauvignon blanc; also very individual Riesling Pfarrleiten.
Josef Bauer, Neufang 52, 3483 Feuersbrunn am Wagram (phone 02738-2309)

Chorherren Klosterneuburg (see Thermenregion)

Fritsch
A good, reliable winemaker, especially renowned for his Eiswein and Auslese, Karl Fritsch is also the leader of the marketing group Wagramer Selektion, which strives not only to give the wines of the region a stronger profile, but also to raise their quality. His Riesling and Grüner Veltliner are well made and recognized as being among the best in the area. The reds tend to be less exciting, though his 1997 Pinot noir was a very interesting wine.
Karl Fritsch, Oberstockstall 24, 3470 Kirchberg am Wagram (phone 02279-274, fax 02279-2830)

Grill
Franz Grill produces dense wines with good fruit. His Grüner Veltliner Auslese is especially remarkable.
Franz and Gertrude Grill, Untere Marktstraße 19, 3481 Fels am Wagram (phone 02738-2239, fax 02738-2239-4).

Kolkmann

The wines of the Kolkmann estate were among the discoveries of my 1999 tasting tour. A Neuburger Spätlese showed complexity and denseness, and the Grüner Veltliner Spätlese had good, ripe fruit aromas. There was a remarkably harmonious Grüner Veltliner Eiswein as well. The real surprise, however, was a beautifully smooth and elegant barrique-aged Zweigelt Spätlese that showed real depth and potential and had no problem whatsoever in dealing with its new oak.

Familie Kolkmann, Flugplatzstraße 12, 3481 Fels am Wagram (phone 02738-2436, fax 02738-2436-4).

Leth

Franz Leth has a relatively large estate (33 ha) and produces well-structured wines, especially Sauvignon blanc, Roter Veltliner and Traminer. The emphasis here is not on power but on elegance and balance, which are achieved very successfully. In recent years he has also made good red wines such as a remarkable 1997 Cabernet Sauvignon and a fine Grüner Veltliner BA.

Franz Leth, Kirchengasse 6, 3481 Fels am Wagram (phone 02738-2240, fax 02738-224017).

Litana

Toni Söllner is a stylish wine grower who took over this traditional estate from his father in 1990. His family have been making wine in the Wagram area for five generations, and his father is the owner of the Wachstum Söllner estate (see below). Toni Söllner's ecological philosophy is evident in every part of the production process, and is rewarded with some Rieslings and Roter Veltliners of real individuality and charm. He is also trying to advance the style of the region's wines by experimenting with new cuvées. His expertise is soon to be supplemented by the input of his younger brother, who is currently working for Willi Bründlmayer. The Grüner Veltliner Hengsberg shows beautifully ripe aromas, while the Roter Veltliner-Grüner Veltliner Auslese cuvée 1998 is opulent and dense and perhaps his best wine yet. There is also a very interesting cuvée of Welschriesling and Riesling. Söllner cultivates his wines according to organic principles and tries even in the cellar to interfere with them as little as possible. A very promising estate.

Daniele Vigne and Toni Söllner, Berggasse 1, 3482 Gösing (phone and fax 02738-3201).

Winzerhaus Ott

Bernhard Ott is a young wine grower for whom 1997 was the first year to bring more than average success. His Grüner Veltliner expresses good, typical Veltliner fruit with plenty of spice and good structure. Riesling and Sauvignon blanc are not yet as successful.
Bernhard Ott, Neufang 36, 3483 Feuersbrunn (phone 02738-2257, fax 02738-2257-22, e-mail winzerhaus.ott@aon.at).

Stadler

A traditional estate which produces mainly Grüner Veltliner, as is customary in this area. Also good Zweigelt and Pinot blanc.
Ferdinand and Elisabeth Stadler, Großwiesendorf 15, 3701 Großweikersdorf (phone 02955-7430).

Wachstum Söllner

Regardless of the fact that he is now known as 'Toni Söllner's father' rather than as a wine grower in his own right, Toni Söllner *père* is a very respectable producer. While young Mr Söllner makes something of a speciality of his Roter Veltliner, his father leads a more traditional estate with a wider spread of grape varieties, including some red wines.
Toni Söllner, Hauptstraße 34, 3482 Gösing am Wagram (phone and fax 02738-2126).

Wimmer-Czerny

Large, powerful wines, carefully produced. Best here are Grüner Veltliner Weelfel, an almost Burgundian wine, as well as Pinot blanc, Chardonnay and Traminer, with good Eiswein.
Hans Czerny, Obere Marktstraße 37, 3481 Fels am Wagram (phone and fax 02738-2248).

Traisental

Area profile

Vineyards: 696 ha
Soil: loess, loam, granulite and chalky conglomerates
White (88 per cent): Grüner Veltliner, Müller-Thurgau, Chardonnay, Pinot blanc, Riesling, Neuburger
Red (12 per cent): Blauer Portugieser, Zweigelt, Blauburger

Until 1995 part of the region Traismauer-Carnuntum, later Donauland-Carnuntum, the Traisental has won its independence. About seven hundred growers are cultivating as many hectares of land, few with very interesting results. The Traisental is a valley along the river Traisen south of the Danube and north of the town of St Pölten. Most vineyards in this region are situated in a band along the Hollenburger Wald on the west side of the village of Nußdorf, mentioned as a wine growing centre already in 1083. The soils on the right bank of the river are dominated by loess and loam, while the left bank towards the Dunkelsteiner Wald also has some areas of granulite (a relation of granite) and chalky conglomerates.

Almost two-thirds of the wines produced are Grüner Veltliner, with white wines dominating the region and only about 12 per cent red varieties planted. The soils here are mainly loess and loam, with the odd deposit of granulite and some gravel. The latter especially offer very promising conditions for vineyards. The climate of the Traisental is very similar to that of the Donauland – not surprisingly, as the area is only ten kilometres long and a direct continuation of that region. Pannonian influences prevail, while the Danube exercises a regulatory influence on the north of the area, though the influence of the Dunkelsteiner Wald in the west is not conducive to wine production. Annual precipitation is around 520 mm.

That it is indeed possible to produce excellent wines in this area is demonstrated by Ludwig Neumayer, the one grower from here to have claimed some attention over the last few years. His estate is in Inzersdorf, where loam and loess dominate the soil. Neumayer, though, is a great exception: only three per cent of the growers here bottle their own wines and sell them themselves. All in all, the Traisental has so far failed to establish itself on the Austrian wine map.

Top growers

Hoffmann
A recent arrival on the wine landscape, Rudolf Hoffmann used to be a wine dealer in Vienna before turning his attention to making wine himself. He now produces pure wines with an emphasis on fruit, especially a floral Grüner Veltliner Fuchsenrand and a spicy Gemischter Satz.
Rudolf Hoffmann, Özelt-Hof, Oberndorfer Straße 41, 3133 Trais-mauer (phone and fax 0676-3133566).

Kreimel
Herbert Kreimel loves powerful wines and is beginning to produce good, ripe Grüner Veltliners and Rieslings, as well as PI.NO.VI.TA, an unusual cuvée of Grüner Veltliner and Pinot blanc that shows some elegant fruit.
Herbert Kreimel, Bäckergasse 2, 3130 Herzogenburg, St. Andrä/Traisen (phone 02782-85635).

Neumayer
8 ha
Chardonnay, Grüner Veltliner, Pinot blanc, Riesling
St Laurent, Pinot noir
For a long time Ludwig Neumayer was the only wine grower ever talked about in the Traisental. It is all the more astonishing that he manages to produce white wines which can give the best Wachau estates a run for their money. They seem to be almost exclusively a product of Neumayer's intelligence, will and determination, which have even led him to reorganize whole vineyards previously given up as unworkable. It is therefore hardly surprising that the

wines themselves are eccentric, too, and that he sometimes vinifies them in ways otherwise frowned upon, such as a barrique-aged Grüner Veltliner, a beautifully complex wine made partly from overripe grapes and seemingly designed specially to baffle the experts.

His best wines are called *Der Wein vom Stein* ('wine from the rock'), a refreshing change from the more fanciful designations used by some of his colleagues. Among these rocks, the Grüner Veltliner is mighty and complex, almost too overpowering when young, with notable oak and often in the Spätlese region. The Riesling has deep fruit notes and good mineral characteristics. The Riesling Rothenbart is, if anything, slightly better than its colleague Vom Stein. There is also very good Pinot blanc, Chardonnay and Sauvignon blanc. Eiswein and a good cuvée from St Laurent and Pinot noir complete the picture.

Ludwig Neumayer, Inzersdorf ob der Traisen 22, 3130 Herzogenburg (phone and fax 02782-82985).

Styria

Area profile

Situated on the same latitude as France's Côte d'Or, the south-easterly part of Styria (Steiermark) offers perfect conditions for winemaking. It has only recently come to international attention, although some of the wines made here have been cult objects in Austria for some time.

In about 400 BC the Celts started to make wine here, followed by the Romans, who had an important city here, Flavia Solva, capital of their province Noricum. After the Romans, the history of the region was marked by a series of invasions by peoples such as the Marcomanni, Quadi, Vandals, Ostrogoths, Huns and Slovenes. During the eighth century it became part of the Slovenian Duchy of Karatia, was taken by Bavaria in 772, then by Charlemagne and finally, at the beginning of the tenth century, by Hungary. It reverted to German rule after the Battle of Lechfeld in 955 and remained unstable, riven by territorial disputes, changes of ownership and revolts.

A number of imposing fortresses still testify to this violent history, first and foremost the enormous Riegersburg, which today houses some fine vineyards within its walls. This borderland existence is still very much in evidence, and strolling through the vineyards it is difficult to know when one is in Austria, and when in Slovenia or Hungary. The people, though, claim to have little in common with their neighbours, and Austrians often profess never to have met even those who live literally across the road.

The capital of the region, Graz, was first mentioned in 1115. Styria was then ruled by Slavs, who were only driven out by Rudolf I of Habsburg in 1276. A period of stability followed and large parts of the region became Hungarian (while remaining, of course, within the Habsburg Empire). Unrest once again blighted Styria during the sixteenth and seventeenth centuries with peasant revolts, the attack on Protestant communities, culminating in their expulsion in 1596, and the repeated assaults of the Ottoman armies, which continued until 1699. The region slowly recovered, but it was not until the beginning of the nineteenth century that its fortunes improved dramatically.

Styria's benefactor was the legendary and somewhat tragic Archduke Johann (1782–1859), the *enfant terrible* of the Vienna court, who horrified the imperial family by marrying a commoner, the daughter of a postmaster. Practically exiled from court, he put his energies into developing the education and the economic base of the area. His special enthusiasm was viticulture, and on his initiative the first systematic research and classification were undertaken on Styria and its wines. His research estate near Marburg (Uailbiz) now lies in Yugoslavia.

Shortly after Johann's death, oidium and phylloxera, the wine plagues of the nineteenth century, swept across the principality. Vineyards had to be pulled out, at times guarded against rebelling growers by the army. The replanting of the Styrian vineyards, however, benefited the area considerably, as only varieties of high quality were allowed to be planted and other, less viable grapes vanished from the map. As already mentioned, the growing of wine directly from American rootstocks was the origin of that Styrian wine curiosity, Uhudler.

The landscape of Styria can be lovely and is often compared to that of Tuscany. Some parts are quite idyllic, with undulating hills, slim poplar trees swaying in the wind on the hilltops as far as the eye can reach, and picture-postcard sunsets. Other parts, to the east, are enveloped in dense forest and are reminiscent of a different period of European history. Particular landmarks are the rattling windmill wheels, or *Klapotetz*, which are designed to scare off birds feasting on the grapes. This early form of pest control is, in Fritz Hallgarten's words, 'more attractive to tourists than frightening to birds', and has become an emblem of Styrian wine production.

Though spread over a large area, only 3,600 ha of Styria are planted with wines, making it the second smallest wine-growing region after Vienna. Some of the country's smallest growers also operate here, with an average plot size of well under a hectare, though most of them sell their grapes to other producers.

Styrian vineyards are often situated on very steep slopes with inclines of up to 60°, where only vines will grow. Working these vineyards is as arduous as it is perilous, but the results of these labours are often very impressive. While Styria enjoys the warmest summers in Austria, hail can be a major hazard for the vineyards.

Being extremely rural – Graz is the only city and Vienna seems more than just two hundred miles away – Styrian viticulture can be traditional and quite unexciting. Those few who have broadened their horizons in the outside world, however, are producing wines which are slowly but surely gaining an exceptional reputation, and a very considerable potential may still lie dormant in vineyards which at the moment are used mainly for simple country wines.

Different conditions shape different wines, and Styria, though mainly a white wine country, is for once not dominated by Grüner Veltliner. The main varietal here is Welschriesling, with Pinot blanc and Chardonnay (here called Morillon) in hot pursuit. There is some Zweigelt here, and also Müller-Thurgau, Sauvignon blanc, Schilcher, Traminer, Muskateller, Ruländer, Pinot gris, St Laurent and Riesling.

In recent years especially, the Chardonnay and Sauvignon blanc have made the name of the region, though the white Pinot varietals can also be very successful here, and it seems to me that the Pinot gris is generally underestimated. Most growers vinify their wines in two distinct styles, the 'classical' Austrian involving steel tanks and no malolactic fermentation, and a more international style with oak ageing. As already indicated, both can be very successful, though nowadays the best wines are usually made in the international style.

Many growers still operate *Heurige* and have sidelines such as fruit schnapps, which is often excellent, and the ubiquitous pumpkin seed oil. Despite its small production, Styria covers a large area and is therefore usually considered as divided into three parts.

SOUTH STYRIA

Vineyards: 1,902 ha
Soil: slate, sand, marl
White (93 per cent): Welschriesling, Sauvignon blanc, Chardonnay
Red (7 per cent): Zweigelt, Uhudler

With 1,900 hectares, Southern Styria is the largest of the three
Styrian wine growing areas. Wine has been grown here since the
fourth century BC, and even at the end of the nineteenth century,
the Lower Styria of the Habsburg Empire had 35,000 hectares
under vines, some of which now lie in Slovenia. In modern Austria,

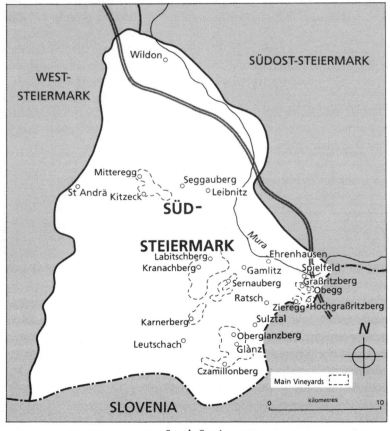

South Styria

Southern Styria is the farthest corner of the country and few people saw much incentive to move and work here. It is only recently that the true potential of the vineyards has been unlocked once more.

Southern Styria is on the rim of a hill formation made up of gneiss and glimmer slate. It was never heavily overlaid by glaciers during the Ice Age, and so rivers formed the face of the landscape and its soil, depositing chalk, sand, clay and loam sediments and cutting regular valleys through the area.

The climate here is influenced not only by the Pannonian but also by southern European weather systems, and at 800 to 1,000 mm the annual precipitation is double that of the Burgenland. On these hills, middle and high vineyards are best, especially as they escape the constant danger in the valleys of frost damage, which comes from the stagnant cold air collecting there, while the hilltops are exposed to cold winds. The very bottom and top of the hills are often used for orchard plantations. The vegetation period here is 240 days, with an annual mean temperature of 9.2° C, higher than that of any other Austrian wine-producing area.

The most northerly pocket of the region, Kitzeck, has a little more than 100 hectares of mainly slate soil, on which Riesling, Pinot blanc, Pinot gris and Welschriesling grow in vineyards such as the Annaberg, Altenberg, Einöd (with an inclination of 80° surely one of the steepest vineyards in the world), Gauitsch, Langriegel and Trebien. Neighbouring St Andrä has 36 hectares of vineyards, among them the Harrachegg, the chalky Sausaler Schlößl (an experimental vineyard during the last century) and the Wilhelmshöhe, a high, south-facing *Ried* on which Chardonnay, Sauvignon blanc, Sylvaner and Zweigelt grow on weathered primary rock.

Travelling south from Kitzeck, we find the largest area under vine in Southern Styria, 350 hectares to the south of Gamlitz. The south slope of the Kranachberg (406 m) contains some hundred individual *Rieden*, and varies from sandy soils through chalk to marl. Sauvignon blanc, Pinot blanc and Pinot noir are the most important grape varieties here. The Pfarrweingarten, south of Gamlitz, with its loamy sands on a coral base, the Sernauberg, with loamy sand and gravel on coral deposits, and the Karnerberg are important individual crus.

The Czamillonberg, part of another, larger area of *Rieden*, is one of the finest vineyards in the area. Sauvignon blanc, Chardonnay and Muskateller mature on this south-facing vineyard with its silicate deposits and brown sediment soil.

The easternmost corner of South Styria, between the villages of Spielfeld and Ratsch, contains a concentration both of excellent vineyards and distinguished wine growers. Here some of the very best wines of Styria are made. The area, site of the eleventh-century Ehrenhausen castle, rises to between 360 and 470 metres above sea level and has about 80 hectares of vineyards, many of them very steep. Like most vineyards here, the Nußberg faces south. Its chalky, marl soils with silicates and sand are an ideal foundation for Chardonnay, Sauvignon blanc, Pinot blanc, Welschriesling, Muskateller and Pinot gris, while the graphite and marl soils of the Untere Anzried are used to grow Sauvignon blanc and Morillon, the great successes of the area.

With the *Rieden* Zieregg, Graßnitzberg and Hochgraßnitzberg, we come to some of the grands crus of Styria. Zieregg is an enclosed cru of some 12 hectares, stretching seamlessly into Slovenia. Drainage has been installed at huge cost to prevent erosion. The soil of the upper and best part is made up of fossil chalk on a marl subsoil which comes to the surface in places. The Graßnitzberg is composed of several soils and microclimates and consists of low parts, south-east facing hillside and some north-east facing plots. It, too, is dominated by fossil chalk at the top of the cru, turning into loam and sand as one goes down the hill. The Hochgraßnitzberg is an enclosed hillside with sandy loam and weathered fossil chalk up to one metre down. It faces south and south-west. Obegg, a neighbouring *Ried*, is made up of sandy and chalky soil.

Top growers in South Styria

Groß
15 ha
Chardonnay, Muskateller, Pinot blanc, Pinot gris, Sauvignon blanc, Traminer
Zweigelt
Like his wine, Alois Groß is a quiet star, not out to dazzle and impress but to create a deeply satisfying glow. With vineyards on very different soil types, one of which is in neighbouring Slovenia, it is his ambition to make wines in accordance with their character. The result is that Groß is another grower successfully to marry

technology and tradition in a newly equipped winery gleaming with steel. His wines are often described as 'shy' and philosophical, two adjectives that also apply to their creator: they open up only gradually, in a slow evolution of ripe fruit aromas. Especially the Sauvignon blanc and Gewürztraminer fulfil his aim of mirroring the countryside from which they originated, particularly his best vineyards, the *Rieden* Wussberg and Kittenberg.

Alois Groß, Ratsch an der Weinstraße 10, 8461 Ehrenhausen (phone 03453-2527, fax 03453-2728).

Harkamp

The Harkamp empire is run by Hannes, the winemaker, and Heinz, a chef, who offers excellent regional dishes in a nearby restaurant that also functions as a showcase for his brother's wines. Because of their typically high alcohol content and the uncompromising use of oak, Harkamp wines are sometimes thought of as being untypical for the Steiermark, but that does not detract from their considerable quality.

Hannes Harkamp, Flamberg 46, 8505 St Nikolai (phone 03185-2280, fax 03185-22804).

Lackner-Tinnacher

13 ha
Chardonnay, Welschriesling, Pinot blanc, Pinot gris, Sauvignon blanc, Muskateller
Zweigelt

Franz Tinnacher is known for his ambition to produce good sweet wines as well as dry ones, both of which he does regularly. His estate is set among idyllic rolling hills, which means that he has to work on some frighteningly steep vineyards. The wines regularly reward these labours with their delicate fruit and acidity, though I personally was less impressed with the sweet wines. The dry Pinot gris, though, was especially memorable, as was a Sauvignon blanc Auslese. Tinnacher is also famous for his fruit schnapps.

Wilma and Franz Tinnacher, Steinbach 12, 8462 Gamlitz (phone 03453-2142, fax 03453-4841).

Maitz (Rebenburg)

True to Austrian tradition, Wolfgang Maitz produces almost all conceivable Styrian wines on just 6.5 ha of land. Equally traditionally, he does not go in for malolactic fermentation or oak casks.

His wines are therefore 'classically' Styrian, with plenty of reductive fruit and acidity, a formula which proves especially successful in the case of his Sauvignon blanc and Pinot blanc, and also in a very good Traminer Auslese.

Wolfgang Maitz, Ratsch an der Weinstraße, 8461 Ehrenhausen (phone 03453-2153, fax 03453-21537).

Platzer

Good cask-aged wines, dense and well defined, especially Traminers, Welschrieslings and red wines.

Manfred Platzer, Pichla 25, 8355 Tieschen (phone 03475-2331, fax 03475-23314).

Polz

45 ha
Chardonnay, Pinot blanc, Sauvignon blanc, Riesling, Pinot gris, Traminer, Welschriesling
Cabernet Sauvignon, St Laurent, Zweigelt

The sheer energy, charm and enthusiasm of the Polzes, a team of three brothers and a sister, can sweep you off your feet. They preside over a considerable estate of almost Californian dimensions, and with the characteristics of a small village. They also oversee a second winery, the Rebenhof, which has 23 ha of vineyards. Their wines may not always be quite as sophisticated as the very best Styrians, but they are beautifully made and have about them an exhilarating air of innovation. These are wines made on an international last. Among their single-vineyard wines, the Obegg and Hochgraßnitzberg are consistently fine, as are those from Graßnitzberg. The Polz winery produces a whole range of wines, both traditional and internationally oriented, and I was most taken with the excellent Pinot gris and the Sauvignon blanc Hochgraßnitzberg, aged in steel tanks for six months. The Chardonnay Hochgraßnitzberg is elevated in large barrels for six months, while the Chardonnay Obegg is aged in barriques for eighteen months and in bottles for another year before reaching the market.

Walter and Erich, the driving force behind the wines, are forever experimenting in order to produce more than 'just' clean, well-produced wines; most recently with wines that were fermented and elevated exclusively in wood. They have already established themselves as one of the best producers of the region and it will only take a little more to catapult them to the very top.

Erich and Walter Polz, Graßnitzberg 54a, 8471 Spielfeld (phone 03453-23010, fax 03453-23016).

Prünte

On a small estate, Klaus Prünte takes the greatest trouble in caring for his vines, planted on some of the steepest vineyards around. The results of his labours are less distinct, less modern in style than other Styrians, but occasionally he produces a wine that is a real gem.

Klaus Prünte, Graßnitzberg 14, 8471 Spielfeld (phone 03453-4126, fax 03453-4936).

Riegelnegg

A surprise new entry into the Styrian hall of fame, Otto Riegelnegg has produced a Sauvignon blanc Sernauberg 1998 which made some of his colleagues pale with envy. Though not a young man on the make, he may still be an old fox who has learned new tricks, and this is definitely an estate to watch.

Otto and Theresia Riegelnegg, Olwitschhof, Steinbach 62, 8462 Gamlitz (phone 03454-6263, fax 03454-6263-6).

Sabathi

Still in his twenties, Erwin Sabathi is one of the rising stars of Styria. With 9 ha he is a medium-sized producer, and his estate can boast seventeenth-century cellars, in which he vinifies wines that are beautifully clear and made from fully ripe grape material. He pays special attention to the Burgundian varietals, and his cask-aged Chardonnay especially is very promising. The Sauvignon blanc and Muskateller are also fine.

Erwin Sabathi, Pößnitz 48, 8463 Leutschach (phone and fax 03454-265).

Sattlerhof

13 ha
Chardonnay, Pinot blanc, Pinot gris, Riesling, Sauvignon blanc, Welschriesling
Pinot noir, St Laurent, Zweigelt

The Sattlerhof, a complex of winery and restaurant on the top of a hill, is thought of as respectable rather than excellent, but I was very impressed by these wines (and, incidentally, the food). Like many local growers, Willi Sattler has to battle with unimaginably steep slopes. Old Mr Sattler used to make wine not in Styria but in the Wachau, at the Freie Weingärtner. He moved to Gamlitz after what is sadly a recurring phenomenon on the steep slopes of Styria: his brother-in-law met with a fatal accident and Mr Sattler jumped into the breach.

The Sauvignon blancs from the Sattlerhof are as typical as any single-variety wine can be, full and fruity but lean at the same time, with astonishing gooseberry, grass and capsicum aromas, despite their occasionally very high alcohol content. All Sattler's wines show exemplarily clean fruit and fine judgement. The 1998 series is of overwhelming intensity.

These may not be wines for every palate, but the style and sheer concentration of their fruit makes them exceptional, nonetheless, and the single-vineyard wines such as Kranachberg, Pfarrwein-garten and Sernauberg are perhaps more French than Austrian in orientation, the Sauvignon blanc with overtones of the Loire, the Chardonnay, aged for eighteen months in small oak, reminding one of Burgundy. Wood is used skilfully and never to excess, and there are older wines on sale as well, showing the consistent ageing potential of Sattler's wines.

Willi Sattler, Sernau 2, 8462 Gamlitz (phone 03453-2556, fax 03453-5732).

Scheucher
A small estate producing very good Roter Traminer and good Sauvignon blanc in an attempt to marry traditional styles and modern technology.

Gottfried Scheucher, Labuttendorf 20, 8423 St Veit a. V. (phone and fax 03184-2252).

Silberberg
The Steiermärkisches Landesweingut Weinbauschule Silberberg, to give it its full title, is not only a wine school in which many of the local growers receive their education, but also a consistent producer of good Sauvignon blanc, Chardonnay, Pinot blanc and Zweigelt, the sale of which partially finances the institution.

Werner Surma, Kogelberg 16, 8430 Leibnitz (phone 03452-82329, fax 03452-8233917).

Skoff
Walter Skoff has just built himself a gleaming new winery in which he attempts to vinify every vintage according to its specific charac-

teristics. Until now the results have been clean, well balanced and very competent rather than overwhelming, but perhaps the new gear will make the estate shift into another gear as well. Skoff tries to achieve top results by harvesting late and treating the grape material as carefully as possible. The fermentation is temperature-controlled, which has the usual effect of lifting the overall standards of the production, but occasionally inhibits the expressiveness of individual wines. His best wines are sold under the label Edition, and he also makes sparkling wine.

Walter and Evelyn Skoff, Eckberg 16 and 99, 8462 Gamlitz (phone 03453-4243, fax 03453-424317).

Söll

One of the up-and-coming Styrian growers, Johannes Söll produces good, clean wines according to natural methods and with very little chemical fertilization. Eiswein and Strohwein are among his specialities.

Maria and Johannes Söll, Sernau Steinbach 63a, 8462 Gamlitz (phone 03454-6667, fax 03454-66677).

Tement

25 ha
Chardonnay, Pinot blanc, Sauvignon blanc, Traminer, Welsch-riesling
Blaufränkisch, Cabernet Sauvignon, Zweigelt

If Styria were to have a wine king, there is no doubt that it would be Manfred Tement. The estate curiously enough owes its existence to two misfortunes in his father's life. Initially, Tement *père* had wanted to become a priest, but lack of money forced him into making wine for the order of Carmelites. A stretch as a prisoner of war in France broadened his wine horizons and he came back with new ideas. Under his son Manfred, the estate the father bought in 1960 has not only broadened its horizons but also risen to a quality that allows it happily to stand comparison with many of the great wines of the world.

Knowing that he is on to a good thing, Manfred Tement has recently almost doubled the size of his vineyard through judicious buying-up of some of the best *Rieden* around. He vinifies a whole range of varietals and styles, with Sauvignon blanc, Chardonnay and Pinot blanc as his main grape varieties.

These are truly fine wines, which manage to combine power and

elegance, fruit and structure in a way that is very close to ideal and clearly take their bearings from international rather than local styles. One third of the Sauvignon blanc Zieregg is aged in 300-litre barriques, blended with steel-elevated wine and then aged either in steel or in large barrels. This is one of Tement's flagship wines: concentrated, elegant and complex fruit, a commanding performance with enormous potential for the future – a great wine. The second lead is played by the Morillon (Chardonnay) Zieregg, a powerful and concentrated giant of a wine, aged for at least fourteen months in new oak, with enormous promise for those few patient enough to lay it down in their cellars, where it will be able to assimilate the wood perfectly. On the Graßnitzberg Tement makes Pinot blanc and Sauvignon blanc, which are also very fine. A sweet Sauvignon blanc Auslese complements the dry varieties. Other beauties include a honeyed Roter Traminer and a wonderfully aromatic Pinot gris with plenty of backbone. If these wines illustrate the potential of Styria, the region will surely rise even further beyond its already considerable status. In addition to his own wines, Manfred Tement is also one of the three conspirators, together with Tibor Szemes and F. X. Pichler, behind Austria's most publicized red wine, the Arachon.
Manfred Tement, Zieregg 13, 8461 Berghausen (phone 03453-4101, fax 03453-410130).

Tscheppe
Part importer and part producer, Eduard Tscheppe makes mainly easy-drinking wines on his 45 ha, the largest Styrian estate. Tscheppe wines are still mainly commercially orientated, offering every grape variety that a client can want in different quality ranges. At their best they can be elegant and clean, but they tend to lack the concentration of other Styrians.
Eduard Tscheppe, Pössnitz 168, 8463 Leutschach (phone 03454-205, fax 03454-29350077).

Tschermonegg
Good wines in traditionally Styrian garb, especially the Sauvignon blanc Superior and the Traminer Trio, a cuvée from Gelber, Roter and Gewürztraminer (what Tschermonegg calls his Gelber Traminer is Weißer Traminer in the eyes of most ampelographers, Gelber Traminer being a synonym for Gewürztraminer). Erwin Tschermonegg took over this estate in 1993 after serving his

apprenticeship in New Zealand (on the Seifried Estate, run by an Austrian compatriot on South Island), which may help to explain his interest in Sauvignon blanc. One of the young growers now making a big noise in Styria.

Erwin Tschermonegg, Glanz an der Weinstraße 50, 8463 Leutschach (phone 03454-326, fax 03454-32650).

Wohlmuth

A very energetic and enthusiastic winemaker, Gerhard Wohlmuth has succumbed to the fashion of giving his wines names like Elitär and Summus, which seems like tempting Providence. They are clean, typical examples of the Styrian style. Intrigued by the idea that he might have a Jewish ancestor, Mr Wohlmuth is also thinking about making a kosher wine, certainly the first in Styria.

Gerhard Wohlmuth, Freising 24, 8441 Kitzeck (phone 03456-2303, fax 03456-2121).

SOUTH-EAST STYRIA

Vineyards: 1,205 ha
Soils: basalt and volcanic soils, sand, loam
White (75 per cent): Welschriesling, Pinot blanc, Traminer, Riesling, Chardonnay, Pinot gris
Red (25 per cent): Zweigelt, Blauburger, St Laurent, Blauer Wildbacher

Very much larger than South Styria, the south-east has fewer distinguished wine growers, although it is certainly possible to grow excellent wine there. Its 1,200 hectares of vineyards are a good third less than those of its southerly neighbour.

The soil here is very different from anything found near by: basalt and other volcanic stones, partly overlaid by fossil chalk. Like all of southern Styria, it lies between the Pannonian and Mediterranean climatic zones of influence. It has an annual mean temperature of almost 10° C and a little under 1,000 mm annual precipitation.

In contrast to Southern Styria, this area has traditionally cultivated Traminer, which takes well to the basalt soils. As this variety has gone out of fashion in recent years, it has often been replaced by red varieties, mainly Zweigelt.

The 80 hectares around Straden in the west of the area benefit from frequently very warm climatic conditions and can produce wines with beautiful fruit. The best *Rieden* of the area are Morafeitl, protected by forest and with deep loam soils, ideal for Sauvignon blanc and Chardonnay; Saziani, with sandy, light humus soils on basalt; and Steintal.

Kapfenstein Castle is an ancient defensive structure partly dating back to the eleventh century. As archaeological finds show, the basalt tuff rock on which it was built to overlook the land (the name derives from an early form of *gaffen*, 'to look out') has been settled since 3000 BC. Today the vineyards around Schloß Kapfenstein – all belonging to the Winkler-Hermaden family, which also owns the castle itself – produce good Chardonnay, Pinot blanc and Pinot gris, and remarkable red wines. The *Ried* an der Kapelle, with its gravelly and sandy soils on basalt, is planted mainly with Chardonnay and Pinot gris, while Kirchleithen, with its sand and sandy loam, has mainly Traminer, Sauvignon blanc, Welschriesling, Pinot blanc and Pinot gris. Rosenleithen – sand and sandy loam again – has Pinot blanc and Chardonnay. A remarkable *Ried* is Winzerkogel, on whose gravelly and loamy sands not only white but also red grapes ripen well. The Zweigelt and Blauburger produced here are called Olivin after the volcanic stone found here.

The vineyards around Klöch are both relatively extensive and old – the Romans made wine here. Another castle, now a ruin, overlooks the area and bears testimony both to its former strategic importance and its turbulent history. The basalt, tuff and sandy loam of the Klöchberg offer ideal growing conditions for the Traminer grape, which ripens here better than anywhere else in Austria.

Another part of South-East Styria and another castle: the Riegersburg. Situated on a steep basalt rock (460 m), the Riegersburg is one of the largest strategic buildings of the Middle Ages in Europe and has been extended several times during the Renaissance and the baroque periods. It is an impressive structure which now belongs to the Princes of Liechtenstein. Most of the vineyards here are within the large defensive wall systems and benefit from the microclimate created by the sheltering and sun-retaining qualities of the massive walls. The Süd-Bastei and Burggraben are especially famous, and benefit from the heat retention of both rocks and walls.

Top growers in South-East Styria

Fürwirth

Next to typical Styrian white wines, Morillon (Chardonnay) and Pinot blanc, Fritz Fürwirth produces good Gewürztraminer, which is especially remarkable as a Spätlese.

Fritz and Marianne Fürwirth, Deutsch-Haseldorf 46, 8493 Klöch (phone and fax 03475-2338).

Hutter

Very good Chardonnay/Pinot blanc cuvée, also good Roter Traminer Auslese and Sauvignon blanc.

Franz Hutter, Reiting 2, 8330 Feldbach (phone and fax 03152-4422).

Neumeister

13.5 ha
Chardonnay, Pinot blanc, Pinot gris, Riesling, Sauvignon blanc, Traminer, Muskateller
Zweigelt

Another fine grower – and another building site. In 1998 Albert Neumeister was busy building a winery into a hillside, with the idea that the transport of the grape material would be powered by gravity only, from the vineyard right to the bottle. The building project was a huge investment, but I realized that it was worth every penny when I tasted the wines.

Few people manage to produce truly individual wines with the aid of computer-controlled fermentation, but Albert Neumeister is one of them. One of the rarities is a Roter Traminer, which I found elegant, complex and quite beautiful. Neumeister also excels among the more standard grape varietals. The Sauvignon blanc Morafeitl Selektion pretty much defines what can be done with this grape in Styria and throws down the gauntlet to international competitors. The Chardonnay (here called Morillon) Morafeitl Selektion and the Pinot gris Saziani Selektion were also excellent, with fine structure, well-integrated wood and fruit all living in beautiful harmony.

Albert and Anna Neumeister, 8345 Straden 42 (phone 03473-88308, fax 03473-83084).

Platzer

Manfred Platzer makes solid, traditional wines that are always a pleasure to drink. There are varieties such as Welschriesling, Gewürztraminer and Pinot gris, which are vinified with all due care, as well as Sauvignon blanc and Riesling. These wines are in a simpler category than the great Styrians, but they are well made and can have beautiful fruit.

Manfred Platzer, Pichla 25, 8355 Tieschen (phone 03475-2331, fax 03475-2331-4).

Riegersburg

The Riegersburg is a magnificent old pile, one of the largest medieval and Renaissance castle complexes in Europe, perched on an almost unassailable hill and reachable only on foot. It is now owned by the Princes Liechtenstein, and the vineyards within its monumental walls, which possess a unique microclimate, are tended by Andreas Tscheppe, who also has vineyards outside the castle confines. The main grape varietals are Pinot blanc and Chardonnay, voluminous and fruity wines, if less focused than the best Styrians. They are excellent exponents of the 'classical' Austrian line, with a very pleasant interplay of clean fruit and acidity.

Andreas Tscheppe, Glanz 75, 8463 Leutschach (phone 03454-391).

Winkler-Hermaden

16 ha
Chardonnay, Pinot blanc, Pinot gris, Riesling, Sauvignon blanc, Traminer, Welschriesling
Cabernet Sauvignon, Pinot noir, Zweigelt

Situated underneath the medieval castle of Kapfenstein, which belongs to the family, Georg Winkler-Hermaden's winery suffers from only one problem: the wines are sold out so fast that he has to turn away many a hopeful customer. Unusually for Styria, Mr Winkler-Hermaden concentrates a great part of his efforts and resources on his Zweigelt, which he vinifies in oak casks and calls Olivin, in recognition of his mineralogist uncle. In good years, this can be a smooth, smoky and tannic wine with good length. The cellars in which these wines ripen, with beautiful cross-vaulting dating back some 300 years, are the special pride of their master.

Among the white wines, the Traminer Ried Kirchleitern is particularly fine – definitely a wine with a future. The Sauvignon blanc and especially the Morillon (Chardonnay) Ried Rosenleiten also display good muscle and structure. These wines are ideally drunk accompanying the excellent cooking of Mr Winkler-Hermaden's brother Martin in the atmospheric castle restaurant just up the hill, which also doubles as a hotel and runs wine seminars.

Georg Winkler-Hermaden, Schloß Kapfenstein, 8353 Kapfenstein 105 (phone 03157-2322, fax 03157-23224).

WEST STYRIA

Vineyards: 480 ha
Soil: gneiss, slate
White (30 per cent): Welschriesling, Pinot blanc
Red (70 per cent): Blauer Wildbacher, Zweigelt

With no more than 480 hectares under vines, West Styria, though beautiful, does not on the whole have a wine production that is remarkable in terms of quality or quantity, though wine was produced here by the Celts and Romans, and there is evidence of winemaking as early as 400 BC.

The most important traditional grape of West Styria is the Blauer Wildbacher, or Schilcher, which is vinified *en rosé* and made into a light, acidic and fruity summer wine. Schilcher does not only have fans, however. When Pope Pius V visited the Habsburg Emperor Joseph II he complained about being served 'a pink vinegar which they call Schilcher'. A wine book of 1845 also mentions that Schilcher was often made by adding blackberry juice to white wine. Schilcher is supposed to be acidic, even astringent.

The soil of West Styria is dominated by crystalline gneiss and slate, often covered by sediment soils. Many vineyards are situated on steep hills and are higher than those in other parts of Styria, usually between 420 and 600 metres, in order to escape night frosts in the valleys. Wind is less of a problem here than in eastern Styria, as the area is protected by the foothills of the Alps.

The best *Rieden* of the area are Hochgrail and Engelweingarten near Stainz, both planted entirely with Schilcher, and Burgegg below Landsberg castle, a *Ried* which in the 1920s was one of the first to carry the newly bred grape Zweigelt.

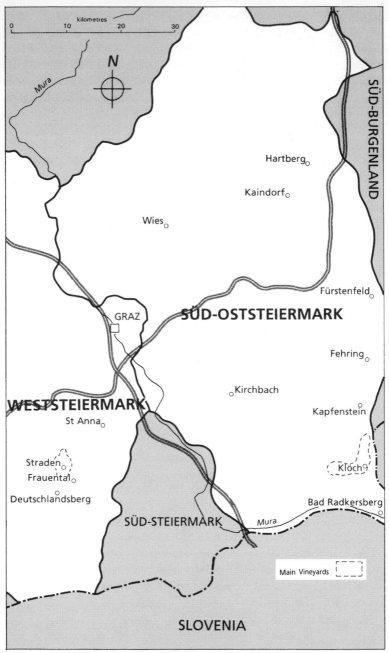

West and East Styria

Top growers in West Styria

Domaine Müller

43 ha

Chardonnay, Welschriesling, Sauvignon blanc, Pinot blanc, Pinot gris, Schilcher
Zweigelt, Cabernet Sauvignon

An estate with a name like Domaine Müller should really be in Alsace, and there is indeed a foreign connection. Some of the world's best wines are lying in Günter Müller's cellars: Mr Müller is also the main importer into Austria of some of the finest French wines. Before he took over the estate, and also took the lease on the nearby Prinz Liechtensteinsche Weingut, he worked as a wine dealer in France and California.

With benchmarks like these so distressingly close at hand, one could forgive him for not being unduly ambitious with his own wines, but on the contrary, he has just built an ultra-modern winery with a plethora of ingenious inventions designed to drive up the quality of his wines even further. As if this were not enough, he is determined to move mountains in order to produce good wine: when I last visited him he was engaged in 'correcting' an entire mountainside in order to optimize its orientation towards the sun. Günter Müller is not a timid man. His neighbours in the valley regard this maverick grower and importer with some degree of suspicion, and his wines are rarely rated very highly by Austrian journalists, but I found some of them, especially his Sauvignon blanc and Pinot gris, quite impressive, with beautifully balanced structure, judiciously used wood and excellent ageing potential. With his French background, it is not surprising that the style of these wines is unashamedly international, with plenty of new oak being used. Günter Müller is also ambitious about his red wines, especially a Cabernet Sauvignon, which might well hold considerable promise for the future. With a bow to local tradition, he also produces a Schilcher, clean and fresh, but by its nature not a wine I could ever warm towards.

Günter and Eva Müller, Gussendorf 5, 8522 Groß St Florian (phone 03463-2234, fax 03463-211625).

Vienna

Area profile

Vineyards: 731 ha
Soil: slate, gravel, loam, loess
White (86 per cent): Grüner Veltliner, Riesling, Pinot blanc, Chardonnay, Welschriesling, Müller-Thurgau, Gemischter Satz
Red (14 per cent): Zweigelt, Pinot noir, St Laurent, Blauburger

Vienna's wine pedigree is impeccable. Indeed, as Hugh Johnson remarks, no other capital has as intimate a connection with wine as this one. The Celts already made wine in their settlement of Vedunia, and the Romans elaborated this practice in their military harbour of Vindobona. Ever since then, wine has been made, sold and drunk in Vienna. Until the late seventeenth century wines were sold directly in the town houses, but the reorganization of the city after the Turkish siege in 1683 meant that the sale of wines was largely pushed out into the periphery.

The next important date for Viennese wine culture came in 1784, when Emperor Joseph II officially recognized the custom of local growers of selling wine and food produced on their estates to members of the public in small inns called *Heurige*, most of which are scattered around the wine-growing areas in the outskirts of the city. As the name *Heurige* ('this year's') suggests, the wines sold in these places are largely from the current vintage, though an *Alter* ('last year's wine') is usually also available. Traditionally (and despite the English saying that good wine needs no bush), the public is alerted to the sale of wine by a bush of fir trees hung above the door of the *Heurige*, which also explains their alternative name, *Buschenschank*.

In 1784 this was already a time-honoured practice, said to go

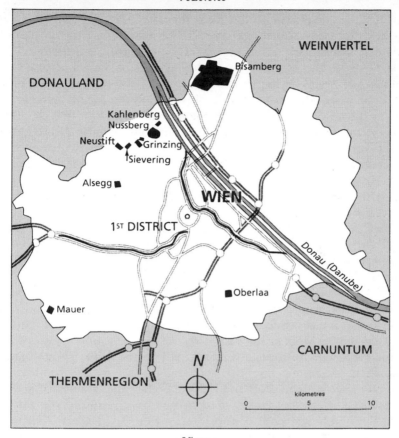

Vienna

back to Charlemagne, and it is still one of the best-loved aspects of life in the city. Hugh Johnson gives a lovely sketch of *Heurige* moods: '*The atmosphere in their leafy taverns varies from idyllic to hilarious. In most of them Beethoven wrote at least a concerto.*' Today, many of these *Heurige* are veritable tourist traps in which people are delivered by the busload to be filled up with cheap wine and pushed out for the next lot, but it is still possible to find small, beautiful *Heurige* used only by locals – an effort well worth making. Wine is sold by the jug or the glass and can at its best be utterly enchanting: greenish gold, fresh and crisp, a wine that, to me, seems to capture women and song in a glass.

The Viennese have always liked their wine. During the Middle Ages they drank up to six times more wine than they do now, which means that the average annual consumption in the city was well above 200 litres. In 1815 the annual consumption was 87 litres per head. Owing to rising taxes and the phylloxera catastrophe, wine consumption and cultivation in the capital collapsed dramatically, and at the end of the nineteenth century the people of Vienna had more than halved the amount of wine they drank per year. This figure has declined even further: today Austrians drink around 30 litres of (mainly Austrian) wine per year per head. The nation has definitely sobered up.

The climate of Vienna is influenced by two things in particular: the Pannonian plains in the east and the river Danube. The river is an important tempering factor and protects the region against late frosts and the other extremes of the Pannonian climate that makes itself strongly felt here: summers are hot while winter temperatures are consistently around freezing point. The annual vegetation period is 255 days, and the annual mean precipitation around 660 mm.

Vienna is surrounded by vineyards to the north and small parts of the south. Most of the vineyards are in the historic eighteenth and nineteenth districts, and across the Danube, in the twenty-first district. Among the vineyards surrounding the city, the Nußberg, Bisamberg, Stammersdorf and Kahlenberg are well known for producing good quality wines, though they have lost the fame they had until the eighteenth century. Some of the best vineyards are in Döbling, where the soil is particularly rich in chalk.

There are about 760 hectares under vines, around half of the area cultivated before 1950. Now, however, new vineyards are being planted again. Wines are still not commonly identified with *Rieden* here, though some individual vineyards have been known since the Middle Ages. Especially noteworthy in Nußdorf are the Nußberg with its chalky soil, the neighbouring *Rieden* Burgstall and Collin with more loamy and sandy soils, and the *Rieden* Preussen, Rosengartl and Schoß. In Grinzing, the Hungerberg, Reisenberg and Schenkenberg, all sandy loam, and the heavier, stonier Sommereck and Steinberg have made names for themselves.

On the left bank of the Danube there are some 250 hectares of vineyards with *Rieden* like Hochfeld with black earth on loess, Herrenholz and Hochfeld with light sediment soil, Kirchberg with black soil and loess, and In den Rothen, the most highly rated *Ried* here, with chalky loess soils and an especially warm microclimate, ideal for Riesling.

The majority of the wines growing around Vienna are produced for *Heurige* consumption and the emphasis is on uncomplicated wines for early drinking. A quarter of the total production is Grüner Veltliner; Riesling and Pinot blanc are also popular. Other common varietals are Chardonnay, Welschriesling, Müller-Thurgau, Neuburger, Traminer, Zweigelt, Pinot noir, St Laurent, Blauburger, and Blauer Portugieser, and Gemischter Satz, a mixed planting of several grape varietals. The epicentre of production lies in Döbling, the further reaches of Vienna's rather *haut bourgeois* nineteenth district, which dissolves into vineyards. Another important, and incomparably less aristocratic, wine growing district is Stammersdorf, the twenty-first district.

With increasing urbanization, winemaking in Vienna has long been in decline. Here, the beneficial effects of the 1985 scandal also produced a new awareness and a resurgence of wine production and standards, so that today it is possible to say that Viennese winemaking is alive and well.

Top growers

Bernreiter

Peter Bernreiter has his *Heurige* in Jedlersdorf, hardly the most romantic part of Vienna. The *Heurige* itself, however, is beautiful, and Bernreiter's clear and well-structured Pinot gris is famous well beyond Vienna.

Peter Bernreiter, Amtsstraße 24–26, 1210 Wien-Jedlersdorf (phone 01-2923680, fax 01-29236804).

Fuhrgassl-Huber

A good *Heurige*, one of the larger ones and beautifully situated. Good Grüner Veltliner.

1190 Neustift am Walde 68 (phone 01-441405).

Hengl-Haselbrunner

Heurige open all year. Good Riesling from different vineyards; traditionally Austrian but clean red wine.

Ferdinand Hengl, Igasegasse 10, 1190 Wien-Döbling (phone 01-323330).

Kattus

No Viennese society ball is complete without the Hochriegl Sekt by Kattus, and the house is indeed a venerable institution, as demonstrated by its Biedermeier cellars in Döbling. There is a range of sparkling wines from semi-sweet to dry produced here, the best being Alte Reserve and Großer Jahrgang. As wines, these offerings are rarely remarkable, but there is a great amount of tradition and nostalgia invested in them.

Am Hof 8, 1011 Wien (phone 01-3684350, fax 01-3692477).

Kierlinger

A refreshingly unpretentious and untouristy *Heurige* producing some of the best Viennese Pinot blanc and Riesling.

Kahlenbergerstraße 20, 1190 Wien (phone and fax 01-3702264).

Klager

Leopold Klager has made a good name for himself with his Gemischter Satz, a solid Riesling and an accomplished barrique-aged Chardonnay.

Leopold Klager, Stammersdorfer Straße 18, 1210 Wien (phone and fax 01-2921356).

Mayer am Pfarrplatz

25 ha

Grüner Veltliner, Chardonnay, Sauvignon blanc, Gelber Muskateller, Riesling, Traminer

Pinot noir

This is a *Heurige* with important connections: Beethoven lived in the house in 1817 and stayed here longer than at most of his thirty-odd other Viennese addresses. He may have written part of his Ninth Symphony here, and he certainly composed his Heiligenstadt Testament in this house, partly consoled, no doubt, by local wine. A second connection is political. During the 1980s Franz Mayer was a driving force in the restoration and reinvigoration of Viennese winemaking, and he is still leading by example. There is good and intense Riesling from the *Rieden* Alsegg and Preussen, and interesting Chardonnay, both with and without new oak. An old-style Viennese wine is the Gemischter Satz (mixed set), which is predominantly Grüner Veltliner. Franz Mayer also makes a good Pinot noir. For those interested in the ageing potential of these wines, there is a large archive cellar.

Franz Mayer, Beethovenhaus, Pfarrplatz 2, 1190 Wien (phone 01-373361, fax 01-374714).

Reinprecht
A very traditional *Heurige* producing excellent Pinot gris Ausbruch, Gewürztraminer and a very good Chardonnay. The Welschriesling and Pinot noir are also very good.
Hugo Reinprecht, Cobenzlgaße 22, 1190 Wien (phone 01-32014710, fax 01-320571322).

Schilling
A very active grower committed to driving up the quality of his wines. Good Pinot blanc, Riesling and Chardonnay, as well as St Laurent.
Herbert Schilling, Langenzersdorffer Straße 54, 1210 Wien-Strebersdorf (phone 01-2924189, fax 01-2928266).

Schmidt
Josef Schmidt loves Sauvignon blanc, which he vinifies in three different styles: in steel, in barriques and as botrytis wine. He also has a Welschriesling with good bite and fruit, and some Gemischter Satz.
Josef Schmidt, Stammersdorfer Straße 105, 1210 Wien (phone 01-2926688, fax 01-2926688-4).

Wieninger
14 ha
Grüner Veltliner, Chardonnay, Riesling, Bouvier, Pinot blanc, Sauvignon blanc, Welschriesling
Cabernet Sauvignon, Merlot, Zweigelt, Pinot noir
Fritz Wieninger used to be the archetype of the yuppie winemaker. Well dressed, articulate and never far from his mobile phone, he continued where his father had left off and changed the image of his estate from just another *Heurige* to Vienna's most exciting wine producer, highly spoken of among his colleagues. Meanwhile, both he and his wines have matured a little, and he is now occasionally spotted without his mobile and in serious mood. He makes good Grüner Veltliner, but his heart is in producing what some think are the best Chardonnays in Austria. I found these, the Select and the Grand Select, to have beautiful balance and fruit, though not the complexity I had been expecting. Wieninger also makes very good red wines, among which are a fine Pinot noir and a Cabernet

Sauvignon/Merlot cuvée, both of which will profit from some ageing.

Fritz Wieninger, Stammersdorfer Straße 80, 1210 Wien (phone 01-2901012, fax 01-29010123).

Wachau

Area profile

Vineyards: 1,448 ha
Soils: primary rock, loess, gneiss, crystalline slate, sand
White (90 per cent): Grüner Veltliner, Riesling, Chardonnay, Pinot
blanc, Muskateller, Müller-Thurgau
Red (10 per cent): Zweigelt, St. Laurent, Blauer Portugieser

If there is any area in Austria which is seen as *the* wine-growing
region and which has consistently produced fine wines, even before
1985, the Wachau must surely be it. As if this were not enough, it
is also graced with great natural beauty and charm. Set along the
Danube, its steep wooded hills rise upwards with a peculiar mixture
of grace and dramatic sweep. Set into the hillsides are the baroque
towns of Loiben, Dürnstein, Weißenkirchen, Joching and Spitz on
one side of the river, and Mautern on the other.

A natural passageway between east and west, the Wachau has
seen many migrations and its fair share of battles. The first evidence
of human culture here, the Willendorf Venus, a small stone figurine,
dates from 20,000 BC. The Celts probably began to produce wines
in much of the Wachau. They were supplanted by the Illyrians,
who in their turn failed to stem the invasion of the Roman army.
In AD 15 the Danube became the northern border of the Roman
Empire, and the occupiers erected a permanent camp, Favianis,
near the modern village of Mautern on the southern bank of
the Danube. The first evidence of wine production, grape seeds
excavated from tombs, also dates from Roman times.

In 791 Charlemagne defeated the Avars and enfeoffed the area
to Bavarian monasteries, who were to control it for much of the

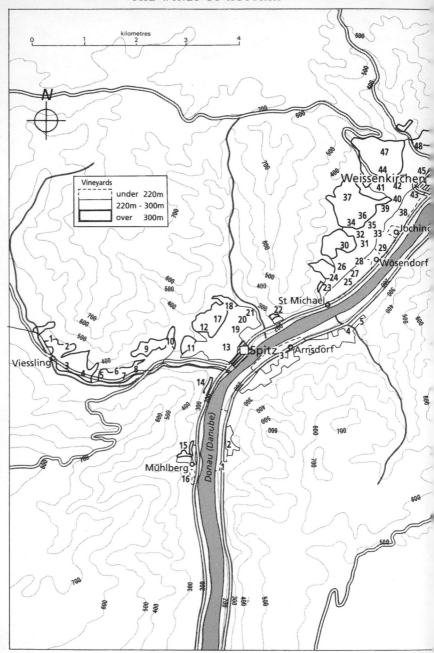

Wachau

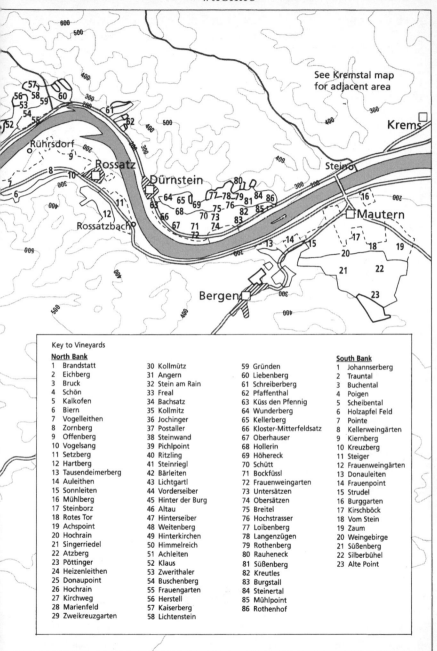

WACHAU

See Kremstal map for adjacent area

Krems

Rührsdorf

Rossatz

Dürnstein

Steino

Mautern

Rossatzbach

Bergen

Key to Vineyards

North Bank

1	Brandstatt	30	Kollmütz
2	Eichberg	31	Angern
3	Bruck	32	Stein am Rain
4	Schön	33	Freal
5	Kalkofen	34	Bachsatz
6	Biern	35	Kollmitz
7	Vogelleithen	36	Jochinger
8	Zornberg	37	Postaller
9	Offenberg	38	Steinwand
10	Vogelsang	39	Pichlpoint
11	Setzberg	40	Ritzling
12	Hartberg	41	Steinriegl
13	Tausendeimerberg	42	Bärleiten
14	Auleithen	43	Lichtgartl
15	Sonnleiten	44	Vorderseiber
16	Mühlberg	45	Hinter der Burg
17	Steinborz	46	Altau
18	Rotes Tor	47	Hinterseiber
19	Achspoint	48	Weitenberg
20	Hochrain	49	Hinterkirchen
21	Singerriedel	50	Himmelreich
22	Atzberg	51	Achleiten
23	Pöttinger	52	Klaus
24	Heizenleithen	53	Zwerithaler
25	Donaupoint	54	Buschenberg
26	Hochrain	55	Frauengarten
27	Kirchweg	56	Herstell
28	Marienfeld	57	Kaiserberg
29	Zweikreuzgarten	58	Lichtenstein

59	Gründen
60	Liebenberg
61	Schreiberberg
62	Pfaffenthal
63	Küss den Pfennig
64	Wunderberg
65	Kellerberg
66	Kloster-Mitterfeldsatz
67	Oberhauser
68	Hollerin
69	Höhereck
70	Schütt
71	Bockfüssl
72	Frauenweingarten
73	Untersätzen
74	Obersätzen
75	Breitel
76	Hochstrasser
77	Loibenberg
78	Langenzügen
79	Rothenberg
80	Rauheneck
81	Süßenberg
82	Kreutles
83	Burgstall
84	Steinertal
85	Mühlpoint
86	Rothenhof

South Bank

1	Johannserberg
2	Trauntal
3	Buchental
4	Poigen
5	Scheibental
6	Holzapfel Feld
7	Pointe
8	Kellerweingärten
9	Kiernberg
10	Kreuzberg
11	Steiger
12	Frauenweingärten
13	Donauleiten
14	Frauenpoint
15	Strudel
16	Burggarten
17	Kirschböck
18	Vom Stein
19	Zaum
20	Weingebirge
21	Süßenberg
22	Silberbühel
23	Alte Point

next thousand years. The first time the name of the region is mentioned – 'ad Uachaouuam' – is in a document from 823.

In the fifth century St Severin had founded a hermitage 'by the vineyards', a good place for spirited meditation. He seems to have started something of a tradition here, because some of today's Wachau growers still like to meditate over, and on, their wines. At the end of the twelfth century, King Richard Coeur de Lion was imprisoned in the fortress above Dürnstein, the ruins of which still command the hill. It is quite easy to believe that the good King actually found his sojourn in this beautiful part of the world a welcome respite from the stresses of defending Christianity, and that he might have stayed here voluntarily, in a blissful, wine-induced stupor.

As a feoff of Bavarian monasteries and of the archbishop of Salzburg, the Wachau delivered wine from its rocky terraces, some of which have been cultivated ever since. The now famous appellation 'Vinea Wachau Nobilis Districtus' was recorded in a document by Leuthold I of Kuenring in 1285. Three difficult centuries followed, with trade limitations, religious disputes, the Turkish campaigns of 1529 and 1683 and the Thirty Years War.

After this period of strife the region recovered, but it was to be the scene of major fighting in 1805, when Napoleon's army was beaten near Dürnstein in a battle which again caused considerable devastation. The bones of those killed during this battle can still be visited in the atmospheric local church of St Michael, founded in 987 and featuring a bone house as well as some Celtic ornamental stones built into the fabric of the church, bearing testimony to an earlier history. A memorial to the battle in the middle of the vineyards serves as a further reminder of this time and as a landmark.

At the beginning of the twentieth century the Wachau was not especially known for great wines, but more for its orchards, especially apricots, cherries, and apples, and it was not until the 1950s that the first great wines began to emerge from the ancient vineyards; ironically, this was partly because of the declining price of fruit and the reorientation of many growers. With the introduction of the confederation 'Vinea Wachau Nobilis Districtus' in 1984, the Wachau gained a sharper profile and could dictate its own wine policy. The organization was founded by four Wachau growers, Wilhelm Schwengler (of Freie Weingärtner Wachau),

Franz Hirtzberger, Franz Prager and Josef Jamek. Today it has about 170 members and covers some 85 per cent of the area under vines in the Wachau.

Understanding the wines, soils and climate of the Wachau is a lifelong task and a source of endless discussions and research. Like all of eastern Austria, the Wachau is a meeting point of western European and Pannonian climatic influences. Atlantic air meets warm, continental currents flowing into the area from the eastern, Pannonian Plains. The continental character of the climate (hot, dry summers, severe winters) is offset by the effect of the Danube, which balances out the differences in temperature to some extent. The extensive water surface also reflects the sun and aids the generation of sugar in the grapes through photosynthesis.

Microclimatic factors, such as the cool air streaming down the hills and the aromatic air from the forests in the north, increase the temperature difference between day and night, especially during the weeks leading up to the harvest (September/October), thus intensifying the aroma of the wine, especially in the higher vineyards. The 'cool' fruit and the exotic characteristics of Wachau wines are a result of this particular climatic combination.

The steep hills have a great influence on all climatic parameters. Close to the banks of the Danube (at 250 m), the annual mean temperature is about 9° C. From 250 m to 450 m it is 8–9° C, and from 450 m to 600 m 7–8° C. Annual rainfall in the Wachau is lower than in any other wine-producing area in Austria (500 mm; 580 mm in Spitz, 520 mm in Loiben), and the terraces in particular need irrigation during the summer months. The vegetation period is around 245 days, less in the higher vineyards.

Around Loiben, the influence of the Danube is less strongly felt, making the vineyards sensitive to frost, while in the area of Wösendorf and Spitz air circulation is bound more effectively by the river, lessening the threat of frost. Towards Krems, where the valley opens up to the east, the arid Pannonian summers assert themselves slightly more than in the remainder of the Wachau.

The key to the *Rieden* in the Wachau is, of course, the soil. It consists largely of granite, gneiss and crystalline slates, and loam, loess and sand in the lower regions. These are the oldest rock formations in Austria. Towards the east of the region, near Krems, there is also some yellow loess, as well as loamy soils around Weißenkirchen and some slate in the westernmost corners.

Seen from the river, the soils very roughly follow an ascending order of loess and sandy soils near the banks of the Danube, larger loess deposits further up the hill, and finally the weathered gneiss, granite and slate soils in the top vineyards, which also tend to produce the best wines. Yields from these top vineyards tend to be lower than 30 hl/ha, and they require an amount of labour disproportionately greater than vineyards on the plain. While a vineyard with a light incline might take three to four hundred hours of labour per hectare every year, the upkeep of the terraces and the strenuous (and overwhelmingly manual) work on the slopes pushes up this figure to 2,000 hours.

The terraced vineyards of the Wachau have never taken to the Lenz Moser system of training vines, as it is still almost impossible to use any kind of machines here. Within the terraces, the number of vines per hectare is between 7,000 to 7,500 compared to fewer than 5,000 in vineyards organized according to Lenz Moser.

The Wachau is the only wine-growing area in Austria with a sense of, and passion for, terroir and a cru structure similar to that of Burgundy – including the mystique attached to some of the more famous vineyards. Individual plots are well known, and jealously protected, for their special characteristics reflected in the wines.

Going from west to east on the left (northern) bank of the Danube, the *premiers* and *grands crus* of the Wachau are as follows: the *Rieden* Schön and Kalkofen both face south-west. The soils here are weathered granite and slate. Some of the finest *Rieden* of the Wachau can be found in Spitz itself. These are: Tausend-Eimer-Berg, or Burgberg, a hill rising just behind the town with steep, south-facing terraces of crystalline soils on Palaeocene para gneiss; Hochain and the adjacent Singerriedl, again with weathered gneiss and brown soil rich in silicates, a vineyard which benefits from maximum exposure to the sun, renowned for its finely-chiselled Rieslings; Rotes Tor, just to the south of the Singerriedl; and Steinborz, a miniature plateau. Another outstanding cru is Honivogl at the foot of the Singerriedl, with crystalline soil overlaid by brown soil.

At Wösendorf and Weißenkirchen, eight kilometres further downstream, the main *Rieden* are: Hochrain and Kollmitz, characterized by deep para gneiss soils with a top layer of sandy loess;

Pichlpoint; and Ritzling, with loamy sands on weathered granite. The Hinterseiber and Vorderseiber are further up the hill and once again characterized by para gneiss. To the east of Weißenkirchen, the *Ried* Achleiten is renowned for its distinctive *stinkerl*, the mineral note it communicates to many of the wines grown on it. The stone walls of the terraces which secure the soils date back to the twelfth century. At the top of the hill, the soils are made up mainly of Gföhl gneiss. At the lower end dark, often amphibolitic stones with slate emerge from the subterranean rock. Next to it is the almost equally famous *Ried* Klaus, again mainly gneiss and some slate and a famous Riesling vineyard.

Following the river, we come to the charming village of Dürnstein with the castle ruin on the hill above it. Here Hollerin and Kellerberg are recognized as particularly fine. Both are situated on the south-eastern side of the castle hill, the soils of Hollerin dominated by weathered gneiss and sand, and those of Kellerberg by crystalline gneiss and slate (it also benefits from the influence of the wooded hilltops immediately surrounding it). The Loibenberg, under vines since the fourteenth century, rises to 420 metres and offers soils from weathered gneiss and slate to sandy loam and some loess to the east. The Mühlpoint nearby has similar soils, while up the hill the *Ried* Steinertal is purely crystalline, a small, sheltered spot. The *Ried* Schütt was mentioned first in 1379; it demarcates the border between Dürnstein and Loiben and is separated into two vineyards, the Dürnsteiner Schütt, with weathered gneiss and sand soils and a pronounced microclimate, and the Loibner Schütt, which faces south-west.

The village of Mautern on the south side of the Danube has conditions which are very different, and its vineyards are much flatter than the terraced hills across the river. The *Ried* Burggarten, once apparently the site of Charlemagne's camp, is slowly being eaten up by building activity. Its soils are gravel and sand. The Silberbühel, below the magnificent Göttweig Abbey, has some crystalline soils and gravel, mostly covered by sandy loess. At its foot the *Ried* Vom Stein, a former gravel pit, is planted exclusively with Riesling.

The Wachau is a white wine area par excellence, and the undisputed main varietals are Riesling and Grüner Veltliner, which can here produce intensely concentrated and powerful wines with enormous ageing potential. Other common varieties are Chardonnay (in the Wachau called Feinburgunder), Müller-Thurgau, Muskateller, Pinot blanc and Sauvignon. In his journal *The Vine*, which has given a good deal of attention to fine Austrian wines, Clive Coates writes about the Wachau Chardonnay, Müller-Thurgau *et al.*: 'Few of these are of note. The growers should concentrate on their two classic varieties and forswear the rest.' I would respectfully submit that especially Muskateller and Pinot blanc can evolve into beautifully elegant wines which add an important hue to the Wachau palette.

Priding itself on its status as an area of great tradition and great wines, the Wachau operates its own system of wine classification, denoting not only grape variety, year and often plot, but also three steps of quality. Steinfeder, named after a plant growing in the vineyards, denotes the simplest, lightest wines with low alcohol (up to 11 per cent), best drunk *en primeur*. The second step is Federspiel, named after a device used in falconry to lure the hawk back to the glove. These wines have about 12 per cent alcohol, are more substantial, and need to lie for about two years. The third and highest step is named Smaragd, after the little emerald-green lizards sunning themselves between the vines in summer. Elsewhere in Austria, these wines would be called Auslese. They are made from the best and ripest grapes and can have very considerable alcohol content. They are made to last and should be given plenty of time. At their best, they are among the best white wines made anywhere in the world.

Top growers

Alzinger
7 ha
Grüner Veltliner, Chardonnay (Feinburgunder), Riesling
Leo Alzinger is a quiet, retiring man, not given to great perorations. His curse has always been to live cheek by jowl with two of the greats of the Wachau, F. X. Pichler and Emmerich Knoll. Despite these forbidding neighbours, Leo Alzinger's wines are very impressive indeed, with fine and complex aromas, all harvested from the work-intensive terraces that dominate wine-growing in the Wachau. Alzinger has reached his position among the very best (not only in terms of his neighbours) within a single decade.

Until 1930 his family were coopers, and afterwards they produced grapes for a co-operative. This has all changed now, and Alzinger is, despite his unassuming manner, one of the fixed stars in the Wachau firmament. His wines marry elegance and opulence and can be very stylish indeed. Care is the watchword in the production of these wines: yields are severely restricted, the unfiltered must is not disturbed by pumping, and a pneumatic press ensures the least possible stress on the grapes. Like most Wachau winemakers, Alzinger relies on natural yeasts. His best *Rieden* are Liebenberg, Loibenberg, Steinertal and Hollerin. The 1997 Grüner Veltliner Liebenberg is a vindication of Mr Alzinger's care and determination, with wonderfully complex fruit aromas and great power, while the Riesling Loibenberg from the same year shows great class and the beautiful almond tones often associated with its *Ried*. In botrytis years, he also produces BA and TBA wines from his Veltliners and Rieslings.

Leo and Anni Alzinger, Unterloiben 11, 3601 Dürnstein (phone and fax 02732-77900).

Bäuerl

A small and traditional producer, making not so much spectacular as finely judged wines from vineyards in some of the most famous *Rieden*. These wines may not be of the calibre of the superstars, but Wolfgang Bäuerl does not strive for power. Instead he tries to work as closely as possible in accordance with natural rhythms, such as the phases of the moon, and creates wines which are ideal with food, and beautifully elegant and harmonious. This approach brings increasing dividends, and his finely spun Grüner Veltliners and Rieslings have made a considerable name for themselves with their elegance, fine fruit, and length.

Wolfgang Bäuerl, Loiben 28, 3601 Dürnstein (phone 02732-75555, fax 02732-755554).

Dinstlgut Loiben
400 ha
Grüner Veltliner, Riesling, Chardonnay, Müller-Thurgau, Blauer Portugieser, Zweigelt

The Dinstlgut is a traditional house; indeed, it can look back on a thousand-year history. In recent decades it was known as solid but a little boring until, in 1994, Walter Kutscher took over, a man known to Austrian wine lovers as a writer and collector, not as a producer. Under his aegis the Dinstlgut has improved in leaps and bounds and has now taken its place among the top producers in the Wachau. It is a very complex organization, part-owned by 520 growers. It is not surprising that most of the wines produced here are moderate and rather simple, though always of good quality. The cellars of the estate, hewn into the rock in 1002, also offer some rather better wines though, especially from 1997, a year that demonstrates the much higher expectations that can now be had of the wine. Among the Grüner Veltliners, the Spätlese 'L' from the Loibenberg shows good depth and great power, while the Riesling from the same *Rieden* showed more finesse and dryness on the palate, despite a good deal of residual sugar. Other Grüner Veltliners and Rieslings were fine, but competition in the Wachau quickly makes tasters snobbish. The Riesling TBA, however, was excellent, if perhaps a little jammy, but the acidity which is also present should secure it a considerable potential.

Dr Walter Kutscher, Unterloiben 51, 3601 Dürnstein (phone 02732-85516, fax 02732-8551625).

Donabaum
A new face in Wachau winemaking circles, Sieghardt Donabaum is making a good name for himself with some spectacular Rieslings, very well made Grüner Veltliners and also good Muskateller.

Sieghardt Donabaum, Zornberg 4, 3620 Spitz (phone 02713-2287, fax 02713-2287-4).

Freie Weingärtner Wachau
600 ha
Grüner Veltliner, Riesling, Neuburger, Pinot blanc, Chardonnay, Sauvignon blanc, Müller-Thurgau
Zweigelt
It is conventional wisdom that nothing good can ever come from a wine-growers' co-operative. This one is proof that this is not always the case. Situated outside the villages, in a tiny and lovely baroque château which almost makes one forget the very modern production facilities surrounding it, this co-operative produces year on year some of the best wines around, along with large quantities of very good wines for local consumption. There are 778 members holding shares in the Freie Weingärtner Wachau.

The co-operative can trace its history back as far as 1137, when Hadmar I of Kuenring made local peasants work on the vineyards belonging to the Bavarian monasteries. In 1715, the provost Hieronymus Uebelbacher, who has become a local legend, built the Kellerschlössel, a baroque gem in the middle of the vineyards, on top of the co-operative's cellars. He decorated the interior of the building with a very eccentric collection of prints, which are pasted to the walls in a gigantic and bucolic collage. In 1938 the lease-holders of the Herrschaften Dürnstein and Thal Wachau bought out the vineyards and winery from its owner, Ernst Rüdiger Fürst von Sternhemberg. In 1990 the co-operative called itself Freie Wein-gärtner Wachau ('Free Wine-growers of Wachau'). The secret of its present success seems to lie in the inspired leadership of Willi Klinger and Fritz Miesbauer, who never seem to tire and certainly never make any compromises in quality.

It is bound to be a good sign that the Freie Weingärtner, while being the third-largest producer in Austria in terms of hectares, is sixth in terms of quantity of wines produced, with a yield of about 50 hectolitres per hectare and considerably less for some more prestigious wines. Their newly completed press houses have a unique layout and guarantee the most careful processing of the grapes, aided by the best technology available – including, for instance, computer tagging of consignments of grapes in order to ensure the best possible match of ripeness and sugar for the wines. The cellars are infinitely more traditional, a century-old labyrinth of vaults and barrels in which one would be quite happy to be lost. According to legend, a massive tasting table in one of the vaults, overlooked by a long row of elaborately carved vats, was the scene of some of the copiously lubricated negotiations between the then Austrian foreign minister, Leopold Figl, and Colonel Molotov that resulted in Austria not being part of the Soviet bloc.

Willi Klinger is famous for the fact that, if prodded tactfully after a long tasting session, he will go to the piano and play any song that comes into his head; in a former incarnation he was a musician. His previous, wider interests are still in evidence when one finds that one can discuss with him not only wines, both Austrian and international, but also literature, music and seemingly every topic under the sun. Fritz Miesbauer is the younger and quieter part of the team, and also the oenologist.

The Freie Weingärtner have vineyards in the famous *Ried* Ach-leiten, and it is not surprising that the Achleiten Rieslings and

Grüner Veltliners belong to their most famous wines, with good, concentrated fruit, strong mineral characteristics and the well-known Achleiten *stinkerl* ('pong'). The wines from other locations, such as Kellerberg, Loibner Loibenberg, Singerriedel, Tausend-Eimer-Berg and Terrassen Spitz, can also be very considerable. There can be an astringent acidity in some wines, but I found most of the wines produced here (including the simpler ones) beautifully made and often underestimated. It was also here that I had a rare opportunity to peek into the past, and into the future, by tasting wines dating back as far as 1969. They all held up beautifully, and had become 'wiser' and mellower without losing any of their structure and presence. If Austrian wine ages like this – there are very few old bottles around, and production methods and expertise have improved out of all recognition – the future is very rosy indeed, not only for the Freie Weingärtner, but for the wine country as a whole.

Willi Klinger and Fritz Miesbauer, 3601 Dürnstein 107 (phone 02711-371, fax 02711-37113).

Hirtzberger
12 ha
Grüner Veltliner, Riesling, Pinot blanc, Pinot gris
Together with F. X. Pichler and Emmerich Knoll, Franz Hirtzberger is one of the Wachau Trinity, the three mighty growers whose wines have achieved legendary status among wine lovers. Visiting his enchanting baroque domaine is a pleasure in itself, but tasting his wines and taking some of them back is the true purpose of pilgrims from far and wide. They have to be quick, though: true to Wachau form, his wines are sold out by February, when the faxes come pouring in. Hirtzberger is obsessive about the quality of his wines, and it shows. In his winemaking he, like several of his colleagues, relies more on intuition than on the latest technology, and what others may do with computer-controlled temperature regulation is achieved here with an electric blanket wrapped around a tank at critical times. All this obsessive behaviour, though, creates white wines of astounding depth, complexity and ageing potential, though what impresses me again and again about them is the focus they achieve. It is easy to wax lyrical about the elegance, fruit and mineral structure of these wines, and I simply cannot find fault with them, especially in years like 1997.

Among the 'big four' of the Wachau – Hirtzberger, F. X. Pichler, Prager and Knoll – his wines are, in some vintages, the most elegant and focused.

In Hirtzberger's hands the Grüner Veltliner can become a great grape variety, able to overwhelm when young and to mature for thirty years and more without losing any of its structure and power, almost longer than his equally outstanding Rieslings. His Burgundian varieties, too, are famous. The most famous *Rieden* to look out for are Rotes Tor, Honivogl, Singerriedl and Hochrain. Being made with enormous care and often on some of the steepest terraced slopes of the Wachau, these bottled miracles do not come cheap, but they are surely worth it. Hirtzberger's wines have very little sugar residue and are very clear in style, mighty wines with beautifully differentiated aromas and enormous potential.

Franz and Irmgard Hirtzberger, Kremser Straße 8, 3620 Spitz an der Donau (phone 02713-2209, fax 02713-2405).

Högl
4.5 ha
Grüner Veltliner, Riesling, Chardonnay (Feinburgunder), Muskateller

Though Josef Högl is one of the rapidly rising stars of the Wachau, finding his estate is a bit of a challenge. His tiny farm is tucked away in a side valley off the Danube valley. Here, seemingly, presentation is nothing, wine is everything. Formerly sorcerer's apprentice to F. X. Pichler, Högl creates beautiful wines of great concentration and clarity in tiny quantities and in a cellar that is hewn right into the mountain. It is a joy to discuss them with him, even if that requires some knowledge of the local dialect. The idiom of his wines, though, is instantly and internationally comprehensible: a finely judged balance of fruit and structure, especially with the Grüner Veltliner (*Ried* Schön, *Ried* Steinertal) and the Riesling, combined with powerfully concentrated fruit and great finesse. It may be that these wines are not quite as polished as the greatest Wachau ones, but their combination of energy and elegance is a delight. It is well worth going out of one's way to find this hidden gem.

Josef Högl, Vießling 31, 3620 Spitz/Donau (phone and fax 02713-8458).

Holzapfel

Karl Holzapfel did his apprenticeship in California and is increasingly highly thought of for his Grüner Veltliners and Rieslings. Holzapfel has vineyards in some of the best *Rieden*, including Achleiten and Klaus. His Grüner Veltliner and Riesling can have picture-book fruit, with lovely, elegant structure, though they are not as mighty as other wines from these *Rieden*. The Müller-Thurgau cuvée is also remarkable. Apart from the wine estate, there is also a good restaurant and Holzapfel's famous schnapps, which he distils himself from blackcurrant and apricot.
Karl Holzapfel, 3610 Joching 36 (phone 02715-2310, fax 02715-23109).

Hutter

Known until recently for his 'good drinking wines', Friedrich Hutter has invested a great deal of work in his vineyards, and this is beginning to pay off, especially with his very promising Rieslings. With vineyards on both sides of the Danube, his wines can be quite diverse in character. Wachau rarities such as Pinot gris and St Laurent can also be found here.
Friedrich Hutter, St Pöltener Straße 385, 3512 Mautern (phone 02732-83004, fax 02732-830044).

Jäger

In their historic cellars, father and son Jäger are making wines which have for some time been among the 'secrets' of the Wachau wine world, less defined perhaps than typical Wachau wines, but nonetheless well worth tasting. Their wines from the famous *Ried* Achleiten especially can be of great concentration and mineral depth. These wines do not necessarily advertise their virtues while they are young, but they promise great things for the future.
Manfred and Roman Jäger, 3610 Weißenkirchen 1 (phone and fax 02715-2535).

Jamek

25 ha
Grüner Veltliner, Riesling, Chardonnay (Feinburgunder), Muskateller, Pinot blanc
Josef Jamek, the octogenarian *éminence grise* of Wachau wine, with his short-cropped hair, his moustache and ceremonious courtesy, is a relic of the Habsburg era, and it is curiously this fact which

allowed him to help make the wine of his part of the world what it is today. After the war, he did not go in for the usual sweetish style but stuck with the dry, pre-war wines while steadily increasing their quality. Today the estate is led by his daughter and son-in-law, Jutta and Hans Altmann, but he is still very much in evidence. On my first visit, old Mr Jamek made a point of taking me into the vineyards and showing me every one of them, politely and with the knowledge of a lifetime explaining their geological and climatic peculiarities, including two *Rieden* which are legendary here, Klaus and Achleiten.

Mr Jamek's wines now also seem slightly old-fashioned, broader and less focused than some other Wachauers. While other Wachau growers are working more reductively and with more emphasis on fruit, his wines are still intended to be drunk with a good meal, preferably on his own domaine, which doubles as a well-known country inn and fine rustic restaurant. Though his Rieslings and Grüner Veltliners are good, his Pinot blancs often steal the show with their beautifully concentrated fruit and length. Mr Altmann, who has taken over in the cellar, is now beginning to emphasize the acidity of the wines, and perhaps Jamek wines will in future be able to stand at the very top of the Wachau again.

Jutta and Hans Altmann, Joching, 3610 Weißenkirchen (phone 02715-2235, fax 02715-223522).

Knoll

11 ha
Grüner Veltliner, Riesling, Chardonnay (Feinburgunder), Muskateller

Like the baroque statue of St Urban on his labels, Emmerich Knoll is today something like the patron saint of Wachau wine, a shy and contemplative man who is happiest in his cellar, where he produces famous wines with a minimum of modern technology. When I first visited the estate, I found that he had fled into the vineyards and had left me in the capable hands of his son. The cellar of the Knoll estate is still dominated by large barrels, many of which are traditionally embellished with wood carvings. Steel tanks are standing alongside, somewhat shamefacedly. His reference collection of old wines reaches back into the mists of Austrian winemaking, and he indeed made beautiful and perfectly structured wines long before that 1985 watershed.

Knoll's personal love and attention is devoted not only to the Rieslings from his *Rieden* Kellerberg and Schütt, but also, and especially, to the Grüner Veltliner – his are some of the very best wines made from this grape. Other grape varietals, such as Chardonnay and Muskateller, are dismissed by him as toys which he enjoys experimenting with. His style is more baroque than that of some of his colleagues, more rounded at times, but always profound, never demonstrative, a true union of fruit and mineral characteristics frequently very reminiscent of a Puligny-Montrachet (especially when aged for five years or more).

In good years these wines can be truly symphonic experiences, though his reluctance to interfere in the fermentation process and to drive it on once it becomes hesitant means that in some years (1995, 1997) his wines may retain more residual sugar than one would wish. Still, wines like his Grüner Veltliner Ried Loibenberg or his Riesling Ried Schütt and Ried Loibenberg are legendary in his own country and deserve to be counted among the best. One of his best vineyards, incidentally, *Ried* Pfaffenberg in Krems-Stein, is technically no longer in the Wachau and is therefore labelled without the Wachau name.

Emmerich Knoll's views are those of a far-sighted traditionalist who consciously relies on his instincts rather than on technology (too much of which makes wines anonymous, he says), and at the same time fights the very Austrian habit of drinking wines young, which as far as his wines are concerned is tantamount to pederasty. Wines like his, he believes, should be allowed to mature, ideally for some seven to ten years, though they do have potential for very much more. His cousin Josef has a good restaurant just across the road, which, as one would expect, offers a fine selection of Knoll wines, both young and mature. Emmerich Knoll's son, who is also called Emmerich, is now increasingly working with his father and is bringing his own ideas into the process.

Emmerich Knoll, 3101 Unterloiben 10 (phone 02732-79355, fax 02732-79555).

Lagler
8 ha
Grüner Veltliner, Riesling, Neuburger, Pinot blanc, Chardonnay, Sauvignon blanc
Karl Lagler is something of an institution in his home village of

Spitz. He is also one of the most consistent growers there, and his wines are continuing to rise in quality. His finest wines from the *Rieden* – the Steinborz, Tausend-Eimer-Berg and Hartberg – are beautifully crafted and concentrated, not least among them a remarkable Sauvignon blanc. Like many of his colleagues, Lagler was delivering his harvest to a co-operative for a long time, but these days are over, and he now resides proudly in one of the most beautiful houses in Spitz. He also still runs a *Heurige* together with his vineyard.

Karl Lagler, Rote Tor Gasse 10, 3620 Spitz an der Donau (phone 02713-2516, fax 02713-2950).

Leberzipf

A very small (2 ha) and traditional producer, Walter Leberzipf produces some beautiful Grüner Veltliners which are also available in his own *Buschenschank*. His 1998 Grüner Veltliner Ried Kalkofen was, though light, a perfect example of its kind.

Gabriele and Walter Leberzipf, Gut am Steg, 3620 Spitz (phone 02713-2170).

Lehensteiner

Andreas Lehensteiner attracted considerable attention with some finely judged wines which defy the trend and emphasize finesse and purity over concentration and sheer power. To this end he manages to put his vineyard on the *Ried* Achleiten to good use and produces wines which convince where some more overwhelming Wachau wines fail: with harmony and clarity.

Andreas Lehensteiner, 3610 Weißenkirchen 7 (phone 02715-2284).

Mazza

Ilse Mazza is running a very successful and classy *Heurige*, but she also makes wines which are far above the average, most notably a fine Riesling from the *Ried* Achleiten.

Ilse Mazza, 3610 Joching 124 (phone 02715-2300, fax 02715-230073).

Mittelbach

Opulent, very ripe Grüner Veltliners and Rieslings with characteristic honeyed aromas. Franz Mittelbach has won several international prizes for his wines. With 19 ha he is also among the larger Wachau producers.

Franz Mittelbach, Unterloiben 12, 3601 Loiben (phone 02732-85362, fax 02732-85362-20).

Nikolaihof

The Nikolaihof is one of a few good Wachau wine producers on the 'wrong' or southern side of the Danube. Founded in 985 as a feoff of the diocese of Passau, the Nikolaihof is one of the most traditional estates of the region. Christine Saahs cultivates vineyards on both banks of the river, notably the *Ried* Steiner Hund near Krems, officially no longer part of the Wachau, on which she grows her finest Riesling. All vineyards are tended according to organic principles. On the southern bank, the *Rieden* Vom Stein and Im Weingebirge produce fine Riesling and Grüner Veltliner respectively on gravel and sandy loam. Sometimes these do not have the concentration and elegance of 'proper' Wachau wines from the primary rock to the north, but their ageing potential is considerable. Also good Neuburger and Chardonnay.

Christine and Nikolaus Saahs, Nikolaigasse 3, 3512 Mautern (phone 02732-82901, fax 02732-76440).

Franz and Maria Pichler

Pichler is not a good name to have if you want to stand out in the Wachau. Being called Franz Pichler must be worse, as Franz Xaver Pichler is a wine-grower whose fame has by now spread far and wide. Franz Pichler and his wife Maria have produced very respectable wines since they founded the estate in 1982, though they did not have an easy start, as the name of Franz Pichler *père* was perceived by some more as a liability than an asset. However, they have left all this behind them and have recently attracted considerable attention with their clean and well-structured Grüner Veltliner, Rieslings, and other varietals. Not yet a superstar himself, Franz Pichler is definitely a very interesting winemaker.

Franz and Maria Pichler, 3610 Wösendorf 68 (phone and fax 02715-2307).

Franz Xaver Pichler

8 ha

Grüner Veltliner, Riesling, Sauvignon blanc, Muskateller
'F. X.', as he is called in awestruck tones in his native country, is the pope of Wachau wines and a great winemaker by any standard. An avid opera lover known to fly abroad to hear a particular

performance, he also seems to have assimilated the aura of the great divas, and at times appears to find it mildly insulting that people actually see the need to taste his wines. He, too, started with a *Heurige*, but wonderful vineyards such as the Loibenberg, Kellerberg and Steinertal conspired together with hard work and tremendous intuition to make him into a grower who soon achieved legendary status.

A collector of paintings and baroque sculpture, Pichler sees himself as an artist with his own work as an art form, and his wines bear out this self-perception. Underneath his unshakeable self-confidence (at one blind tasting he was heard saying, 'This is the best Riesling I have ever drunk and the best Riesling I have ever made'), he is far more malleable than many people make him out to be, and usually real interest and a little tenacity are enough to soften his rock-hard exterior. It is certainly worth it.

By common consent, F. X. Pichler does things with Grüner Velt-liner and Riesling grapes that others only achieve rarely, if at all, as he himself knows very well. His Grüner Veltliner 'M' ('Monumental', a selection of the best grapes from various *Rieden*), produced only in the best years, is staggeringly intense and complex, displaying tropical fruit, honey and mineral aromas, powerful yet elegant – a wine, as he says, to meditate on. It is the almost austere mineral base and clarity underlying the layers of evolving richness on the palate which make these truly great wines so impressive. The complex tones of ripe and perhaps overripe fruit come with alcohol contents of up to 14.5 per cent, but Pichler's wines will stand up to this without any problem. Though his Grüner Veltliners may be the real revelation, his highly concen-trated Rieslings and his Sauvignon blanc are equally famous and will age very happily for many years, if not decades. Pichler's best *Rieden* are Kellerberg, Loibenberg and Steinertal.

Pichler shares a distrust of very reductive vinification and high technology with other Wachau growers, believing that these would make his wines too uniform. He ferments them in large wooden barrels and leaves them there for about six months. Industrial yeasts are only used for the first consignment of must; after that, natural yeasts take over.

For someone whose name is synonymous with great white wine, it may be surprising that F. X. Pichler has a real passion for red wines, but he certainly does, for French wines in particular. As red grapes would not be able to reach the same potential as white ones in the Wachau, Pichler has teamed up with Tibor Szemes from the Burgenland and the excellent Styrian Manfred Tement to produce a red wine called Arachon which first hit the market in 1996. It comes as no surprise that this is one of the very good Austrian reds.

F. X. Pichler, 3601 Oberloiben 27 (phone and fax 02732-85375).

Rudi Pichler
5.5 ha
Grüner Veltliner, Riesling, Chardonnay, Pinot blanc, Roter Veltliner
Having unjustly suffered the fate of being 'the other Pichler' for a long time, Rudi has since established himself as one of the finest Wachau winemakers and is steadily building up this reputation. The Rieslings especially are very fine, big powerful wines with wonderfully concentrated fruit and rock-solid structure. His Veltliners and Pinot blancs, too, are very good indeed. Unlike many others in the region, Rudi Pichler is willing to experiment and to bring in modern technology such as temperature-controlled fermentation. From steel tanks some wines even go into small new oak barrels, but they are never overwhelmed by the wood. As a style, though, this is an interesting and indeed beautiful voice in the Wachau ensemble, where barrel-aged Grüner Veltliners with residual sugar are a great rarity. Still, it works astonishingly well and demonstrates once again that this grape is capable of immense transformations and seemingly limitless quality. Rudi Pichler has vineyards in the best terroirs around, among them Hochrain and Achleiten, the latter of which is often distinguished by a characteristic mineral note adding some direction to the fruit. Though less famous than Franz Xaver (the two are not of the same family), his offerings provide some of the best value around, for the time being at least.

Wösendorf 38, 3610 Weißenkirchen/Wachau (phone 02715-2267, fax 02715-22674).

Prager (Bodenstein)
13 ha
Riesling, Grüner Veltliner, Chardonnay (Feinburgunder), Sauvignon blanc
Toni Bodenstein is what Austrian dialect calls a *zuag'raster*, i.e. he

comes from far away – fifty kilometres to be precise. After many years in the Wachau, where he took over his father-in-law's prestigious estate, people think of him almost as a local. Local or not, his wines are very fine. They are also having great success in the USA, especially the Rieslings, which account for more than half his vineyards. Among these, the *Rieden* Achleiten and Dürnsteiner Hollerin are especially remarkable, the Achleiten with the customary bitter almond note, the latter powerful and harmonious. Bodenstein is especially proud of his 1997 Riesling TBA, a great rarity and a wine which perfectly balances power and elegance, sweetness and acidity. One of the few graduates among the Wachau growers, he also has a great interest in history. The term *Urgestein* ('primary rock') so often used to describe the wines around here, is more a reflection of the rugged and impenetrable character of the people than a geological term, he says. The Prager winery has a great name in the Wachau, not least because old Mr Prager was one of the pioneers of what we know today as dry white Wachau wines. As if in deference to this tradition, the modern Prager wines do at times take some time to come into their own properly. It is well worth the wait.

Toni Bodenstein, 3610 Weißenkirchen 48 (phone 02715-2248, fax 02715-2532).

Schmelz
6 ha
Grüner Veltliner, Riesling, Müller-Thurgau
Johann Schmelz learned his craft in the Jamek cellars and is therefore well equipped to produce excellent wines, which he has increasingly done since starting on his own in 1987. He obviously believes in cross-fertilization, as his eldest son is now learning with Gerald Malat, only a few miles away. While still known mainly as a *Heurige*, the Schmelz estate is making an excellent name for itself and manages again and again to beat better-known producers in blind tastings.

Johann and Monika Schmelz, Joching 14, 3610 Weißenkirchen (phone 02715-2435, fax 02715-2605).

Schmidl
Franz Schmidl is well known, but not for his wine. It is as a baker that he is famous. He also produces very good Grüner Veltliners, Rieslings and Pinot blancs, and his estate not only boasts vineyards

in some of the best *Rieden* around but also a three-hundred-year-old wine cellar.
Franz Schmidl, 3601 Dürnstein 21 (phone 02711-224, fax 02711-2249).

Schneeweiß

After a lean patch, Peter Reiter – Anton Schneeweiß's son-in-law – has revived this estate and not only restored its good reputation, but raised great expectations for its future. The wines can be dense, and with plenty of clean fruit and their plots in *Rieden* like Vorderseiber, Steinriegl, Ritzling and Achleiten, this should allow them to go on to even greater things.
Anton Schneeweiß, 3610 Weißenkirchen 27 (phone 02715-2227, fax 02715-2644).

Karl Stierschneider

The wines of the Kartäuserhof are powerful beasts, still struggling to combine their sheer strength with consistent style and clarity. Occasionally, however, a surprisingly fine Riesling or Grüner Veltliner comes from this estate. Karl Stierschneider's special interest is BA and TBA wines made from Grüner Veltliner, and he has made himself quite a reputation for these.
Karl Stierschneider, Kartäuserhof 6 (phone 02715-2374, fax 02715-2374-4).

Paul Stierschneider (Urbanushof)

In the family since 1696, the Urbanushof produces expressive wines known for their rich extract even in the lighter wines. *Rieden* such as Loibenberg and Frauenweingarten and small yields are guarantors of good quality. Paul Stierschneider also produces a Wachau rarity, Sauvignon blanc.
Paul Stierschneider, 3601 Oberloiben 17 (phone and fax 02732-72750).

Kamptal

Area profile

Vineyards: 4,189 ha
Soil: primary rock, loam, loess, slate
White (90 per cent): Grüner Veltliner, Riesling, Chardonnay, Pinot blanc
Red (10 per cent): Zweigelt, Pinot noir, Cabernet Sauvignon, Merlot

The Kamptal is a valley along the river Kamp, a few miles to the east of the Wachau, and the first mention of wine-growing in the area dates back to 1082, when the Kamptal was owned by the bishopric of Passau in Bavaria. The centre of the area is the beautiful baroque town of Langenlois, which also claims to have the highest number of vineyards within its confines – a claim which incidentally is disputed by Gols in the Burgenland.

The situation of the Kamptal between the Pannonian plains and the forested areas of the Waldviertel determines the climate. Protected from north winds by the foothills of the Manhartsberg and the hills of the Weinviertel, the south-facing vineyards on the gentle slopes of the Kamptal have excellent conditions. The average annual temperature is 9° C, with a vegetation period of about 234 days and annual mean precipitation of about 580 mm per year, significantly more than in the Wachau. There is a danger of late frosts in May for all vineyards, and of frosts in spring and autumn for the lower ones. Hail in early summer is another hazard, but September usually marks the beginning of a dry period spanning the entire harvest season until November.

Geologically, Langenlois is at the meeting point of several formations. The subsoil is formed largely by gneiss and crystalline slate,

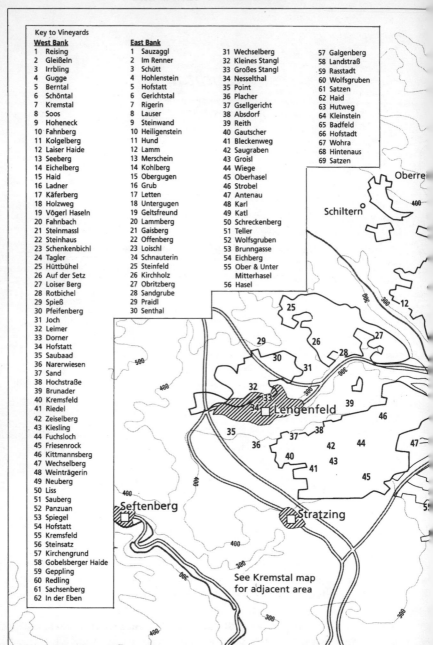

Key to Vineyards

West Bank
1 Reising
2 Gleißeln
3 Irrbling
4 Gugge
5 Berntal
6 Schöntal
7 Kremstal
8 Soos
9 Hoheneck
10 Fahnberg
11 Kolgelberg
12 Laiser Haide
13 Seeberg
14 Eichelberg
15 Haid
16 Ladner
17 Käferberg
18 Holzweg
19 Vögerl Haseln
20 Fahnbach
21 Steinmassl
22 Steinhaus
23 Schenkenbichl
24 Tagler
25 Hüttbühel
26 Auf der Setz
27 Loiser Berg
28 Rotbichel
29 Spieß
30 Pfeifenberg
31 Joch
32 Leimer
33 Dorner
34 Hofstatt
35 Saubaad
36 Narerwiesen
37 Sand
38 Hochstraße
39 Brunader
40 Kremsfeld
41 Riedel
42 Zeiselberg
43 Kiesling
44 Fuchsloch
45 Friesenrock
46 Kittmannsberg
47 Wechselberg
48 Weinträgerin
49 Neuberg
50 Liss
51 Sauberg
52 Panzuan
53 Spiegel
54 Hofstatt
55 Kremsfeld
56 Steinsatz
57 Kirchengrund
58 Gobelsberger Haide
59 Geppling
60 Redling
61 Sachsenberg
62 In der Eben

East Bank
1 Sauzaggl
2 Im Renner
3 Schütt
4 Hohlenstein
5 Hofstatt
6 Gerichtstal
7 Rigerin
8 Lauser
9 Steinwand
10 Heiligenstein
11 Hund
12 Lamm
13 Merschein
14 Kohlberg
15 Obergugen
16 Grub
17 Letten
18 Untergugen
19 Geltsfreund
20 Lammberg
21 Gaisberg
22 Offenberg
23 Loischl
24 Schnauterin
25 Steinfeld
26 Kirchholz
27 Obritzberg
28 Sandgrube
29 Praidl
30 Senthal

31 Wechselberg
32 Kleines Stangl
33 Großes Stangl
34 Nesselthal
35 Point
36 Placher
37 Gsellgericht
38 Absdorf
39 Reith
40 Gautscher
41 Bleckenweg
42 Saugraben
43 Groisl
44 Wiege
45 Oberhasel
46 Strobel
47 Antenau
48 Karl
49 Katl
50 Schreckenberg
51 Teller
52 Wolfsgruben
53 Brunngasse
54 Eichberg
55 Ober & Unter
   Mitterhasel
56 Hasel

57 Galgenberg
58 Landstraß
59 Rasstadt
60 Wolfsgruben
61 Satzen
62 Haid
63 Hutweg
64 Kleinstein
65 Badfeld
66 Hofstadt
67 Wohra
68 Hintenaus
69 Satzen

Oberre

Schiltern

Seftenberg

Lengenfeld

Stratzing

See Kremstal map
for adjacent area

Kamptal

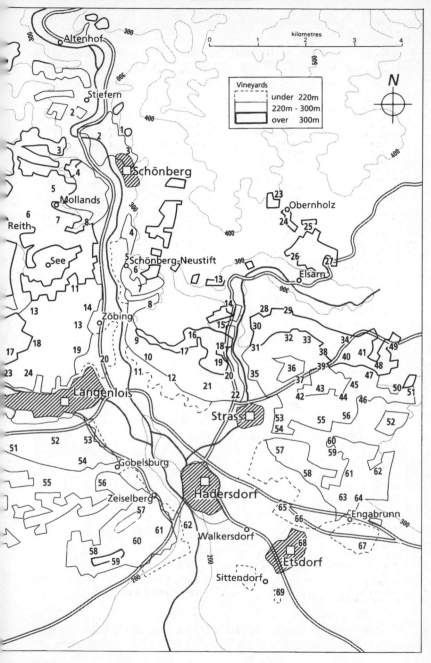

overlaid by marine sediments such as sands and clays. Other influences are the slow southward shift of the bed of the river Danube, which deposited gravel throughout the region, and loess dating from the last Ice Age, giving a soil profile of loess and crystalline soils on hills and hillsides and gravel with loam and sand in lower areas.

By far the most important *Ried* is situated to the north-east of Langenlois: the Heiligenstein ('rock of saints'), which has undergone a remarkable change of name. During the Middle Ages it was known as Hellenstein ('Hell rock'), possibly because of the scorching summer heat in the vineyards. A geographical anomaly, the Heiligenstein is a cone of primeval rock which has pushed through the surrounding area. Its soils consist of weathered crystalline rock, volcanic rock and desert sands. The southern parts of this cru are called Zöbinger Heiligenstein. The entire hill has now been declared a natural monument, and officials seem to be especially concerned about rare grasses growing here. There are plans to plant more grass on the Heiligenstein – for the first time in 250 million years. Apart from rare grass, though, Riesling finds a wonderful expression here.

The *Ried* Letten, adjacent to the Heiligenstein, was originally called Red Letten, because the iron content coloured the soil orange. Apart from Grüner Veltliner, this is also a preferred site for Pinot blanc and Pinot noir. Today it is usually called Kammerner Heiligenstein and vinified together with other sub-vineyards of the Heiligenstein proper. *Ried* Grub continues along the hillside. A natural plateau, it was used 15,000 years ago as a camp site by mammoth and reindeer hunters, as archaeological finds have proved. Whether the prehistoric bones add anything to the quality of the loess is not clear, but the position of the vineyard, protected from three sides against cold winds – which the hunters must have searched out – today benefits the wine.

Underneath the *Rieden* Heiligenstein and Letten is *Ried* Lamm, which has recently distinguished itself with some outstanding Grüner Veltliners and Rieslings. The plot is called Lamm not because it used to be a feeding ground for lambs, but because of the deep loam (spelt as in English in the Kremstal dialect) which makes up its soil.

On the southern side of Langenlois lies the Gobelsburg, a charming baroque castle belonging to Zwettel Abbey, and an excellent wine estate. To the west of the Gobelsburg, the *Rieden* Thal, Hofstatt, Spiegel and Pazaum (Innere, Mittlere and Obere) are situated on a hill, partly with black soil on loam and loess.

The Loiser Berg and the smaller Vogelsang lie to the west of Langenlois. A flat hill, this vineyard can be cool, moist and windy, but the southerly exposure and the absence of frost risk compensate for this; its weathered crystalline soils are ideal for Riesling and very good for Grüner Veltliner and Pinot blanc.

The largest vineyard area is the Schilterner Berg, directly north of Langenlois. Some excellent crus are to be found here. *Ried* Steinmassel (formerly a quarry), is a protected basin sunk into the surrounding countryside. The quarrying has exposed the crystalline slate subsoil, which is very suitable for Grüner Veltliner and Riesling. The *Rieden* Käferberg and Dechant are near the top of the hill, large vineyards with heavy brown and loess soils on primary rock, used especially for Pinot noir and Merlot, but also for Grüner Veltliner. Other *Rieden* here are Hoheneck, Fahnberg, Hozweg, Bockshörndl, Frau Point, Vögerl, Hofstatt, Schenkenbichl and Tagler.

A few kilometres east from Langenlois we come to Straß im Straßertal, another old winemaking village. Loess, brown and black soils predominate here, and the best vineyard is the *Ried* Gaisberg to the east (i.e. close to the Heiligenstein). It benefits from the crystalline soils of the Heiligenstein, but is more overlaid by brown earth and loess. The Wechselberg to the north of the village and the *Rieden* close to it also benefit from crystalline soils with loess and loam, and some brown earth in the lower parts. The *Ried* Hasel to the east of the village is very varied in its exposition, but the loess, gravel and black earth which make up its soil help to produce consistently interesting wines. There are other wine-producing villages, notably Lengenfeld, Schönberg and Hadersdorf, but these are not yet consistently producing very interesting wines.

The main grape varieties in this area are Grüner Veltliner and Riesling, with other Austrian varietals such as Neuburger, and increasingly more international ones, such as Chardonnay, Pinot blanc and even Sauvignon blanc. There is some red wine being made here, too: Zweigelt of course, but also surprisingly good Pinot noir. Kamptal wines can be very distinguished indeed, more opulent and perhaps broader than those of the Wachau, but also more varied in style.

Top growers

Aichinger

With their 'gourmet *Heurige*' and wine production, Anna and Josef Aichinger are faithful to their origin as chef and sommelier respectively. Their wines have established an excellent reputation independent of the *Heurige*, the Grüner Veltliner being rated especially highly. Aichinger wines frequently are slightly sweeter than other Kamptal wines, but the sugar is well integrated.

Josef and Anna Aichinger, Hauptstraße 15, 3562 Schönberg am Kamp (phone and fax 02733-8237).

Brandl

Johann Brandl does not mind seeking publicity, but fortunately his wines can stand up to the occasional spotlight trained on them. His Grüner Veltliner and Riesling Exclusiv and Riesling Zöbinger Kogelsberg have made a name for themselves with their complexity and power, which promise wonderful possibilities of maturation for both wines and winemaker. The first harvest of his best vineyard, Zöbinger Heiligenstein, was in 1993.

Familie Brandl, Heiligensteinstraße 13, 3561 Zöbing (phone 02734-2635-0, fax 02734-2635-4).

Bründlmayer

60 ha

Grüner Veltliner, Riesling, Pinot gris, Chardonnay, Pinot blanc Cabernet Sauvingon, Merlot, Pinot noir, Zweigelt

At first glance Willi Bründlmayer seems too good to be true: not only charming, courteous, stylish and one of Austria's very best and most consistent winemakers, he is also one of the few top growers to produce significant quantities. As if this were not enough, he also makes Austria's best sekt. The first thing one notices when talking to Bründlmayer is that he takes nothing for granted. When most of his colleagues imported Allier oak barrels at a rate of knots, he got together with a local cooper and had him make up barrels from Austrian, Russian and French oak as well as acacia and other woods in order to see which ones would really be most suitable for his purposes. He still works with local craftsmen, using both acacia and French and Austrian oak, which he suits to the characteristics of individual wines and vintages.

Bründlmayer's beautiful traditional cellar is complemented by a large hall of tanks and wine presses which is all agleam with steel and with the newest technology. He uses ambience yeasts: yeast from his own vineyards which he keeps frozen and then ferments with a small quantity of wine harvested one week early as a catalyst for fermentation of the main harvest. Gentle presses and careful treatment of the unfiltered must are further hallmarks of his winery.

The spirit of innovation, though, starts in the vineyards. His best vineyards are cultivated following the Lyre method advocated by the French viticulturist Alain Carbonneau: a high training with maximum leaf surface on both sides of the vine, which according to Bründlmayer may be more laborious to look after but also gives the wines significantly more concentration. The majority of his wine then matures in his large cellars.

The result of all this scrupulous care is that not a single mediocre wine leaves the Bründlmayer estate, from his simple Leicht & Trocken ('light and dry'), up to his heavy guns. Bründlmayer's Grüner Veltliner and Riesling, as well as his Chardonnay, set a yardstick for every vintage. They have less of a mineral backbone than the offerings from neighbouring Wachau, but they are still beautifully structured, with fruit, depth and length very well balanced.

His Grüner Veltliner Alte Reben (*vieilles vignes*) is one of the very few wines of this grape variety to be matured in new oak barrels, but since it is rich in extract the wood does not overwhelm it, creating instead a deep and powerful wine, with many layers of gradually evolving fruit aromas, that can be seen as the flagship of the estate. The Grüner Veltliner Ried Lamm, aged in large wood for nine months, can also be extraordinary; with its 14.5 per cent alcohol the 1997 vintage is a wine and a half, almost too powerful. The Riesling Zöbinger Heiligenstein, aged for up to one year in large vats, is a great wine, grown on the primary rock soils of the most famous *Ried* of the area. Its dense fruits and powerful structure require time to mature fully.

Every now and then, in vertical tastings, one comes to understand that whites from as far back as 1947 still drink beautifully. Bründlmayer's red wines are also very respectable, though they necessarily pale (if not in colour) next to the whites. The Bründlmayer sparkling wines are made, as Willi Bründlmayer himself says, according to the classical *méthode champenoise*, and are marvellously true to the grape varietals used (Pinot blanc, Pinot noir, Chardonnay) without compromising their complexity.

Willi Bründlmayer also plays the part of advisor and co-investor of the excellent estate Schloß Gobelsburg.

Willi Bründlmayer, Zwettler Straße 23, 3550 Langenlois (phone 02734-21720, fax 02734-3748).

Dolle

A very traditional estate, currently run by Peter Dolle III. The emphasis here is on Burgundian varieties such as Pinot blanc, but the Grüner Veltliner is also regarded as very good. There are some big wines, such as the 1998 Riesling Gaisberg, which combines high alcohol with high residual sugar, but some of them seem to be a case of ambition winning over substance. The Cuvée Année from Cabernet Sauvignon and Pinot noir, which is vinified in small oak, has good structure but does not achieve individuality.

Peter Dolle, Herrengasse 2, 3491 Straß (phone 02735-2326, fax 02735-2857).

Burgi Eder

As proprietor of the Eder estate, Notburga Sedlmayer has found it a good idea to be known in the wine world as Burgi Eder. The estate possesses some of the legendary Zöbinger Heiligenstein, but so far has not managed to capitalize on this by making Rieslings or Grüner Veltliners that maintain the standard of some other growers who have vineyards there. She does, however, produce good, fragrant Muskat Ottonel, a rarity in these parts. Also Neuburger.

Notburga Sedlmayer, Mühlplatz 1, 3484 Grafenwörth (phone 02738-2301, fax 02738-2301-30).

Ehn

Hidden away behind a bakery, Ludwig Ehn specializes in wine rarities and individual wines, such as ripe, round Grüner Veltliners with a distinct gooseberry nose (1998) and citrus-scented Rieslings, as well as Pinot blanc and Pinot noir. It is remarkable how Ehn manages to create aromas in almost all his wines that few others find, and the wines themselves are always highly interesting.

Ludwig Ehn, Bahnstraße 3, 3550 Langenlois (phone 02734-2236, fax 02734-22364).

Schloss Gobelsburg
32 ha
Grüner Veltliner, Riesling, Zweigelt
Pinot noir, St Laurent, Merlot

Schloß Gobelsburg is a beautiful baroque castle belonging to the monastery of Zwettl and surrounded by the proverbial rolling countryside. It has still very much an eighteenth-century feel to it, especially in the upper floors, which double as a museum of ceramics. As befits a castle, Gobelsburg has a long and varied history, which also holds true for the wine production. Starting in 1074, production was taken over by Zwettl Abbey in the late seventeenth century after the then owner had ruined itself with an ambitious (and charming) renovation programme and had joined the order on condition that it took over his debts together with his possessions.

During the twentieth century there was a good spell followed by a steep decline, halted abruptly in 1996 when Michael Moosbrugger and Willi Bründlmayer leased the castle and vineyards. Moosbrugger is not a child of wine-growers. He studied philosophy and music until he was forced to help in the family hotel after the death of his father. It was here that his fascination with wine awoke, a fascination that led him first to Lausanne and then as assistant at the Salomon and Jamek estates, where he learned his craft. When the Gobelsburg announced that it was looking for a new winemaker and a change in fortunes, he knew that his chance had come.

Today this is an exemplary wine producer, rapidly ascending to the very top. As a gesture to its owners, Gobelsburg produces some Messwein, i.e. wine supposedly used for Holy Communion, which in itself could make many an agnostic well-disposed towards Catholicism. The real Gobelsburg top wines, however, are in a different league from this agreeable but rather simple offering, and the Grüner Veltliner Ried Grub and especially Ried Lamm are truly outstanding specimens, powerful, complex and long, with very considerable potential. The Riesling Zöbinger Heiligenstein, too, is excellent. When I last visited Schloß Gobelsburg, I found a surprise tucked away in the cellars: a few barrels of Merlot which

Michael Moosbrugger was very apologetic about. He needn't have worried. This was an unexpected joy and makes one believe that the red wine potential of the Kamptal is far from being recognized and exploited. Schloß Gobelsburg, though, has only just started, and more wonderful things are to be expected of it.

Michael Moosbrugger, Schloßstraße 16, 3550 Gobelsburg (phone 02734-2422, fax 02734-242220).

Haas

Another estate which is being increasingly recognized for dense and complex Grüner Veltliner and Rieslings and for a good barrique-aged Chardonnay. Almost totally unknown until recently, this is a rising star.

Michaela and Erich Haas, Weingut Allram, Herrengasse 3, 3491 Straß (phone and fax 02735-2232).

Hiedler (Rosenhügel)

Calling some of your wines 'Maximum' can be a risky business. The 1996 seemed to locate the maximum not very high, but the 1997 was a marked improvement, especially for the Pinot blanc. Ludwig Hiedler is a grower in the ascendant, beginning now to profit from the hard work he has put in over the last decade and a half. His special interests are the Burgundian varietals and in his hands they may well reach their optimum.

Maria Angeles and Ludwig Hiedler, Am Rosenhügel 13, 3550 Langenlois (phone 02734-2468, fax 02734-24685).

Hirsch

16 ha

Grüner Veltliner, Riesling, Chardonnay
Cabernet Sauvignon, Pinot noir

For a long time the wines of Josef Hirsch and his son Hannes were a well-kept secret and a rare commodity. Nowadays, they are not secret any longer but just as hard to find. Father and son are anything but parochial. An ardent climber, Josef has climbed the Himalayas and the Turkish mountains, while the forays of his son were more concentrated on wine, with working visits to California, Australia, Chile, New Zealand and South Africa. It comes as little surprise that some of this adventurousness has transferred into the vineyards; Hirsch senior has experimented extensively, and quite successfully, with red grape varieties, especially Cabernet Sauvignon and Pinot noir. The glories of the estate, however, are the Grüner Veltliners and Rieslings, and among the latter it is the Zöbinger Heiligenstein that often stands out, followed by Ried Zöbinger Gaisberg and a delicately fragrant Grüner Veltliner Ried Kammerner Heiligenstein. These are beautifully weighted and full-bodied wines, often with a little residual sugar which keeps modestly in the background, adding richness without making the wine seem sweet. The Rieslings are vinified in the 'traditional' manner, i.e. without wood.

Josef and Hannes Hirsch, 3493 Kammern 25 (phone and fax 02735-2460).

Jurtschitsch (Sonnhof)
50 ha
Grüner Veltliner, Riesling, Chardonnay, Pinot blanc, Sauvignon blanc
Pinot noir, Zweigelt, Merlot

The Sonnhof is run by three brothers, which is worrying because they all look very similar. They also talk a good deal, but this does not distract them from working on an estate which is not only one of the big players, but also one of the consistently good ones. The most astonishing thing about the estate itself is its enormous system of cellars, replete with gigantic barrels. Above ground, things are very modern, with a newly refurbished tasting room decked out in glass, steel and designer lamps. The assortment of wines produced here is very impressive and reaches from solid drinking wines to top growths which are regularly in contention for prizes and medals. To some, these wines have less individuality than those of comparable producers in the vicinity, but there is no denying the fact that wines like the Sauvignon blanc Ried Fahnberg and especially the Grüner Veltliner Ried Loiserberg and Alte Reben are fine wines, with good structure, fruit and ageing potential. The Jurtschitsch brothers also make a very respectable red wine, the Rotspon, a cuvée of Zweigelt, Pinot noir and Merlot.

Josef Jurtschitsch, Rudolfstraße 37–39, 3550 Langenlois (phone 02734-2116, fax 02734-211611).

Kirchmayr
The Kirchmayr estate has vineyards all over the place: in the Wachau, the Kremstal, the Kamptal, the Weinviertel and the Burgenland. Many of these grapes are made into sparkling wine, but

there also some decent Grüner Veltliners, Pinot blanc, Riesling and Sauvignon blanc with good, dense fruit and well-balanced structure.

Hans Kirchmayr, 3351 Weistrach 123 (phone 07477-42173, fax 07477-42173-4, e-mail kirchmayr@wein-erlebnis.at).

Leithner

Good Grüner Veltliner and Traminer, usually not large but finely structured.

Thomas Leithner, Walterstraße 46, 3550 Langenlois (phone 02734-2552, fax 02734-25524).

Loimer

17 ha
Grüner Veltliner, Riesling, Chardonnay, Pinot blanc, Pinot gris Cabernet Sauvignon, Pinot noir

Fred Loimer is a tireless perfectionist who for his pains has been hounded by bad luck for some years, culminating in a near-fatal fall. Austrian wine was spared losing one of its most promising younger growers, who has quickly developed something of a cult following. He seems determined to make up for lost time and produces some fine Grüner Veltliner and Riesling, as well as some of the best Pinot gris in the area. Loimer invests obvious love and devotion in his wines, and it shows. I sometimes found the residual sugar too high, the wood a little pronounced and perhaps not quite integrated in his Veltliners and Chardonnays, but Austrian experts disagree strongly, saying that the structure of these wines is just about perfect. Perhaps age will tell, for these are wines to keep. Even the young wines, though, drink beautifully, with a good balance between fresh fruit and a certain baroque roundedness.

Fred Loimer, Zeigelhofengasse 12, 3550 Langenlois (phone 02734 2239, fax 02734-2208).

Metternich-Sàndor

This name is not only redolent of the old Austria-Hungary, it is also indicative of some very solid Kamptal wines, especially Grüner Veltliner and Sauvignon blanc.

Metternich-Sàndor, Talstraße 162, 3491 Straß im Straßertal (phone 02735-2393, fax 02735-5070).

Retzl
At Erwin Retzl's estate, wine is made in a traditional way, giving preference to natural yeast over others and to large oak barrels over steel tanks. Tradition is very much in evidence here, with wines dating back as far as 1901 in his cellar. The recent relatives of this Methuselah are clean and crisp Rieslings, as well as Welschrieslings, Sauvignon blancs and Grüner Veltliners.
Erwin Retzl, Heiligensteinerstraße 9, 3561 Zöbing (phone 02734-2251, fax 02734-22514).

Schneider
A rare adherent of a vine training system different from Lenz Moser, Gerald Schneider prefers an arched training and treats his vineyards with exclusively organic fertilizers. The result of this approach is some Burgundian-seeming Grüner Veltliners, beautifully clean and typical Rieslings and Pinot blancs.
Gerald Schneider, Cobaneshof, Weinstraße 37, 3550 Gobelsburg (phone 02734-2564, fax 02734-2564-4).

Topf
15 ha
Grüner Veltliner, Riesling, Pinot blanc, Chardonnay, Sauvignon blanc
Zweigelt, Cabernet Sauvignon
Johann Topf is brimming with enthusiasm. He is among the younger growers in the area and has already managed to make his mark with characterful, dense wines and innovative methods. In the vineyard, he champions natural methods and a minimum of chemical warfare – as do, incidentally, many of his good colleagues. His Topf Grüner Veltliners are vinified in steel, whereas the Chardonnays spend their fermentation in small wood. The Pinot blanc and Sauvignon blanc have good, typical aromas, the former nicely rounded, the latter crisp and clean. The Topf trademark is their instantly recognizable fruit, without, though, compromising the structure, as is so often the case with Austrian wines. These wines are very interesting and bound for even bigger and better things.
Johann Topf, Herrengasse 6, 3491 Straß im Straßertal (phone 02735-2491, fax 02735-249191, e-mail johann.topf@aon.at).

Weixelbaum
Good Grüner Veltliner, also rarer varieties such as Roter Veltliner and Malvasier.
Heinrich Weixelbaum, Weinbergweg 196, 3491 Straß im Straßertal (phone 02735-2269).

Zottlöderer
Some very good Rieslings, also good Sauvignon blanc and Grüner Veltliner.
Franz Zottlöderer, Sauerbrunngasse 49, 3491 Straß im Straßertal (phone and fax 02735-5252).

Kremstal

Area profile

Vineyards: 2,438 ha
Soil: primary rock, loess, sand, gravel
White (90 per cent): Grüner Veltliner, Riesling, Chardonnay, Roter Veltliner, Müller-Thurgau, Neuburger
Red (10 per cent): Zweigelt, Pinot noir

The town of Krems, picturesque as most are in this area, is situated by the banks of the Danube on the eastern edge of the Wachau, and also marks the beginning of the Kremstal to its east and north-west. Krems is one of the oldest Austrian settlements documented – mentioned first as 'urbs chremisa' in 995 – and has always played an important role in winemaking and the wine trade. During the Middle Ages, three-quarters of the population of the town lived off cultivating vines. A number of fine Gothic and baroque buildings bear testimony to its historical wealth. A school of viticulture was founded here in 1975 and is still carrying on with its work.

In terms of climate and soil, the Kremstal, a slice barely fifteen kilometres wide, is very similar to the Kamptal, with loam and loess soils, some deposits of sand and gravel and a mild microclimate, though the fact that continental and Pannonian climates are meeting here can produce great differences between individual hills and their vineyards. The town's proximity to the river results in the presence of large gravel deposits in lower vineyards. Chalky loess terraces are another characteristic of the area.

Protected by hills and by the Waldviertel to the north-east, the Kremstal benefits from warm, Pannonian air, while winter temperatures can be very low, especially away from the river banks. Annual mean temperatures are around 9° C (5–6° C on the hills), while

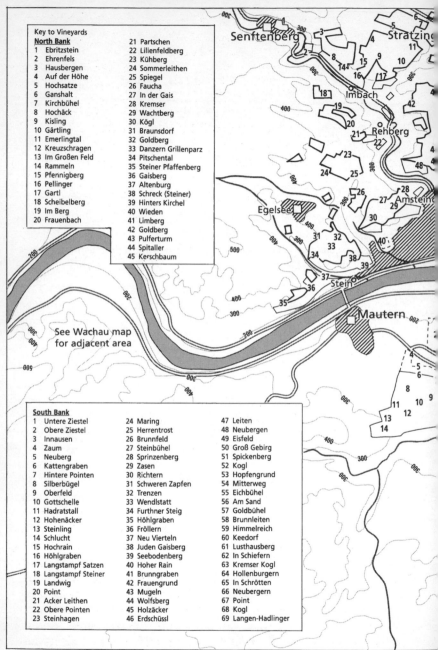

Key to Vineyards

North Bank

1	Ebritzstein	21	Partschen
2	Ehrenfels	22	Lilienfeldberg
3	Hausbergen	23	Kühberg
4	Auf der Höhe	24	Sommerleithen
5	Hochsatze	25	Spiegel
6	Ganshalt	26	Faucha
7	Kirchbühel	27	In der Gais
8	Hochäck	28	Kremser
9	Kisling	29	Wachtberg
10	Gärtling	30	Kögl
11	Emerlingtal	31	Braunsdorf
12	Kreuzschragen	32	Goldberg
13	Im Großen Feld	33	Danzern Grillenparz
14	Rammeln	34	Pitschental
15	Pfennigberg	35	Steiner Pfaffenberg
16	Pellinger	36	Gaisberg
17	Gartl	37	Altenburg
18	Scheibelberg	38	Schreck (Steiner)
19	Im Berg	39	Hinters Kirchel
20	Frauenbach	40	Wieden
		41	Limberg
		42	Goldberg
		43	Pulferturm
		44	Spitaller
		45	Kerschbaum

See Wachau map
for adjacent area

South Bank

1	Untere Ziestel	24	Maring	47	Leiten
2	Obere Ziestel	25	Herrentrost	48	Neubergen
3	Innausen	26	Brunnfeld	49	Eisfeld
4	Zaum	27	Steinbühel	50	Groß Gebirg
5	Neuberg	28	Sprinzenberg	51	Spickenberg
6	Kattengraben	29	Zasen	52	Kogl
7	Hintere Pointen	30	Richtern	53	Hopfengrund
8	Silberbügel	31	Schweren Zapfen	54	Mitterweg
9	Oberfeld	32	Trenzen	55	Eichbühel
10	Gottschelle	33	Wendlstatt	56	Am Sand
11	Hadratstall	34	Furthner Steig	57	Goldbühel
12	Hohenäcker	35	Höhlgraben	58	Brunnleiten
13	Steinling	36	Fröllern	59	Himmelreich
14	Schlucht	37	Neu Vierteln	60	Keedorf
15	Hochrain	38	Juden Gaisberg	61	Lusthausberg
16	Höhlgraben	39	Seebodenberg	62	In Schiefern
17	Langstampf Satzen	40	Hoher Rain	63	Kremser Kogl
18	Langstampf Steiner	41	Brunngraben	64	Hollenburgern
19	Landwig	42	Frauengrund	65	In Schrötten
20	Point	43	Mugeln	66	Neubergern
21	Acker Leithen	44	Wolfsberg	67	Point
22	Obere Pointen	45	Holzäcker	68	Kogl
23	Steinhagen	46	Erdschüssl	69	Langen-Hadlinger

Kremstal

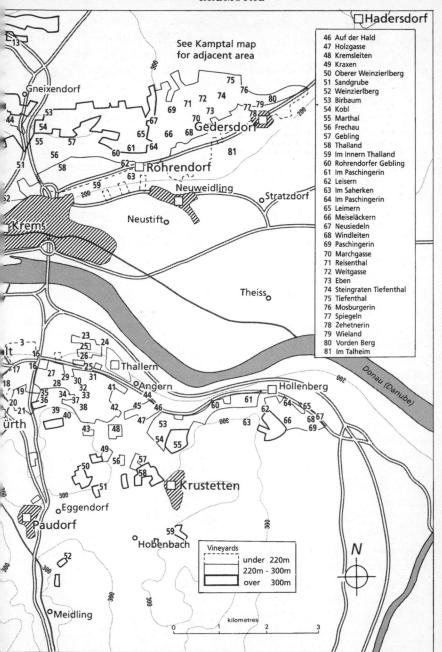

Hadersdorf

See Kamptal map
for adjacent area

46 Auf der Hald
47 Holzgasse
48 Kremsleiten
49 Kraxen
50 Oberer Weinzierlberg
51 Sandgrube
52 Weinzierlberg
53 Birbaum
54 Kobl
55 Marthal
56 Frechau
57 Gebling
58 Thalland
59 Im Innern Thalland
60 Rohrendorfer Gebling
61 Im Paschingerin
62 Leisern
63 Im Saherken
64 Im Paschingerin
65 Leimern
66 Meiseläckern
67 Neusiedeln
68 Windleiten
69 Paschingerin
70 Marchgasse
71 Reisenthal
72 Weitgasse
73 Eben
74 Steingraten Tiefenthal
75 Tiefenthal
76 Mosburgerin
77 Spiegeln
78 Zehetnerin
79 Wieland
80 Vorden Berg
81 Im Talheim

Gneixendorf

Gedersdorf

Rohrendorf

Neuweidling

Stratzdorf

Krems

Neustift

Theiss

Thallern

Angern

Hollenberg

Donau (Danube)

Krustetten

Eggendorf

Paudorf

Hobenbach

Meidling

Vineyards

under 220m
220m - 300m
over 300m

N

kilometres

0   1   2   3

the annual mean precipitation increases as one goes up, from just under 550 mm by the river to 750 mm on the hilltops.

The best vineyards around the city of Krems itself are Pfaffenberg to the east, part of which officially belongs to the Wachau, though the soil is identical on both sides. Most of the wines grown on this site are still bottled anonymously by co-operatives.

Steiner Goldberg and Steiner Hund are on opposite sides of the same hill. While Goldberg is more dominated by sandy soils on crystalline subsoil, the latter is more pronounced on *Ried* Hund, where the sand becomes sandy loess. The Kremstaler Kreuzberg is known for its Grüner Veltliner, which grows on gravel and crystalline soil.

The crus to the north-east of the village are not as distinguished and usually larger. Two of the most important ones are Thalland and Weinzierlberg, both dating back to the Middle Ages. Thalland has black earth on loess and gravel, while Weinzierl is dominated by loam, loess, gravel and even clay. The Sandgrube is not, as the name would suggest, exclusively sandy, but dominated by loam, gravel, and loess.

Rohendorf, away from the Danube and towards Langenlois, is home to the gigantic Lenz Moser winery. The village has some good vineyards, especially Rohrendorfer Gebling with weathered terraces, loess, and gravel. *Ried* Paschingerin has loess soil, as does Thalland.

Senftenberg is to the north-west of Krems. The vineyards are largely cultivated by part-time wine-growers, with one glorious exception: Martin Nigl, who makes some very remarkable wines here. Loam, loess and gravel dominate here, with some weathered crystalline rock soil. Good vineyards are Ehrenfelser, Emmerlingtal, Gartl, Stratzingbach, Hochäcker, Kremsleithen, Pellingen and Rammeln.

About a third of the Kremstal vineyards are on the southern bank of the Danube, around the villages of Furth, Thallern and Hollenburg. Most of these are at the foot of the hilly landscape which blends into the Traisental, and loess soils tend to make up the best vineyards, though there are also sandy soils, gravel and loam. The more distinguished crus in this area are Spiegeln, Vordern Berg, Kogl and Hochrain.

Top growers

Berger

Erich Berger heads a fairly large, traditional estate which has been in the family since 1818. He has just acquired five terraced vineyards with up to thirty-year-old Grüner Veltliner vines, which might well prove to be a decisive factor for an estate that is already producing good, classical Grüner Veltliner and Rieslings. There is also some sparkling wine.

Erich Berger, Wiener Straße 3, 3494 Gedersdorf (phone 02735-8234, fax 02735-8234-4).

Buchegger

Walter Buchegger has the curious distinction of supplying wines to the Olympic Games, but at home his reputation is spreading slowly. He is very much a rising star, though, and has a ream of awards to prove it. Unusually for Austrian growers, he makes just two white and two red wines, Grüner Veltliner, Riesling, Zweigelt and Cabernet Sauvignon. Among these, it is especially the Grüner Veltliner that is very fine and puts him near the top league. The red wines are matured in French oak.

Walter Buchegger, Weinbergstraße 9, 3494 Gedersdorf (phone and fax 02735-8969).

Forstreiter

Meinhard Forstreiter attracted attention with his 1997 Grüner Veltliner Exklusiv, which is indeed a fine example of the species. His Neuburger and Pinot gris are also interesting, if perhaps not quite as harmonious.

Meinhard Forstreiter, Hollenburg 13, 3506 Krems-Hollenburg (phone 02739-22960).

Geyerhof

Mainly Grüner Veltliner, but also good Malvasier are vinified by Ilse Maier. Also good Zweigelt.

Ilse Maier, Oberfucha 3, 3511 Furth (phone 02739-2259, fax 02739-22594).

Domäne Baron Geymüller

Run by the Dinstlgut Loiben, this estate produces a good range of clean and typical wines with modern methods of vinification. The sweet wines are especially renowned.

Hollenburg 57, 3506 Krems (phone 02739-2229, fax 02732-8581625).

Hagen
Very good Riesling Weinzierlberg, also good Grüner Veltliner.
Anton Hagen, Seilerweg 45, 3500 Krems-Rehberg (phone 02732-78160).

Weingut der Stadt Krems
With 32 ha, this estate is one of the largest in the area; it is also one of the oldest. As far back as 1210 the Babenbergers founded a hospice here, which acquired vineyards, largely through legacies. This estate was eventually united with the vineyards belonging to the town of Krems, some of which date back to 1452. The former hospice estate was acquired by the town fathers in 1915, enabling them to process the grapes from their vineyards and cellar the wines. After being run by a co-operative for some time, the town estate is today run by Heinrich Redl, who has striven hard to improve standards and has begun to vinify wines from his best vineyards, such as the Kremser Sandgrube, separately. The Sandgrube is Veltliner territory, while Riesling is made on the Weinzierlberg and the primary rock of Steiner Grillenparz. Recently (1999), Redl has been granted more of a free hand in vineyard and cellar, which may well prove the making of an estate that has been performing below its very considerable potential. This is not to say that the wines of the Stadtweingut are poor: there are Veltliners which can be both peppery and honeyed, as well as well-constructed Reislings. The red wines are less remarkable.
Stadtgraben 11, 3500 Krems (phone 02732-801440, fax 02732-801442, e-mail stadtweingut@krems.gv.at).

Winzer Krems
This co-operative deserves a mention because of its sheer size: it has a total area of 990 ha under contract – more than 900 different vineyards altogether, cultivated by 1,700 wine-growers. The co-operative can trace back its origins to the thirteenth century. Eighty per cent of its vineyards are in Kamptal and Kremstal, and the rest are outside, in the Traisental and Donauland. Half the wines of the Winzer Krems originate from vineyards around Krems. The director of the co-operative is Franz Ehrenleitner, who has overseen a continuous rise in standards. The chief oenologist is Franz

Arndorfer. The wines produced so far are almost invariably simple and unremarkable, with Grüner Veltliner leading the fray, though some Winzer Krems wines were admitted to the Austrian Salon of fine wines. The age-old loess cellar of the co-operative houses a wine archive going back in an unbroken line to 1947. Winzer Krems also produce sparkling wine from Riesling.

Sandgrube 13, 3500 Krems (phone 02732-85511, fax 02732-855118).

Malat
30 ha
Grüner Veltliner, Pinot blanc, Riesling, Chardonnay
Cabernet Sauvignon, Merlot, Pinot noir, St Laurent

Gerald Malat used to be a rally driver and has taken this fascination with gleaming steel and ingenious devices into his cellar, where he is constantly constructing improvements and gadgets. This concerted modernism is transplanted into vineyards which were already cultivated by the Romans, and is combined with traditional vinification methods, such as fermentation of some wines in larger oak barrels. Malat's Trockenbeerenauslesen are considered to be among the very best in the country, and as if to emphasize the fact that they are great wines, some of them are filled into magnums. The Malat winery, however, also produces remarkable dry wines, especially his Das Beste vom Veltliner ('the best from the Veltliner'), usually an Auslese, and a very crisp Sauvignon blanc. The Grüner Veltliners may not have the sheer structure and power of those in nearby Wachau, but they make up for much of this with fruit and mellowness. The red wines also contribute to Malat's excellent reputation, especially his Cabernet Sauvignon and Pinot noir, which is one of the few Austrians to approach Burgundian style and finish.

Gerald Malat, 3511 Furth-Palt/Krems (phone 02732-82934, fax 02732-8293413).

Mantlerhof
A traditional, high-quality estate, a champion of the Roter Veltliner grape, which Josef Mantler makes into beautiful, clean and yet complex wines.

Josef Mantler, Hauptstraße 50, 3494 Brunn im Felde (phone 02735-8248, fax 02735-8916).

Mayr (Vorspannhof)
10 ha
Grüner Veltliner, Riesling, Sauvignon blanc, Chardonnay, Gelber
Muskateller
Initially known as one of Austria's most romantic *Heurige*, the
Vorspannhof has made wines of increasingly high quality.
Especially the Grüner Veltliner Kermser Sandgrube and Riesling
Kremser Marthal are remarkable wines, with fruit very typical for
the area and good length. In some years, the Gelber Muskateller
is particularly fine. These wines are produced in very small quanti-
ties. This is an estate to watch.
Familie Mayr, Herrengasse 48, 3552 Droß bei Krems (phone
02719-2342).

Moser
50 ha
Grüner Veltliner, Chardonnay, Pinot blanc, Riesling, Sauvignon
blanc
Pinot noir, Cabernet Sauvignon, Zweigelt, Cabernet Franc
One of the larger Kremstal growers, Sepp Moser also makes some
of its best wines, which seem to transcend their area in character.
His Sauvignon blanc Atriumweingarten and especially his Riesling
TBA are famous among cognoscenti and are thought to belong to
the very best in the country – which is a considerable achievement
in an area which not only has fewer top growers than others, but
also has vineyards which are considered difficult. There is, of
course, a whole palette of wines, ranging from Grüner Veltliner to
Riesling and also some very interesting red wines. Many of the
vines are imported from Montrachet, Chablis, Champagne and
the Rhine to provide the best material possible. The wines are
vinified using very up-to-date technology, after considerable investment in the cellar in 1997. Sepp Moser also has an estate in
Apetlon, by the Neusiedlersee, where he makes exclusively red
wines.
Sepp Moser, Untere Wiener Straße 1, 3495 Rohrendorf bei Krems
(phone 02732-70531, fax 02732-7053110).

Lenz Moser
It is not easy to understand the workings of this estate, which
boasts hardly 5 ha itself, but buys in grapes from some 3,000 small
growers, making it one of the largest wine producers in Austria.

Suffice it to say that it fills an average of 9 million bottles a year. The firm is based on a dynasty of Lenz Mosers, and the current holder is Lenz Moser V. His ancestor, the venerable Professor Lenz Moser III, was a viticulturist who in 1929 developed the method of high vine training still widely used across Austria.

Wine was grown in the eleventh century on an estate on this site, which was then the property of the Benedictine abbey of Ebersberg in Bavaria. The first 'Moser' is documented to have made wine in 1124. In 1849 the estate passed into secular ownership and the Anton Mosers took over the reins.

Lenz Moser wines are omnipresent, both in Austria and abroad. When I visited their headquarters, I was impressed by the fact that they do manage to present clean, very drinkable wines at very moderate prices. However, the increase in quality between these and their top wines is, while clear, not enormous, and they remain very much a middle-of-the-range producer in the classical Austrian style, concentrating on grape varieties such as Grüner Veltliner and Zweigelt. Having said that, their 1995 Beerenauslese was very respectable and received high praise. Lenz Moser also vinifies the wines of the Malteser Ritterorden.

Lenz M. Moser, Lenz-Moser-Straße 1, 3495 Rohrendorf (phone 02732-85541, fax 02732-85900).

Nigl
15 ha
Grüner Veltliner, Riesling, Chardonnay, Müller-Thurgau, Sauvignon blanc
Zweigelt

The name Nigl crops up whenever fine wines are mentioned. Within a very few years, Martin Nigl has advanced from being totally unknown to being one of the top growers for white wines in the area, after he took over the estate, significantly in 1986-7. His Grüner Veltliners and Rieslings especially have attracted a devoted following with their elegance and full body, and they are usually sold out long before they see bottles. Situated at the northern tip of the Kremstal, Nigl's vineyards are mainly primary rock around the Senftenberg and loess in the plots around the city of Krems. His wines are mainly vinified in steel, with the exception of one oak-aged Chardonnay. His best wines, usually of Auslese quality, are labelled Privat, but fortunately he does not keep them all to himself. Nigl's Grüner Veltliner Alte Reben benefits from seventy-year-old vines which produce wine of wonderful compactness and complexity with great depth of fruit. The wines from the Senftenberger Piri vineyard are not far behind in style and concentration, and can be even better in some years. The Riesling Hochäcker can also be good – a more robust example of this variety than those produced in nearby Wachau, but still very fine. Although Nigl wines are wonderful for drinking in their youth, they have a considerable ageing potential.

Martin Nigl, Priel 7, 3541 Senftenberg (phone 02719-2609, fax 02719-26094).

Proidl
10 ha
Grüner Veltliner, Riesling, Müller-Thurgau
Cabernet Sauvignon, St Laurent, Zweigelt
Their labels may look old-fashioned, but for a family making wine here for nine generations that is understandable. The wines of the Proidl estate are examples of the generational change that has taken place in Austria. The current holder of the staff, Franz, has put in an enormous amount of hard work, recultivating steep slopes which had been given up as too difficult, and turned the estate around from a co-operative grower to a little gem, a process which involved many a fight with the authorities. With these trials behind him, he now concentrates on making beautiful Grüner Veltliners and also, surprisingly, elegant Müller-Thurgau TBA, as well as very good Rieslings and Malvasiers. There is also some good St Laurent and Zweigelt.

Franz Proidl, Oberer Markt 5, 3541 Senftenberg (phone 02719-2458, fax 02719-24584).

Salomon (Undhof)
20 ha
Grüner Veltliner, Riesling, Traminer
The Undhof Salomon is remarkable in many ways. Not only did Erich Salomon restore a historic estate with Gothic chapel and vaults which would otherwise have lain in ruins, but his father was also one of the true pioneers, the first to import Pinot blanc into Austria and to popularize it; he was also the first to export his wines to the USA, where they are highly regarded today. His son Erich has reinvigorated the fortunes of the estate, put some cellar

problems well behind him and produces beautifully typical wines, often with a characteristic understated elegance. These are not among the spectacularly alcoholic giants which are at times popular in Austria, but classical wines whose filigree fruit has earned many admirers. As they are usually in the Auslese range, they are also extremely long-lived. The Rieslings Kremser Kögl Reserve and Pfaffenberg especially are remarkable. Erich Salomon's brother Berthold, incidentally, is the indefatigable boss of the Austrian Wine Marketing Board.

Erich Salomon, Undstraße 10, 3504 Krems-Stein (phone 02732-83226, fax 02732-8322678).

Schmid
Dense and fruity Rieslings and Chardonnays, at times very good indeed.

Josef Schmid, Obere Hauptstraße 89, 3552 Stratzing bei Krems (phone 02719-8288).

Türk
Good, clean Grüner Veltliner and a powerful but not sophisticated top wine, Erlesenes vom Veltliner. Also clear, classical Riesling Kremser Weinzierlberg.

Franz Türk, Kirchengasse 86, 3552 Stratzing (phone 02719-2846, fax 02719-2846-4).

Dr Unger (Kelleramt Göttweig)
38 ha
Grüner Veltliner, Riesling, Müller-Thurgau, Malvasier, Chardonnay, Neuburger
The Kelleramt Göttweig and its vineyards have produced wine for many centuries, and when the hotel owner Wolfgang Unger bought it in 1987 it was one of the most traditional estates of the era, not only in terms of its history, but also of its winemaking. Much has changed since then, and the four-hectare Kelleramt has been transformed into an estate producing classically pure wines on 38 hectares, seven of which are in the Wachau. Especially famous for its Eisweins, which have started a trend in the area, the estate now also produces the best oak-aged Chardonnay in the area. The mainstays of the estate are, of course, Grüner Veltliner and Riesling, finely structured and pure wines which seem like school examples of good, typical Kremstal and Wachau wines, rarely at the very

top of the table, but setting an impressively high standard none-theless.
Dr Wolfgang Unger, Kirchengasse 14, 3511 Furth bei Göttweig (phone 02732-85895).

Walzer
The year 1998 has given Ewald Walzer two TBA wines, of which the Grüner Veltliner is fine. His Grüner Veltliner Alte Reben and Riesling Marthal are also very well made, compact and with good body.
Ewald Walzer, Gneixendorfer Hauptstraße 16, 3500 Krems (phone and fax 02732-87148).

Zimmermann
A young grower making promising Riesling and Grüner Veltliner.
Obere Hauptstraße 20, 3494 Theiß (phone 02735-8209, fax 02735-82094).

Above and Beyond

———

Though the overwhelming majority of Austrian wine is produced in the eastern part of the country, there are some wine-growers in other areas. Most of them work on one hectare or less and therefore cannot be considered for this book. For the sake of completeness, though, here a few general remarks.

Vorarlberg

Vorarlberg, at the very western tip of Austria on the Swiss border, boasts a long winemaking history. The Romans brought vines to this province, and in the fourteenth century two-thirds of all farmers here made wine. The greatest expansion of vineyards was reached in the seventeenth century, when the area had 700 ha under vines. From there, however, wine production went downhill and the phylloxera blight spelled the beginning of the end of Vorarlberg winemaking. At the beginning of our century there were a mere 65 ha and during the 1980s less than one hectare was left. Today, Vorarlberg has about 15 ha of vineyards, with Grüner Veltliner, Burgundian varieties, Müller-Thurgau, Bouvier, Riesling, Traminer, Blauer Portugieser, Zweigelt, Cabernet Sauvignon and Merlot.

Owing to the low average temperatures, Vorarlberg vineyards are situated on south-east or south-west facing hills, on the upper slopes and therefore away from the cold air accumulating in the valleys. The warm Föhn wind in late summer and autumn helps the ripening of the grapes.

The only producer with more than two hectares of vineyards is the Möth family in Bregenz with 6.5 ha. Other producers are Franz

Nachbaur (who even got his wine into the Austrian Salon league of critically approved wines), Heinz Otto Fulterer and Peter Summer.

Heinz Otto Fulterer, Naflastraße 3, 6804 Feldkirch-Altenstadt (phone 05522-72203, fax 05522-72203-17).

Familie Möth, Langenerstraße, 6900 Bregenz (phone 05574-47711).

Franz Nachbaur, Zehentstraße 4, 6832 Röthis (phone 05522-43251).

Peter Summer, Fober 26, 6820 Frastanz (phone 05522-53671).

Wine-growing in Upper Austria is negligible, despite the presence of the Stiftsweingut Krems-Stein, whose 20 ha of vineyards are in the Wachau. Some wine is made in Carinthia and in Tyrol, but here the largest producer, Karl Reinhart, has only one hectare under vines.

Karl Reinhart, 6170 Zirl (phone 05238-2600).

Appendices

APPENDIX I

Useful Addresses

Austrian Wine Marketing Board
Gumpendorferstr. 5
A-1060 Vienna
Phone 0043-1-587 4767
Fax 0043-1-587 4767 32
E-mail austrian.wine@inmedias.at
http://www.austrian.wine.co.at/
wine

PR for Wine (UK)
Victoria Morrall and Emily
Wilkinson
41 Crofton Road
London SE5 8LY
Phone 020-7708 5195
Fax 020-7708 4822

A selection of UK importers:

Berry Bros & Rudd
3 St James's Street
London SW1A 1EG
Phone 020-7396 9600
(Helmut Lang, Bründlmayer)

F & M Cressi Ltd
1 Red Lion Court
Alexandra Road
Hounslow
Middx TW3 1JS
Phone 020-8607 6110/1
Fax 020-8570 9129

E-mail cressi@d4web.com (or
sales@cressis.clara.net)
(Metternich-Sàndor, Esterházysche
Schlosskellerei, K+K Kamptal)

Forth Wines Ltd
Crawford Place
Milnathort
Kinross-shire KY13 7XF
Phone 01511-863668
Fax 01577-865296
(Lenz Moser, Malteser
Ritterorden)

FWW Wines
241 Banstead Road
Banstead
Surrey SM7 1RB
Phone 020-8786 8161
Fax 020-8393 3313
(Freie Weingärtner Wachau,
Helmut Lang, Engelbert Prieler)

Ben Ellis Wines
The Brockham Wine Cellars
Wheelers Lane
Brockham
Surrey RH3 7HJ
Phone 01737-842 160
Fax 01737-843 210

(Schloß Gobelsburg, Manfred
Tement, Willi Bründlmayer,
Krutzler, Zens)

Lay & Wheeler
6 Culver Street West
Colchester CO1 1JA
Phone 01206-764 446
Fax 01206-560 002
(Feiler Artinger, Gernot Heinrich)

Richard Nurick Wines
2–10 Whitchurch
Pangbourne
Berkshire RG8 7BP
Phone 01189-842 565
Fax 01189-845 954
(Juris/Stiegelmar)

Richards Walford & Co
The Manor House
Pickworth
Lincs PE9 4DJ

Phone 01780-460 451
Fax 01780-460 276
(Nikolaihof, Bründlmayer, Knoll,
F. X. Pichler, Steindl)

T & W Wines
51 King Street
Thetford
Norfolk IP24 2AU
Phone 01842-765 646
Fax 01842-766 407
(Opitz, Umathum)

Noel Young Wines
56 High Street
Trumpington
Cambridge CB2 2LS
Phone 01223-844 744
Fax 01223-844 736
(Willi Bründlmayer, Alois Kracher,
Krutzler, Nekowitsch, Wieninger)

APPENDIX II

Austrian Wine in Sober Numbers

CLIMATE: ANNUAL AVERAGE VALUES

	Height above sea level (m)	Annual mean °C	Max °C August mean	Min °C January mean	Annual rainfall mean	Sun hours per year
Neusiedlersee						
Illmitz	117	10.9	29	−12	595	1832
Neusiedl	129	10.3	32	−12	597	1862
Middle Burgenland						
Deutschkreuz	192	9.9	32	−13	594	1830
South Burgenland						
Wörterberg	402	9.4	30	−12	754	n/a
Bernstein	615	8.4	28	−12	749	n/a
Neusiedlersee-Hügelland						
Eisenstadt	159	10.4	32	−12	619	1859
South-East Styria						
Graz	366	9.5	30	−12	838	1844
West Styria						
Deutschlandsberg	410	9.3	31	−14	1153	1874
South Styria						
Leibnitz	275	9.5	32	−16	917	1639
Weinviertel						
Hollabrunn	245	9	32	−15	519	1778
Falkenstein	302	9.2	33	−14	509	1655
Retz	256	9.2	32	−14	435	1651
Traisental						
St Pölten	272	9.4	33	−12	696	1717
Thermenregion						
Baden	260	10	32	−11	596	1712

	Height above sea level (m)	Annual mean °C	Max °C August mean	Min °C January mean	Annual rainfall mean	Sun hours per year
Bad Vöslau	230	9.8	32	−13	611	1741
Carnuntum						
Schwechat	178	9.9	32	−13	543	1773
Donauland						
Tulln	174	9.5	32	−14	641	n/a
Kremstal						
Krems	203	9.6	32	−12	521	1721
Kamptal						
Langenlois	210	9.2	32	−13	481	1667
Wachau						
n/a	n/a	n/a	n/a	n/a	n/a	n/a
Vienna						
Hohe Warte	202	10.3	32	−10	607	1771

Source: Austrian Meteorological Service. Measuring period: 1961–1990

PRODUCTION QUANTITIES BY WINE GROWING REGION (IN HECTOLITRES)

	total	hl/ha	Lower Austria	Burgenland	Styria	Vienna
1990	3,166,290	57.6	1,717,299	1,291,974	133,571	23,230
1991	3,093,259	56.2	1,858,737	1,070,231	135,127	28,967
1992	2,588,215	48.3	1,599,132	842,682	125,865	20,087
1993	1,865,479	37.0	1,238,341	452,249	150,668	23,909
1994	2,646,635	53.0	1,665,645	800,098	150,211	23,089
1995	2,228,969	45.9	1,359,105	739,084	111,077	19,056
1996	2,110,000	43.5	1,394,962	547,433	133,481	28,377
1997	1,801,747	37.8	921,032	713,351	148,546	14,868
1998	2,703,170	56.4	1,609,853	932,430	137,238	23,263

Source: Austrian Wine Marketing Service

AREAS UNDER VINES BY WINE
GROWING REGION (IN HECTARES)

Lower Austria	**30,688**
Wachau	1,350
Kremstal	2,214
Kamtal	3,858
Donauland	2,755
Traisental	713
Carnuntum	1,012
Weinviertel	16,263
Thermenregion	2,518
others	4
Burgenland	**16,029**
Neusiedlersee	8,332
Neusiedlersee-Hügelland	5,348
Middle Burgenland	1,912
South Burgenland	437
Styria	**3,668**
Southern Styria	1,902
Western Styria	531
South-Eastern Styria	1,230
others	6
Vienna	**620**
Others	**21**
Carinthia	1
Upper Austria	2
Salzburg	0.5
Tyrol	5.5
Vorarlberg	12

Source: Austrian Wine Marketing Service

STRUCTURE OF WINE PRODUCING ESTATES

Size of Estates	<1 ha	1–2 ha	2–3 ha	3–5 ha	>5 ha
Number of Estates	21,196	5,724	2,869	3,266	2,814
% of total	59.12	15.95	8.0	9.1	7.8

Source: Austrian Wine Marketing Service

APPENDIX II

NUMBER AND SIZE OF ESTATES BY AREA

Region	Lower Austria	Burgenland	Styria	Vienna	Others
Number of estates	20,181	11,342	3,950	377	19
Average Size in ha	1.67	1.82	0.81	1.83	0.74
% of Austrian total	57.86	35.42	5.5	1.18	0.02

Source: Austrian Wine Marketing Service

APPENDIX III

Important Austrian Wine Associations and Marketing Groups

———

The Austrians are very fond of clubs and associations, especially if they come with titles for their distinguished members. This phenomenon has also taken hold of the wine world and there is an embarrassment of riches in this respect. The names most likely to pop up on the labels of the wines discussed are the following: a small selection from the almost thirty different associations currently in existence, each of which comes with its own standards of quality and vinification. It will be very much in the interest of exporting producers to clear up this tangle of names.

Cercle Ruster Ausbruch
Fifteen members; dedicated to reviving the classical Rust Ausbruch, a sweet, elegant wine. These wines must mature in barrels for at least one year and in bottles for another six months before being sold.

Kamptal Klassik
145 members. Marketing association of growers around Langenlois, aimed at promoting both the wines and an Austrian style of vinification, as well as 'natural' methods of cultivation.

Pannobile
Small association in Burgenland (seven members), dedicated to developing wines of high quality with a character typical for the area, using indigenous grape varietals. White wines are assembled from Neuburger, Pinot blanc and Chardonnay, red cuvées from Zweigelt, Blaufränkisch and St Laurent. This is an interesting group, making interesting wines which may well be an indication of what future wines from this area could taste like.

Renommierte Weingüter des Burgenlandes (RWB)
Ten members; a very exclusive, self-regulating association of some of the best producers in the Burgenland. A good guideline for quality in this region.

Die Thermenwinzer
Eight members; hoping to raise quality and typicality of their wines through regular tastings.

Traditionsweingüter Österreich
Twenty members; aimed high initially, but has become somewhat uncritical in its admission criteria. Is lobbying for a change in the wine law similar to the French system.

Vienna Classic
Not an inspired name, but a laudable goal: improving the quality and image of Viennese wines.

'Vinea Wachau' Nobilis Districtus
Founded by Wilhelm Schwengler (of Freie Weingärtner Wachau), Franz Hirtzberger, Franz Prager and Josef Jamek. 170 members; important association which includes all important producers in the Wachau, with the exception of the Dinstlgut Loiben. Its members cover about 85 per cent of the area of the Wachau. Oversees Wachau classification of Steinfeder, Federspiel and Smaragd. It is an effective organization and has helped markedly to create a strong image for Wachau wines. It is a pity, though, that the wines are only classified by alcohol content and not by quality, meaning that poor producers can also label their heftiest wines with the prestigious word Smaragd. The Latin phrase making up the name of the association, incidentally, is not a modern marketing ploy but the designation given to this region by one of its former rulers, Leuthold I von Kuenring (1243-1312).

Wagramer Selektion
Association of fifty growers seeking to improve the quality of the wines of Wagram/Donauland.

Die Weinviertler
Eight members; goal is the quality control and marketing of Weinviertel wines. Roman Pfaffl at the helm gives this aim credibility.

APPENDIX IV

Vintage Chart

During the last fifteen years the Austrian wine landscape has changed beyond all recognition. Standards have risen, new styles and methods of vinification have been popularized and new grape varietals planted. On the whole, wines produced today age much better than those made twenty or thirty years ago (though there are always surprises to be found). Because of this, there is little point in describing older vintages in much detail. If they are still available (and Austrians like to drink their wines young), they may be very different indeed from their more recent cousins.

1990 Good weather conditions produced an excellent harvest. A warm winter was followed by a very dry summer and only naturally moist or artificially irrigated vineyards could escape damage. Most other grapes did not reach full ripeness at the time of harvest. The area around Krems was also hit by hail in May. An uneven year: good in South Burgenland and in some parts of Styria. Some wines have good acidity and fruit; red wines especially are compact and have good potential, if perhaps less than those from the previous year.

1991 A difficult year. Growth in the vineyards was delayed after the coldest winter since records began. Heavy rains in June were followed by hail and then high temperatures in July. Parts of the Wachau were flooded. An early frost made great difficulty for many growers who had failed to prune their vines rigorously enough. A good year for botrytis wines (despite some involuntary botrytis) and for some red wines, especially in Neusiedlersee-Hügelland. Here, growers who used malolactic fermentation fared best, because of the high acidity of the grape material.

1992 The jury is still out on this vintage, which had been declared, prematurely, a vintage of the century. After a mild and dry winter, spring brought much-needed rain, though not quite as much as in previous years. The development of the plants was early. The summer was extremely hot and ripening proceeded rapidly, only to be stunted by prolonged drought. Those hoping for quantity rather than quality were often victims of these dry conditions. Rains just before harvest salvaged much of what had already been written off, but after the long dry period the grapes did not assimilate as much water as was feared. In many regions, the harvest had already finished in September, even for high gradations of wine. Unsurprisingly, this year produced a large number of Spätlese and Auslese wines, though as always high sugar content was no guarantee of good quality. Botrytis did not occur, but this lack was compensated for in part by a good harvest of Eiswein. A good year also for red wines, with relatively low acidity and high alcohol content.

1993 Extreme weather conditions characterized this year. A long winter with temperatures as low as -20° C was followed by a warm spring, though there was a sudden frost in late winter which caused widespread damage in the vineyards, especially in Neusiedlersee-Hügelland and the Thermenregion. Summer was disappointingly cool, but the rapid ripening of the grapes in spring nevertheless meant that harvesting was on average fourteen days earlier than in other years, though the yield was much lower than in the previous year. Those who gambled on a later harvest had to contend with heavy rainfalls. Many of the wines of this year were more elegant than those from 1992, with good balance between fruit and acidity. There was sufficient botrytis for producing Auslese wines. 1993 red wines are still much talked about and in many ways it was this year which first demonstrated the qualities of new-style Austrian reds. Some of these wines are by now part of Austrian wine folklore, especially those from the Burgenland. Also a fine year for Wachau Grüner Veltliner. With the relatively low alcohol content, often near-perfect structure and high extract of its wines, 1993 was an exceptional year.

1994 After initial severe frosts which damaged vines in the Thermenregion and around the Neusiedlersee, a warm spring brought good budding. Spring was followed by the hottest summer on record in Austria. Good rainfalls in June and July, which spurred on the development of the vines, were followed by a hot and dry period which necessitated irrigation, especially in the Wachau, though thunderstorms brought relief to the vineyards around the Heiligenstein in Langenlois. Hail in the Middle Burgenland was devastating, especially for the crops of Blaufränkisch. Wine-growers had to wait until early autumn for significant rain, which was prolonged and interrupted the harvest, dragging it out over a relatively long period. The resulting combination of high sugar content and low acidity in the grapes taxed many growers and often brought out the best in them. The botrytis wines around the Neusiedlersee had a bad year, as conditions in October were too dry for the development of noble rot. As an exception to this rule, the vineyards around Illmitz produced good quantities of botrytis grapes, though little Eiswein. Some excellent wines were produced, especially late harvests such as Spätlese and Kabinett wines, but there was also a higher than usual percentage of mediocre wines. All in all, this was not an opulent vintage, but individual elegant wines were produced. In Lower Austria, Riesling often turned out better than Grüner Veltliner, and the red wines had an especially successful year, though yields were low due to frost and hail damage. A good but uneven year.

1995   A wet but mild winter was followed by a spring with noticeably cold periods in May. A warm summer with an especially hot July was followed by a wet and cool August, which brought oidium and created problems for dry wine producers. The continued wetness during the first half of September led to the widespread rotting of grapes and a lowering of the yield by 30 per cent compared with 1994. While this was bad news for many producers, 1995 did provide a truly great harvest of botrytis wines. In October the cold made way for a prolonged Indian summer and the warmth further helped the development of botrytis. Sugar levels and acidity recovered in most areas. While this was a miraculous year for the growers around Lake Neusiedl, other producers also achieved good results. The vintage is characterized by low yields and wines with good character and acidity, especially among the late harvest wines. While this was an average year in most of Lower Austria, the areas of Wachau, Kamptal and Kremstal produced some truly remarkable dry wines of great opulence, sometimes with botrytis notes, as well as rare botrytis wines. A magnificent October in Styria compensated for much of the poor summer and made it a better than average year there, too. In the hands of the most capable growers, especially in the Burgenland, this was an excellent year for dry wines as well as a record vintage for their sweet cousins. There were celebrations all round (and a shower of international prizes) in Illmitz and surrounding areas. Many also departed from their usual ways and produced sweet wines themselves, as botrytis was almost ubiquitous. A year of great wines and a good many great rarities.

1996   Because of the cold spring, the growth of the vines was delayed by several weeks, but a warm May allowed much of the vegetation to catch up. The summer was cooler than in previous years, and rainfalls in August kept grapes from drying out. Late August and early September, however, were cool and rainy; there were even some hailstorms. The cool and moist atmosphere caused some rotting on the vine, and good work in the vineyards was essential. The best results were to be had with grapes harvested late, allowing them to lose some excess water. This vintage was very much a test of individual ability, and has produced some of the most interesting wines of recent years in estates that took the conditions as a challenge and had the expertise and intuition to deal with them, despite the fact that it was overall an average year. Some growers nevertheless produced remarkable wines by rigorous selection and late harvesting of the grape material (Kremstal). The moist conditions proved excellent for botrytis wines, if not as wonderful as the previous vintage. In general, white wines could ripen to a considerable degree while red wines did not usually reach the concentration of earlier vintages. In general these wines will have to be drunk young.

1997   This year sent many growers into ecstasies of joy, despite the fact that the quantity of the total harvest was a third below average. Harsh, early frosts imposed a natural limitation of quantity, but spring was beautiful and with enough rain and sunshine to produce a record growth of the buds. The early summer was quite wet, but late summer and autumn were warm and dry, though frosts at the end of October damaged some (white) grape material which had been left out for late harvest. This was indisputably the year of the great white wines, especially in Lower Austria and Styria. The grape material was perfectly healthy (bad news for sweet wine producers, who had to wait for Eiswein) with well-balanced extract, high sugar content and perfect acidity. The only problem regularly encountered (especially in the Wachau) was the fact that some wines stopped fermenting and there was a natural sugar residue in what should have been bone-dry wines. In retrospect, this serves to enrich these powerful and wonderfully balanced wines. Red wines, too, made a major step forward this year in terms of quality, style and ageing potential, and indigenous grape varieties such as Zweigelt and Blaufränkisch have shown their true potential in 1997, particularly around Lake Neusiedl and in the rest of the Burgenland, though some very considerable Pinot noirs and cuvées were also produced. One of the great vintages this century in Austria.

1998   A year with a perfect start: early flowering and a hot summer with just the right amount of precipitation seemed to line up the country for another truly great vintage. Heavy rainfalls in September and October, however, somewhat changed the picture. It was now a question of the abilities of individual winemakers to make nature surrender perfect grape material. Some growers were tempted to harvest before the rain, but this resulted in few good wines. In late October and early November the weather became more clement again, and growers who had done good work in the vineyards and had had the courage to wait until after the rain were able to harvest an often exceptionally good vintage. It comes as no surprise that this late harvest produced wines that can have classic German 'Spätlese' character with almost overripe grapes and high sugar content. As a result, wines from this year can be very high in alcohol, low in acidity and less clearly profiled than those of 1997. Some wines have as much as 15 per cent alcohol, and few of them can quite integrate such a massive amount. The best winemakers, however, managed to turn these conditions to their advantage and achieved some very considerable results in all wine-growing areas.

Good earlier vintages: 1834*, 1836, 1868*, 1888, 1900, 1911, 1921, 1929, 1934, 1937, 1945, 1947*, 1949, 1956, 1959, 1961, 1964, 1968, 1969*, 1971, 1973, 1977, 1979, 1981, 1983, 1985*, 1986*, 1989. Excellent vintages are indicated by a *.

Bibliography

There is a substantial number of new publications dealing with Austrian wine every year, most of which are assessments of the current vintage and the current stars in the Austrian wine firmament. Most of them are, of course, in German. I know of only three English books specifically dealing with Austrian wines, one of which is a historical snapshot, not a guide to current winemaking in Austria.

Giles MacDonough, *The Wine & Food of Austria*, London, 1992.

Giles MacDonough, *New Wines from the Old World*, Klosterneuburg, 1997.

S. F. and F. L. Hallgarten, *The Wines and Wine Gardens of Austria*, Watford, 1979.

Among the German publications, a selection may suffice:

E. Bieber, W. Kutscher, R. Sedlaczek (eds.), *Unser Wein*, Vienna (updated annually).

Wolfgang Dähnhard, *Weinparadies Österreich*, Düsseldorf, 1996.

Wolfgang Dähnhard, *Atlas der österreichischen Weine*, Bern, Stuttgart, 1995.

Hans Dibold, Helmut Romé (eds.), *Falstaff Rotweinguide*, Vienna (updated annually).

Horst Dippel, *Die großen Weine der Wachau*, Vienna, 1995.

J. Fally, A. Gebert, *Blaufränkischland*, Deutschkreutz, 1997.

Rudolf Lantschbauer, *Die Weine des Burgenlandes*, Graz, 1993.

Michael Reinhartz (ed.), *Guide GaultMillau Wein & Schnapps 1999*, Vienna, 1998.

Hubert Sandhofer, Tobias Hierl (eds.), *Österreichs Salon-Weine*, Klosterneuburg (updated annually).

Franz Schams, *Vollständige Beschreibung sämmtlicher berühmter Weingebirge in Österreich, Mähren und Böhmen in statistisch, topographisch-naturhistorischer und ökonomischer Hinsicht*, Vienna, 1835.

BIBLIOGRAPHY

Hans Schmid (ed.), *Heine a la carte, der Gourmet-Führer* (updated annually).

Rudolf Steurer, Viktor Siegl, *Österreichischer Weinführer*, Vienna, 1996.

Rudolf Steurer, *Weinhandbuch*, Vienna, 1995.

Eckhard Supp (ed.), *Enzyklopädie des Österreichischen Weins*, Offenbach/Main, 1996.

Christoph Wagner, *Wein-Guide Österreich*, Vienna, 1998.

Glossary

═══

ALTER: in *Heurige* inns, last year's wine – in contrast to *Heurige* wine, which is this year's.

AUSBAU (French: ELEVATION): the process of ageing a wine in the winery. In Austria, the elevation of a wine is done either along traditional lines – in large wooden casks or, more recently, steel tanks (*klassischer Ausbau*) – or in small casks, or barriques, which are usually made from oak and impart particular characteristics to the wine. The latter, more expensive method, is more international in style and is used especially for red and powerful white wines. Styles of elevation differ considerably between individual areas. The duration of the elevation of a wine is usually not shorter than six months, but can extend to two years and more.

AUSBRUCH: sweet wine produced by adding healthy ripe grapes to others affected by botrytis.

BARRIQUE: see Cask ageing

BEERENAUSLESE: a wine made from selected overripe and botrytis-affected grapes.

BEISL: a city inn similar to a *Heurige*, in which local wine can usually be bought by the glass.

BERGWEIN: wine from a slope of more than 26°.

BOTRYTIS (BOTRYTIS CINEREA): noble rot affecting ripe grapes in particularly warm and moist climatic conditions. The botrytis fungus shrivels the grapes, extracting the water content while leaving the sweetness and aromas, and adding a distinctive aroma of its own. Grapes affected by this noble rot are used to make sweet wines such as Auslese, Beerenauslese and Trockenbeerenauslese wines, which are highly sought after.

BUSCHENSCHANK: see Heurige

CASK AGEING: The ageing of wine in barriques, 225-litre casks usually made from oak wood. Fermenting and/or ageing wine in these barrels releases tannins and other compounds such as vanillin into the wine, giving it an added aroma, reminiscent of caramel, and improving its ageing potential. Using barriques in winemaking is an art in itself, as too much new and still tannic wood can overwhelm the wine. Often a mixture of new and old barrels, or new barrels and steel tanks is used. In Austria, barrique ageing was totally unknown until very recently, but has been taken up enthusiastically. Initially somewhat clumsy, it is now producing very interesting results.

CHAPTALIZATION: improving unfermented must that has an insufficiently high natural sugar content by adding sugar or concentrated grape juice in order to attain a higher alcohol content. This practice, named after its inventor, M. Chaptal, is frequently associated with poor vintages or low-quality wines. It does not necessarily produce sweeter wines, as the sugar is converted into alcohol. In Austrian wine law chaptalization is forbidden for wines from Qualitätswein up.

CRU (Austrian: RIED): quality gradation of a vineyard, as practised in France. A cru is a particular plot of land attributed with certain characteristics of soil and microclimate that make the wine distinctive.

CUVÉE: a wine assembled from different vineyards or grape varietals.

EIGENBAUWEIN: Estate-produced wine.

EISWEIN: ice wine, made from grapes that are harvested and pressed when frozen (usually in November), so that the water in the juice is left behind in the grapes as ice and a sweet, rich juice is extracted. In years with little botrytis this is a popular second choice for growers around Lake Neusiedl.

ERZEUGERABFÜLLUNG: estate bottled.

FEDERSPIEL: middle denomination of Wachau wine.

G'SPRITZTER: summer drink, (usually) white wine mixed with soda water.

HEURIGE: a term denoting both 'this year's wine' and the place where it is usually drunk, a country inn in which a farmer is allowed to sell wines he has made himself.

HOCHKULTUR: high training of vines. The Austrian variety of this was developed by Professor Lenz Moser. It was widely adopted as it facilitates better yields and work on the wines, but is also thought not to produce the best qualities. In an effort to raise the quality of the grape material, more ambitious Austrian growers have recently started to abandon this system in favour of others that lead the vine lower to the ground and increase the density of plants.

KABINETT: a wine of high quality according to German wine law. These wines are not allowed to be chaptalized, have to have a high natural sugar content (17° KMW), and may not have more than 9 gm residual sugar and 13 per cent of alcohol.

KMW (KLOSTERNEUBURGER MOSTWAAGE): a system developed in Austria for measuring the sugar content of the must. For a conversion table to Oechsle or Beaumé, see the chapter 'Legal Framework'.

LENZ MOSER: Austrian viticulturist and developer of the eponymous training system for vines, based on wide spacing of the plants and high stems, thus facilitating mechanization. Also one of the largest wine producers in the Weinviertel, though no longer controlled by the Moser family.

LIEBLICH: sweet, according to German wine law.

MALOLACTIC FERMENTATION: a second, bacterial fermentation during which the wine transforms malic (apple) acid into lactic (milk) acid, thereby giving the wine a more mellow, buttery character. Usually induced, though historically it sometimes simply occurred without being controlled. In Austria, malolactic fermentation was totally unknown and is now used for wines made in a more international style, while other wines are made without malolactic fermentation.

MISCHLULTUR (GEMISCHTER SATZ): cultivation of a variety of different grape varietals in the same vineyard, to be harvested together and made into one wine.

PHYLLOXERA: root louse imported from America which devastated European vineyards in the second half of the nineteenth century and was only conquered after grafting European varietals on to American rootstocks. In Austria the plague was at its worst during the 1880s and 1890s.

PRÄDIKAT: late-harvested wine, according to German wine law. Prädikat wines include Spätlese, as well as sweet wines such as Auslese, Beerenauslese, Trockenbeerenauslese, Eiswein, Strohwein and Ausbruch. Chaptalization is not allowed.

REDUCTIVE VINIFICATION: a method of winemaking designed to minimize contact with air during or after fermentation. This process, today usually involving steel tanks, prevents oxidation and creates a style of wine in which more of the varietal fruit and freshness are preserved, though these wines are often less complex and will not age as well as wines which have been allowed some degree of oxidation during fermentation and before bottling: for instance, by being kept in wooden barrels which 'breathe' naturally.

RIED: see Cru

SALON: an annual competition at which the wines submitted by Austrian growers are tasted blind and awarded prizes. The winners are entitled to call themselves Salon wines.

SCHILFWEIN: a Neusiedlersee novelty. Similar to Strohwein, but dried on reed, not straw.

SMARAGD: highest gradation of Wachau wines.

SPÄTLESE: wine made exclusively from fully ripe grapes (no less than 19° KMW), harvested after other wines.

STEINFEDER: lightest gradation of Wachau wines.

STROHWEIN: wine made from grapes which have been dried on straw mats for several months, causing them to shrivel while retaining their sugar content.

STURM: still-fermenting grape juice, often made from Bouvier, drunk throughout Austria during the harvest season.

SÜSS: sweet.

TBA: see Trockenbeerenauslese

TOASTING: Exposing the inside of a cask (barrique) to heat and thus altering the chemical qualities of the wood, an effect much like toasting bread. The degree of toasting of the wood has a significant influence on the kind and amount of chemicals released into wines fermented and/or matured in the cask and is a matter of judgement for both cooper and winemaker.

TROCKEN: dry (in Austria, less than 9 gm residual sugar).

TROCKENBEERENAUSLESE (TBA): a wine made exclusively from grapes affected by the botrytis mould, or noble rot, producing sweet wines of great concentration. The process of selection is very labour-intensive and the wines (usually sold in half-bottles) are correspondingly expensive.

VINIFICATION: the process of making wine

VINTAGE: the year in which a wine was harvested.

VINOTHEK: wine cellar or wine archive. Most Austrian growers have a vinotheque of their own wines. There are also regional vinotheques in which the wines of the area can be tasted and bought.

WEINBAU, WEINGUT: estate.

WEINGARTEN: vineyard.

YEAST: agent of fermentation process during which sugar in the must is transformed into alcohol. Both natural yeast cultures developing in the must and industrial cultures added to it can be used, according to the winemaker's preference.

Index

_____

Figures in italics refer to maps